# Saying Goodbye to Someone You Love

Norine Dresser, BA, MA, is a folklorist and writer. She is the author of *Multicultural Manners: New Rules of Etiquette for a Changing Society* and *Come as You Aren't: Feeling at Home With Multicultural Celebrations,* and she also wrote the 8-year award-winning *Los Angeles Times* column, "Multicultural Manners." She has a BA in anthropology and an MA in folklore/mythology, both from the University of California, Los Angeles (UCLA). She taught for 20 years at California State University, Los Angeles, lectures frequently, and has worked with a variety of government agencies and associations including the New York State Department of Health, Food Stamp and Nutrition Workers; Methodist Hospital of Southern California; Children's Hospital of Los Angeles; and the American Dietetic Association. She is an internationally recognized expert on cultural traditions and rituals from around the world.

Fredda Wasserman, MA, MPH, LMFT, CT, is a Licensed Marriage and Family Therapist, Certified in Thanatology: *Death, Dying and Bereavement.* She is a Clinical Director of Adult Programs and Education at OUR HOUSE Grief Support Center, the leading nonprofit grief center in California. She received her Masters degree in Health Education and Health Administration from the UCLA School of Public Health and her Masters in Clinical Psychology from Antioch University. Fredda presents workshops and seminars on end of life and grief for therapists, clergy, educators, and medical professionals at locations throughout the country including the David Geffen School of Medicine at UCLA and the Keck School of Medicine at the University of Southern California. Recognized as an expert in guided imagery, Fredda has created a series of guided meditation CDs for relaxation and stress management and maintains a private psychotherapy practice in Los Angeles.

OUR HOUSE Grief Support Center provides grief support to thousands of grieving children, teens, and adults each year on their journeys to hope and healing. A nonprofit, nonsectarian agency, OUR HOUSE was founded in 1993 on the premise that grievers need understanding, support, and connection. In addition to age and relationship specific groups offered at our locations, the El Centro de la Esperanza program offers groups in Spanish and the School Program serves students in low-income, under-served areas of Los Angeles County. Postcrisis grief interventions are available to schools, community organizations, and businesses after the death of a classmate, client, or coworker. OUR HOUSE provides continuing education workshops for mental health professionals, clergy, community leaders and educators and is the most recognized grief support center in California. Visit OUR HOUSE on the web at http://www.ourhouse-grief.org/.

OURHOUSE
GRIEF SUPPORT CENTER

# Saying Goodbye to Someone You Love

## Your Emotional Journey Through End of Life and Grief

Norine Dresser

**Fredda Wasserman**
for OUR HOUSE Grief Support Center

OURHOUSE
GRIEF SUPPORT CENTER

**demos**HEALTH
New York

*Acquisitions Editor:* Noreen Henson
*Cover Design:* Carlos Maldonado
*Compositor:* NewGen North America
*Printer:* Hamilton Printing Company

**Visit our website at www.demosmedpub.com**

**Library of Congress Cataloging-in-Publication Data**

Dresser, Norine.
   Saying goodbye to someone you love : your journey through end-of-life and grief / Norine Dresser, Fredda Wasserman.
      p. cm.
   Includes index.
   ISBN 978-1-932603-85-9
  1. Bereavement. 2. Grief. 3. Death. I. Wasserman, Fredda. II. Title.
   BF575.G7D74 2010
   155.9'37—dc22      2010002096

Special discounts on bulk quantities of Demos Health books are available to corporations, professional associations, pharmaceutical companies, health care organizations, and other qualifying groups. For details, please contact:

Special Sales Department

Demos Medical Publishing
11 W. 42nd Street
New York, NY 10036
Phone: 800–532–8663 or 212–683–0072
Fax: 212–941–7842
E-mail: rsantana@demosmedpub.com

Made in the United States of America

10 11 12  13        5 4 3

*To the many dying individuals, supportive loving ones, grievers, and helping professionals who have shared their lives and their experiences with us*

*And to those who are yet to take the emotional journey of Saying Goodbye to Someone You Love*

# Contents

# Foreword

To paraphrase Woody Allen, "I have nothing against death, I just don't want to be there when it happens."

The subject of death and dying is a great taboo in our culture. I have been a hospice nurse for more than a decade and continue to be amazed by the lack of knowledge that surrounds the dying process. People fear death: talking about it, thinking about it, and preparing for it.

Often I find families in a state of paralyzing dismay when I first meet them. They won't even talk about death in front of the patient, and they pretend that the patient is going to get better even when they know it is not true. When they are finally ready to discuss death, they don't know how to begin or what to say.

This book is a comprehensive collection of heartfelt narratives and practical guidelines that demystify the fears and misconceptions people have about death. The true-life stories highlight how others have experienced this most challenging part of life, from the first conversation about death through saying goodbye and grieving.

*Saying Goodbye to Someone You Love* provides a hopeful, positive perspective on facing life's final moments.

*Susan Romo, RN*
*Los Angeles, California*

# Preface from Norine Dresser

"Did you know you were an Aztec?" my son-in-law Julio asks. Astonished, I answer, "What do you mean?" "You surround yourself with artifacts of death just like they did," he nonchalantly explains.

I ponder for a moment and look around my home filled with death objects: masks, coffins, skeletons, vampires. Even my favorite coffee mug bears the logo from the L.A. County Coroner's gift shop. Yes, Julio pegged me right except I don't drink human blood like the Aztecs and there's no way I could ascend their pyramids walking with my cane.

I didn't grow up feeling comfortable about death or being surrounded by death objects. It was an interest acquired later in life. My parents never spoke about their own deaths and they cloistered me from other deaths. I couldn't even attend my grandparents' funerals because I was pregnant each time, and according to some Jewish beliefs my attendance might mark the baby. As a consequence, going to a funeral for the first time as a mature adult was very intimidating.

My attitude toward death was jolted when, as a folklorist and university professor, I attended a traditional Mexican Day of the Dead celebration, which was held annually on November 2, All Souls' Day. The ceremony began in Evergreen Cemetery in East Los Angeles, followed by a procession several blocks long of costumed skeletons, ghouls, and ghosts of famous people. The parade ended at the Self Help Graphics Art Gallery on Brooklyn Avenue where they had created a giant altar that held miniature coffins, skeletons, and spun-sugar candied skulls with names of people in colorful icing. The table was laden with fragrant Day of the Dead bread decorated with skulls and crossbones, bunches of yellow flowers, and framed photos of people who had recently died. The latter were displayed alongside burning candles and offerings of real food the people had enjoyed in life. It was a visual feast.

What really stood out was a life-size cardboard coffin on the floor with a drawstring at the end. Tentatively, children approached and pulled on the string, which caused the upper half of the coffin to open—and up popped a skeleton. Screaming, the children ran away, gathered their courage, and returned to pull the string again.

How healthy, I thought, to play with the artifacts of death. It was different than Halloween. This was more real. Not only that, on the previous day, All Saints' Day, Mexicans and Mexican Americans visit their family graves to spruce them up and adorn them with yellow flowers. To have an annual death event without immediate sorrow impressed me as a healthier attitude toward death than the one with which I had been raised.

From that very first Day of the Dead, I drastically changed my attitude concerning death. I talked with my husband about it often. We purchased our gravesite decades in advance. Since we were on a budget we chose a double-decker plot and frequently joked, "Who'll get to be on top?"

I tried not to protect my children from death, either. Death was a part of life and I thought I was rather enlightened about it, especially after becoming a quasi-expert on cross-cultural death customs. However, I was put to the test regarding my views when my husband of more than fifty years became terminally ill. Caring for him in hospice while he slowly deteriorated over the course of a year challenged my ideas. Nonetheless, living so close to death on a daily basis reinforced the beliefs I had developed since attending that first Day of the Dead celebration.

Shortly after Harold's death I met Fredda Wasserman, a bereavement specialist with extraordinary credentials. We immediately clicked. Our personalities, our concepts of death and dying, and above all our mission—to demystify death and inform others about the importance of being prepared for this inevitable journey—were all in sync. How fortuitous was my meeting with such a compassionate and savvy therapist, who is now a close friend. Together we embarked upon the writing of this book respectfully melding our different backgrounds and perspectives. Our goal has been to support you and others as you face the challenges of saying goodbye to someone you love. We trust that we have been successful.

*Norine Dresser*

# Preface from Fredda Wasserman

As a psychotherapist and thanatologist, I meet with people when they are diagnosed with a life-changing illness, stay with them through their treatments, celebrate with them when they are cured, companion them as they die, and support their friends and families through their grief. I am grateful to the patients and clients who have allowed me to accompany them through life's final moments. The depth and intimacy of our time together has inspired me to co-author *Saying Goodbye to Someone You Love*.

I suppose my comfort with end of life and death stems from my mother's extraordinary compassion and her appreciation of death as a natural part of life. She taught me about death and grief in the same gentle way that she explained how babies are made. (I was the first kid on my block to know the truth about that, too!). My mother and I visited the homes of friends and family when a baby was born, attended funerals, and paid condolence calls as loving demonstrations of our appreciation for life's beginnings and endings.

Throughout my career, my goal has been to bring death, dying, and bereavement out of the closet. My work in the fields of long-term care, cancer, and HIV/AIDS reinforced my passion and commitment. As a Clinical Director at OUR HOUSE Grief Support Center, I have the opportunity to share the journey with hundreds of grieving adults, children, and adolescents, each of whom teach me along the way and continually renew my belief in the healing power of the human spirit.

Writing this book has been a labor of love. I thank my incredible co-author, Norine Dresser, from the bottom of my heart for her talent and her friendship. I treasure the hours we spent "Norining" as we meticulously wrote and revised every word, striving to accurately convey our message.

*Fredda Wasserman*

# Acknowledgments

The following are people who either generously shared their stories with us or connected us with their friends who had stories to tell. We feel honored by their trust to take good care of their precious memories: Lisa Adams, Bereavement Director, Adventist Health Services; Megory Anderson, Executive Director, Sacred Dying Foundation; Selma Anderson; Abby Arnold; Usha Athanikar; Pat Atkinson, Ph.D.; Irene R. Avidon; Samuel M. Avidon; Lisa Barash; Jayne Barbera; Lark Bergwin-Anderson; Debra Bellon; Lee Boek; Barbara Bonner-McGeehan; Chris Boutelle; Cheryl Boyer; Rita Bricker; Julie Brown, MSW San Diego Hospice and Palliative Care; Sylvia Brown; Dee Buchwald; Tom Burbank; Yvonne Cannon; Caryl Carothers; Elaine Clark; Earle Cohen; Rabbi Neil Comess-Daniels, Beth Shir Sholom; Jean Copley; Linda Cano Cramer; Chris Craven; Barbara Crofford; Diane Darling; Lothar Delgado; PJ Dempsey; Michele DeVore; Pat Dolci; Laura Dotson; Madge Dresser; Shirlee Dresser; Susan Edelstein; Joanna Elliott; Robert English; Judith Firestone; Kimra Fleming; Montserrat Fontes; Lydia Fucsko, Griefline, Australia; Marielle Fuller; Howard and Janice Garey; Bonnie Geary; Mary and Bob Georges, Ph.D.; Allison Gilbert; Clarice Gillis; Robbie Gluckson, Executive Director, Premiere Oncology; Galen Goben, Grief Support Coordinator, Forest Lawn Memorial-Parks and Mortuaries; Victoria Gotsha; Paul Gottlieb; Gus Gravot; Talia Green; Ruth Gundelfinger; Gerri Gussman; Bree Harvey, Director of Education and Visitor Services, Mt. Auburn Cemeteries; Monica Hamor; Amy Hashimoto; Alan Hedman, Ph.D.; Helen Hersrud; Susan Hess; Roy Ho, Executive Director, Na Lei Aloha Foundation; Dan Jenkins; Patricia Jimenez; Dawna Kaufmann; David Kessler; Anakria King; Alan Knopf, M.D.; Sandie Knopf; Elizabeth Knox, Founder, CROSSINGS; Julian Kragulman; Reverend Marc Latonce, North Hollywood Church of Religious Science; Ruth Laskowski; Jo-Ann Lautman, Founder OUR HOUSE Grief Support Center; Laura Leff; Stacey Lisk; Joy Lodge; Stan Mack; Stephanie Machado;

Mary-Beth Manning; Eileen Manus; Myrna Marin; Anika Marinelli; Ron Marinelli; Willian Martin, Communications Director, Forest Lawn Memorial-Parks and Mortuaries; Nancy Martinez; Yasmeen Mazer; Loretta Mazorra; Quinn McDonald; Dana Knickerbocker Melching; Greg Metoyer; Meagan Mucciolo; Pat Mulville, Bereavement Director, Corpus Christie Church, Pacific Palisades, CA; Chanell O'Farrill, Funeral Home Manager, Hollywood Forever Cemetery/Beth Olam Cemetery; Bonnie Olson, Buena Vista Hospice Care; Sean O'Regan, Mt. Auburn Cemetery; Priscilla Panzer; Bonnie Perkinson; Matt Pime; Mark Pinto, Shinnyo-en USA; Libby Platus; Karin Polacheck; Leonard Potash, MSW; Carol Potter; Alysia Reiner; Felice Rhiannon; Cheryl Rilly; Antonia Rivin; Alice Roy, Ph.D.; Peggy Roy; Susannah Ryder; Bill Sabo; Rabbi Regina Sandler-Phillips; William Schampeau; Sharon Schlesinger, Susan G. Komen Breast Cancer Foundation; Miriam Schneider; Sharalynn Schulner; Karl Seligman, M.D.; Brian Shapiro; Mickey Shapiro; Margaret Sharp; Anthony Shay, Ph.D.; Noel Siat; Julie Benton Siegel; Marley Sims; Kerry Slattery; Sharon Smartt; Rees Smith, D.D.S.; Aline Smithson; Lori Soroko; Belle Sorotskin; Rachel Spector, Ph.D.; Father Tom Stehle; Jan Steward; Eric Strong; Rhonda Sudbrink; Jonna Tamases; Robert Taub, M.D., Palliative Care Program, Cedars-Sinai Medical Center; Judith Terzi; Elizabeth Titus; Lucia Van Ruiten; Marie Vester; Douglas Vogel; Sherry Vrooman; Anita Wallace, Service Arrangements Supervisor, Forest Lawn Memorial-Parks and Mortuaries, Covina Hills; Bruce Wasserman; Julie Wasserman; Robyn Wasserman; Greg Weger; Patricia Weger; Deb Weintraub, Susan G. Komen Breast Cancer Foundation; Suzanne Wenzlaff, D.D.S.; Susan Whitmore; Patrick Wilkins; Jerry Wilson; J. William Worden, Ph.D.

We salute our special colleagues who gave careful readings to the manuscript and offered constructive commentaries: to Lauren Schneider and Randi Pearlman Wolfson, grief experts extraordinaire, for their counsel and advice; and to Virginia Crane, reader *par excellence,* we dub her the writers' best friend!

Norine offers her gratitude to Harold, the inspiration for this book, in loving memory of the way he accepted his end of life with such grace and good humor; to my children and their spouses for their leads, input, and support: Mark, Carol, Andrea, Barry, Amy, Julio; to my grandchildren for their ideas, sayings, and assistance: Leila, Zachary, Isa, Avidan; and to all my good friends for their understanding when I couldn't come out and play because I was too busy writing.

Fredda offers special thanks to Jo-Ann Lautman, Tiffany Cannis, and the OUR HOUSE Board of Directors for recognizing the value of this project and to the extraordinary OUR HOUSE staff and volunteers who inspire me daily with their dedication and service. To my precious family and dear friends who believed in me and encouraged me throughout, your love and understanding mean more than I can say.

This book would not have been published without the perseverance and commitment of our fabulous agent Janet Rosen of the Sheree Bykofsky Literary Agency. She touched us with her dedication in finding the right home for this work. Janet never gave up and her belief in the value of *Saying Goodbye to Someone You Love* bolstered us. And we give a standing ovation to our fantastic editor, Noreen Henson, who was an enthusiastic cheerleader from the start, was quick to respond to our questions, and provided clear-cut feedback. She is one-in-a-million editor, except for one thing—she spells her first name the wrong way.

# Life's Inevitable Journey

*Saying Goodbye to Someone You Love* guides you through what may be the most poignant experience of your life. If your loved one is ill or dying, you will find suggestions on how to follow your heart and your instincts in your endeavor to say a loving goodbye. If you are the person who is dying, you will gain insight into what lies ahead on your journey. If someone close to you has already died, you will discover ways to navigate through the tidal wave of emotions and reactions of your grief. If you are comforting a griever, you will find guidance on how to be there for him at this crucial time. If you are a health care professional, you will enhance your skills as a compassionate presence. If you are a general reader, you will be better prepared to face life's final chapter with love and dignity.

Each chapter of *Saying Goodbye to Someone You Love* begins with a humorous story. We have included these anecdotes because laughter and tears are closely related. As playwright George Bernard Shaw wrote in *The Doctor's Dilemma:* "Life does not cease to be funny when people die any more than it ceases to be serious when people laugh."

Although the book is filled with true-life stories, some of the vignettes are composites of more than one individual or family. To protect each person's privacy, the narratives have been fictionalized and the names have been changed with the exception of Fredda, Norine, Harold, and those who are identified by both first and last names.

# Saying Goodbye to Someone You Love

# CHAPTER 1

## Elephant in the Room

*Humorist Art Buchwald's recurring dream while he is a hospice patient:*
*I enter the waiting area (at Dulles Airport). The loudspeaker says, "Heaven is at the last gate. There will be intermediate stops in Dallas, Chicago, and Albuquerque. The plane has just arrived."*
*I go up to the desk and ask, "Am I entitled to frequent flyer miles?"*
*The agent says, "You won't need any, because you're not coming back."*

Art Buchwald's *Too Soon to Say Goodbye*

Opening this book is an act of courage. Chances are that you are reading these pages because you or someone you love is dying or someone dear to you has already died.

Although it is universal and affects everyone, talking about death is generally taboo in American society. Consequently, you probably keep your thoughts about end of life and grief a secret. Even as you realize that others must have the same questions, concerns, and fears about death that you have, you do not raise the topic. Though you may long to share details, anecdotes, and precious memories, you keep your thoughts to yourself. Hence the title of this chapter: Elephant in the Room. Death is the elephant. It is large and looming. Everyone knows it is there, yet you move around it, ignore it, and refuse to speak about it. Sooner or later, you discover that denying the elephant's existence is nearly impossible.

What has been your experience? When someone you love is dying, do you talk openly about the possibility of his death or do you skirt around the topic? Does your dear one try to fool you and perhaps even elude death by pretending that, despite evidence that his condition is worsening, he is "just fine"? Or are you able to acknowledge what is happening and say a loving goodbye? When you are grieving, do you show your emotions openly or do you hide your sadness believing that the rest of the world won't understand? How do you express your condolences to a mourner? Your response in each of these situations depends upon what you learned in your family, your community, your religion, and through life experience.

Reading this book will be an emotional journey. You may experience tears, laughter, sadness, fear, passion, anger, joy, tenderness, or nostalgia. Notice how you feel as you begin. Do you find yourself resisting reading even one more word? Or are you drawn to explore further? Regardless of your initial reaction, getting to know more about end of life will demystify the process and prepare you for the time when you must say goodbye to someone you love.

## PERSONAL AND CULTURAL ATTITUDES TOWARD DEATH

### Ricardo Doesn't "Do Death"

Mr. and Mrs. Arellano have three grown sons, and the middle son, Ricardo, is very different from his brothers and parents. He holds very rigid views. For example, Ricardo doesn't "do death," which means that he refuses to attend funerals, even of his own grandparents with whom he is very close. He cannot be dissuaded so his parents shrug their shoulders and assume that he will not attend their funerals, either.

### Leo Doesn't Want to "Give Up"

Tatiana has a tough time when Leo is diagnosed with kidney cancer. Leo is a fighter and has tried every treatment, even experimental ones. He fights his disease for 4 years. When he reaches the terminal stage and hospice is suggested, Leo refuses to accept the concept. To Leo hospice means giving up. He is unwilling to do that.

Leo rails at the thought of relinquishing hope, so much so that he even refuses to sign an Advance Health Care Directive. He will not talk about dying. The family calls in a mediator to open up a discussion, and when the mediator arrives, Leo falls asleep. When he awakes he claims that the discussion has already taken place. Desperate, Tatiana calls in a rabbi, but still Leo will not talk about death. Tatiana believes Leo wants to think positively and not give in to the possibility of his life being over.

His family is so desperate for hospice care that they even type up the agreement in extra large font to make it easy for him to read. He reads and rereads the agreement before he reluctantly signs. Leo denies death until the end, which comes when he is holding on to a trapeze bar that he uses to help change his bed position. His adult daughter is alone with him in the room and simply tells him that he doesn't have to hold on any longer. Leo lets go and is gone.

## A Few More Hugs

When Viv receives her diagnosis of stage 4 cancer, she suspects that she will not have long to live. Thanks to her many years of volunteering at the hospital, death is no stranger to her. Viv speaks with the oncology nurse and immediately joins a support group where she feels understood and shares openly her fears and hopes.

Viv welcomes the discussions about the mind–body connection, healthy eating, alternative treatments, and yoga classes. The support group members laugh and cry about losing their hair, trying on wigs, and adjusting to life with cancer. Viv is also relieved that they talk about death, which everyone thinks about, but no one outside of group seems willing to discuss.

Three weeks after her diagnosis, Viv writes in her journal "Today I'm feeling OK about all this, but I sure wish my siblings wouldn't act as though nothing were happening. I told Roz and Rena that I don't want any gifts for my birthday. What would they give me anyway? I sure wish they'd think to give me a few more hugs."

## I'm Just Fine

Mingya comes from a family who covers up the truth, especially if it is painful or controversial. They believe that through this behavior they are protecting their children.

When Mingya is diagnosed with breast cancer, only her husband knows. For 5 years they keep this secret from their three adult children. Only after Mingya's appearance begins to change and she becomes more frail does she tell her children about her illness. They must promise to tell no one, including the grandchildren.

When Mingya travels out of state, relatives notice her close-cropped postchemo hair, but her facial expressions and body language signal that she doesn't want anyone to ask questions. She pretends to be healthy, despite her breasts being out of alignment. "I'm just fine," she insists.

Whenever her cousins phone to see how she is, Mingya maintains that she is doing well. Not until 48 hours before her death, does she finally admit that her life is about to end after a 7-year battle with cancer. One daughter helps Mingya telephone long distance relatives to say goodbye. Although the relatives have already guessed, they go along with the charade, pretending they did not know.

Mingya's eldest grandson, who has been regularly bringing meals to his grandparents, learns the truth the hard way. As he is in the middle of his high school graduation procession, he is notified of a family emergency. He must leave the ceremony immediately because his grandmother is dead.

After her death, family members express their outrage that Mingya cheated them by not being truthful. It felt to them like a lost opportunity for the matriarch of the family to teach the next generation how to cope with loss and serious illness. Her grandson admits "We honored Nai-Nai's wishes, but ultimately it made it so much more difficult for us."

## A Conspiracy of Silence

The first time in 4 years that Erin and Sergio see their son Nico, who lives out of state, they are shocked by his gaunt appearance. They know that many of his friends have been diagnosed with AIDS but had no idea that this could be happening to their beloved son.

Nico has had multiple hospitalizations and his T-cell count is rapidly dropping. It is 1992, a time when AIDS is the leading cause of death for 24- to 44-year-old men in the United States. Erin and Sergio tell Nico's case worker, "We know that he is dying, of course we do, but don't tell him." They fear that it will cause Nico to give up hope or he will feel that they have. In his individual session, Nico admits to the case worker, "I know I am dying, but don't tell my parents; they couldn't handle it." There is an unspoken conspiracy of silence.

## If We Talk About It, It Will Happen

Cassandra's cancer treatments have stopped working. Exhausted and no longer willing to be poked and prodded, Cassandra recognizes that her death is inevitable. She would like to make her last wishes known to both of her parents, but her father will not tolerate it.

When Cassandra talks about her death with her mother, her father overhears and admonishes, "What's all this talk about death? It's as if you are wishing it would happen. You know, what you talk about and think about comes to pass. We'll be sad enough later, *if* it happens. Please stop talking in such a morbid way. Cassandra has plenty of time to live."


## Steely Resolve

LeeAnn and her husband, Hubert, have been happily married for over 40 years when Hubert is diagnosed with bladder cancer. For 3 years they anxiously endure endless treatments. They even appeal to a U.S. Senate appropriations committee for permission to try an experimental drug that ultimately does not work.

They exhaust all possible avenues for healing, yet despite this, they never talk about death. They focus more on seeing if the next round of treatments will work. Even at the end of his life when Hubert is experiencing severe pain and is on morphine, the topic of death never arises. LeeAnn believes that both of them ignore the subject in an attempt to protect one another.

After Hubert dies, LeeAnn has regrets. She wishes she had asked Hubert about how he wanted her to handle his business projects. She wishes she could have held him more. She wishes he would have talked about the future and what she should do without him. She wishes that he might have written about what he was going through because he was such a gifted writer. And, she hasn't forgiven God for her husband's painful death.

LeeAnn is moved to tears when she reads a letter from her husband's doctor: "...I have never met a man so elegant and quietly courageous.... He faced monster demons with peace and the steely resolve of a true hero...."


## Flower Delivery

The employees at Mr. Woo's bakery learn that their boss's brother has died. They take up a collection to buy a funeral bouquet to show their respect for Mr. Woo. Since they don't know the address of the mortuary, they have the flowers delivered to the bakery and assume that Miss Liu, the manager, will send them to the proper location.

When Miss Liu sees the flowers, she becomes upset and quickly hides them in the walk-in-refrigerator. She explains that according to Chinese beliefs, objects associated with death should not be placed among the living. It is like bringing death and bad luck to the business and to those who work there. She calls the florist and they send their delivery truck to pick up the flowers and redeliver them to the funeral home. The employees feel embarrassed yet relieved that Miss Liu saved them from making a cultural faux pas.

## Alone in Her Grief

When Annabelle returns to school several days after her mother's funeral, she acts as if nothing has happened. Neither Annabelle's classmates nor her teacher acknowledge the death. Taking the cues from her friends who don't seem to want to hear what she is feeling, Annabelle hides her grief.

However, as graduation approaches, Annabelle's composure begins to waver. When the teacher announces the forthcoming mother/daughter senior breakfast, her friend, Joely, notices that Annabelle's eyes fill with tears.

"What's the big deal?" Joely asks casually. "Why don't you just come with me and my mom?"

Speechless, Annabelle shakes her head no. Again, her friends do not understand and Annabelle feels more alone than ever in her grief.

Cultures and religions around the world encompass a broad spectrum of attitudes about death. In the United States, stoicism is the cultural norm. Open communication about death and grief is the exception, rather than the rule.

Most people's attitudes are rooted in family traditions. For example, some families promote the belief that by not talking about death it won't become real, similar to those who whisper rather than speak the word "cancer" or call it the "Big C." Trying to spare others from pain, people pretend that they don't know what they actually *do* know. Keeping secrets can cause everyone to feel alone and isolated and puts up barriers at a time when taking down barriers can be healing. On the other hand, some people find ease and comfort in talking about death and being with the dying. Where do you fit along this continuum?

## Assessing Family Attitudes

- What did you learn about death from your family of origin?
- What is your family's comfort level in talking about the subject?
- How does the family's attitude fit with your views?

## Respecting Others' Attitudes

- Remember that attitudes about death are emotional, not logical.
- Recognize that upon diagnosis of a life-changing illness, virtually everyone thinks about death.

- Try to understand the other person's reactions, beliefs, and fears about death, even if their ideas are very different from yours.
- Encourage open conversation in which everyone can express their feelings.
- Avoid dissuading someone from thinking or worrying about death.
- Remember that acknowledging death does not mean abandoning hope.

## STORIES FROM THOSE WHO WORK WITH THE DYING

### No More Sad Stories

Teresita, who has been a hospice aide for 4 years, loves her work. She is often surprised by the negative reactions from her family. When she begins talking to them about what happened that day at the hospice, they put their hands up to their ears and say, "Please, no more sad stories." To Teresita, they are not sad stories. They are uplifting stories that validate life.

Some of Teresita's friends are decidedly cool when she describes a moment of tenderness at the bedside of someone who lay dying. They say that her conversations depress them. Teresita laments, "I feel like I have thrown a dirty rag on the floor and everyone is watching."

Eventually, a few of her friends drop Teresita from their social circle. Others notice how she has blossomed as a result of this meaningful work and admire her devotion to those who are facing the end of life.

### A Physician's Point of View

As a practicing OB/GYN, Dr. Victor spends the majority of his career delivering babies. He looks forward to his visits with the new mothers after the babies are born. However, it is quite different when he must visit his dying patients. He struggles when he must visit his cancer patients in the hospital. While ordinarily he makes rounds twice daily, he cannot bear to visit those with terminal cancer more than once a day. He feels like a failure because he cannot cure them; he doesn't know what to say to them.

Then, Dr. Victor attends a national meeting of the Fellows of Obstetricians and Gynecologists. Dr. Elisabeth Kubler-Ross, the leading scholar in the new field of death and dying, is the featured speaker. Dr. Victor listens and considers this moment an epiphany. He learns that he is not expected to perform miracles with dying patients. He doesn't have to say anything profound. He just has to be there.

"The most important thing I learned that day," relays Dr. Victor to his colleagues, "was the value of simply holding my patient's hand to show her how much I care."

## Female Embalmer

After a high school classmate's death, Daria receives such comfort from her friend's funeral rituals that she chooses to become a trained and certified mortician. As an embalmer, she treats bodies with great respect and sees her work as a way of honoring the deceased and serving their families.

One day, she receives a phone call at work from Dr. Jellen, her gynecologist. Daria asks the doctor to wait for a moment while she removes her mask and gloves. Curious, Dr. Jellen looks at Daria's chart to see what her occupation is that requires a mask and gloves.

When Daria returns to the phone, the doctor deplores, "I think what you do is horrible!"

The young mortician is stunned by the ignorance of her highly educated physician, especially since Dr. Jellen, too, is in involved with the human body. Thinking about the doctor's own procedures with her patients, Daria thinks to herself, "I think what *you* do is horrible!"

At home, Daria's parents are totally supportive of their daughter's choice of occupation. However, her grandmother, Tzila, is not. Tzila mostly acts embarrassed and does not discuss her granddaughter's profession with her friends until Daria's grandfather dies. When Daria requests permission to bathe and dress her grandfather's body herself, Tzila gains greater appreciation for Daria's work.

## Comfortable With Grief

Justin volunteers at OUR HOUSE Grief Support Center in Los Angeles and discovers that leading grief groups is the most heart-centered, intimate work he has ever done. He is comfortable in the company of grievers. As he proudly talks about his work, friends and family ask, "How can you do that? Isn't it morbid and depressing?"

Justin answers, "Before I began volunteering I feared that doing this work might be difficult. I wondered if being with grieving people would be too painful or heartbreaking. I was wrong. For me, it has been life-affirming."

## Being With the Dying

Throughout her career, Fredda is continually stirred by the soul-to-soul nature of her work with patients who have been diagnosed with life-changing illness and families and friends who are grieving. From diagnosis through the end of their lives, Fredda accompanies her clients as they explore the emotional issues that arise. The deep satisfaction she experiences is sometimes hard for others to comprehend.

After spending the day at Pavan's bedside, Fredda holds her patient's hand as he exhales his final breath. She marvels at the sacredness of the moment. Once Pavan's body has been taken to the mortuary, Fredda returns home, showers, and dresses for a dinner dance that evening.

At the dinner, Fredda recounts to the woman sitting next to her the experience of being with Pavan as he died just hours before and remarks, "This is all very surreal."

"I know what you mean," her table mate nods with understanding. "I can't imagine how strange it must be to be with a dead body."

"No," replies Fredda, "being with dying is the most profound experience imaginable. It's being here that is surreal."

Death does not have to be the elephant in the room. There are many benefits to having an open discussion about end of life. Talking about the inevitability of death when you and your loved ones are healthy paves the way for an easier discussion in the future when death is at hand. Having the conversation when death is imminent strengthens the intimacy between you. Expressing your feelings when you are grieving will help your heart heal. The stories in the following chapter will guide you on how to have a conversation about end of life, no matter where you are along your journey.

# CHAPTER 2

# The Conversation

*When family and friends gather around Issidore Shapiro*
*to sing "Happy Birthday," honoring his eightieth year,*
*Shapiro cheerily announces,*
*"I'm not renewing any more subscriptions!"*

Norine Dresser's father

Having a conversation about end of life and grief may be a new experience for you. Unaccustomed to discussing death, the task seems daunting. Yet the time has come. How will you begin? What thoughts will you share with your loved one? What questions do you have for her? Consider how, before a baby is born, people don't hesitate to inquire: *When do you think it will happen? What do you think it will be like? What are your fears? How are you planning for it?* You might pose these same questions when talking about end of life. Although the dialogue may be hard to initiate, maintaining an attitude of curiosity and wonder will allow each of you to explore your feelings and express your thoughts, fears, and hopes. Your intimate conversation about end of life can be a tender, gentle expression of affection that strengthens the bonds between you and your loved one by making no topic off limits.

You may want to start the conversation when you and your loved one are both healthy. The opportunities to talk about death are ever present: you attend a funeral, a celebrity's death makes the headlines, a distant relative is terminally ill, the family pet dies. Use these moments as springboards to initiate ongoing communication. Allow death to become part of your vocabulary when end of life is not imminent so you don't have to look back later and wonder, "Why didn't we talk about death when we were out fishing or driving in the car having a causal conversation about life?"

While it is ideal to have death become a natural topic of conversation before anyone is ill, chances are that isn't the case. It is likely that you will not begin your dialogue until you or your loved one is diagnosed with a terminal illness. Now, the conversation about end of life becomes more challenging. You hesitate to talk about this delicate subject because you don't know how she will react. Will the discussion ease the tension between you or make it worse? If you talk about death, will she think you have given up hope? What if either one of you cry? Maybe you want to wait to talk about it after she eats her supper? At last, the moment arrives. Your throat tightens. Your heart races. You muster your strength. The words stick in your throat and then tumble out, "As much as I want you to get well, sometimes I can't help but think about the possibility of your dying. Can we talk about it?" Then you wait for the response. You have done the hardest part. The conversation has begun. At times the words flow freely; at other moments there is silence. Your communication deepens through your body language, the tone of your voice, a simple touch, and the expression on your face. You share what you are ready to share.

As your dear one's illness progresses and death approaches, you listen to your heart and allow the conversation to follow its own course. You express your love, your gratitude, and your deepest sentiments as you say a loving goodbye.

After your dear one dies, your grief needs to be shared. You hesitate because you fear you are burdening others with your sadness. And then you discover those people who care deeply about what you are experiencing and are more than willing to listen to your pain, revel in your good memories, and support you in your healing.

## INITIAL CONVERSATION

### Constant Conversation

One early morning, as Harold and I briskly stride around the Rose Bowl in Pasadena, California, I observe single people walking their dogs.

I prattle, "Honey, if you die before I do, here's my plan. I won't want to live alone in the house, so I'll probably get a dog. Labrador Retrievers are a great breed. Maybe, instead of a black or yellow Lab, I'll get a chocolate one, like President Clinton. What do you think?"

Harold retorts, "I don't know about you, but I know that if you die before me, I'm not getting a dog. I'm getting a girlfriend."

Inadvertently, I have set myself up for his punch line, and we both laugh heartily. At the same time, this repartee demonstrates how often I think about death, not morbidly, but just like preparing for a vacation. Harold and I often talk about death. I insist that we say, "When we die," instead of, "If we die."

## Let's Talk About Death

This year as the Dempsey family gathers for the annual Christmas festivities in Washington, the adult children decide it is time to broach the subject of death with their parents. Their mother and father are in their seventies and in relatively good health, so that makes it a bit easier for the eldest son, Alan, to casually say "Dad, we want to talk about your funeral."

Dad smiles. "My funeral? Why? Do you know something I don't know?"

The family members hold their breath. Have they upset their father? Have they ruined Christmas? Maybe they should have chosen another time.

"Actually, I am glad you asked," Dad replies. "I've been wanting to talk about it but did not know how." The children bring their chairs closer together, and even Mom, who generally hides in the kitchen washing dishes, wipes her hands on a dishtowel, comes into the living room, and enters into the conversation.

Despite the gravity of the subject, the family has a good time teasing and joking. The conversation about death is now open, and the children learn about their parents' wishes. They discover that both mom and dad want no heroic measures performed. Dad would like to donate his eyes and has already indicated that on his driver's license. The parents request that Pastor Finnerty officiate at their funerals and that "Amazing Grace" be sung at the services. The Dempsey children feel a great sense of relief that they are hearing this together.

## Minnie's Surprise

Spry and healthy at 87, Aunt Minnie lives alone and is proud of her independence. As the last remaining member of her generation, she is the keeper of the family history and is dearly loved by her many nieces and nephews. Occasionally, the family wonders what will happen if Aunt Minnie gets ill or needs special care. Who will be available to care for her physically and financially?

And then it happens. Minnie falls in her apartment, breaks her hip, and is admitted to the hospital for surgery and rehab. The members of her extended family visit her regularly and focus on keeping her spirits up. Among themselves they worry about whether Aunt Minnie has a will and if she wants to be buried or cremated, but no one has the courage to ask. "I think it's too late, we can't talk to her about it *now*," laments her grandniece, Bella.

But Minnie brings it up herself. At her request, Bill, her oldest nephew, locates important papers in her desk drawer. She advises, "I want you all to know that everything has been taken care of. I made all the arrangements 30 years ago; I picked the coffin and it's paid in full. And, by the way, I want to be buried in the dress I wore to Bella's wedding; you'll find it hanging in my closet." Minnie surprises them again. Her hip heals, and she returns to independent living, moving just a bit more slowly.

## Go Wish Game

Even though her father Bradley is 89, Shelly doesn't know how to approach the topic of death with him. They have never had open conversations with one another and Bradley has always had monosyllabic answers for everything. He's a bit cantankerous and an excellent example of the stereotypical New Englander.

Desperate to talk about death with her father, Shelly plays a card game of "Go Wish" with him. She has heard that this game facilitates a death conversation in an entertaining way. "Go Wish" is a deck of 36 cards each printed with an end-of-life preference, for example, 1) to have my family with me; 2) to not be connected to machines; 3) to feel that my life is complete. Each player reads through the cards and then divides them into three piles labeled: very important to me; somewhat important to me; not important to me.

Shelly is delighted by her father's response to this game. Bradley acts amused by the playful way in which they discussed significant issues.

## Perfect Opening

A dozen medical students gather at OUR HOUSE Grief Support Center for their "What is this thing called grief?" seminar led by Clinical Director, Fredda Wasserman. Each student describes either her experience with death or what she thinks working with dying patients or grieving families will be like. To their surprise, the students discover that each of them has been touched by death, and they are amazed by what they didn't know about one another.

Fredda asks, "How many of you have had these same discussions with your family members or friends?" When most of the students acknowledge that they have not, Fredda suggests, "You probably haven't had the conversation because you didn't know how to begin. Now you have the perfect opening. All you have to do is tell them that you were here today; then you can easily lead right into 'I realize that we have never had a conversation about death,' or you might ask them what it was like when someone they loved died."

As the students leave, they are abuzz with their new perspectives on death and grief. One student expresses, "I never realized that being a doctor means I have to talk about death and grief with my patients. Now I see how important that is. This has been an eye-opening experience."

> Daring to talk about death when there is no urgency may reduce fear and tension. It can be a relief to everyone to know that you have had "the" conversation and death is no longer the unspeakable.

## Opening the Conversation

- Choose a time when there is no urgency.
- Include key family members or friends in the discussion.
- Be sincere and honest with your feelings.
- Allow playfulness and jokes as part of the conversation.

## Phrases You Might Use to Initiate the Conversation

- I can't imagine what my life will be like if you die before me.
- I sometimes think about death and wonder when and how it will happen.
- I was reading the book *Saying Goodbye to Someone You Love* and I realize that you and I have never had a conversation about end of life.
- What are your thoughts about death?
- What was it like for you when someone close to you died?
- What arrangements have you made for your burial or cremation?

# TALKING WITH YOUR DYING LOVED ONE

## Is Today the Day?

After Harold settles in at home under hospice care, our conversations change. No longer hypothetical, we acknowledge that death is close at hand. He must sleep in a hospital bed in the front of the house so that there is more room for visiting attendants to provide the care that Harold now requires. I place family pictures in plain view. We turn the bed so that his vista includes swaying tree tops, soaring red-tailed hawks, and nighttime fireworks from Dodger Stadium when the home team wins.

Despite the beauty of this setting, Harold tells me, "I miss sleeping next to you. I want to die in my own bed." I welcome him back with waiting arms. I've missed him too.

One morning he tells me, "Guess who I dreamed about last night?" After he says that it's Bernie, his best friend who died 35 years ago, I ask, "Is he calling you?" Harold gives me an exasperated look. Another morning, he seems to have extra complaints and I ask, "Is today the day?" He rolls his eyes and impatiently responds, "Not yet." Our dynamics remain the same; we still joke a lot, hold nothing back.

As death approaches, I continue to reassure Harold, "Don't worry about anything, Honey. I am with you every step of the way."

## Am I Dying?

When his doctor gives him the test results that the cancer has spread to his lungs, Lazlo does not want to know his prognosis. "You can tell my wife, Rosalyn, but I don't want to hear it," he instructs.

Lazlo remains silent about his illness, and life goes on as if nothing has changed. Although his daughter, Lindy, visits more frequently lately, their discussions continue to center around sports and politics. They never mention Lazlo's increased difficulty breathing and his escalating pain.

When she and her mom are alone, Lindy asks, "Mom, why don't we ever talk with Dad about his cancer?"

Rosalyn explains, "Dad only has a few months to live, but he doesn't want to discuss it. I'm afraid that talking about it might make his condition worse and speed up his death." Hearing this, Lindy bursts into tears. When Lazlo walks into the kitchen and sees his daughter crying and his wife's red, puffy eyes, he demands, "Well, hell, am I going to live or am I going to die?"

In a raspy voice Rosalyn breaks the news, "Honey, you're dying. I know you don't like to talk about it but I wish you would tell us what you're thinking."

With tears streaming down her face, Lindy crosses the room and puts her arms around her father, "Pop, you don't have to say anything. Just remember that we love you."

## What Would I Do Without You?

"I've been thinking a lot about death lately," Magda announces to her husband Damian, while doing the dinner dishes, a few days after she is diagnosed with breast cancer.

Shaken, Damian protests, "But Dr. Fellows says your cancer is curable. Why are you thinking about dying?"

"Darling, my mother and my sister died of breast cancer," Magda reminds her husband. "Neither of them ever admitted how seriously ill they were, and I hated pretending nothing was happening. I'm not going to let it be that way with us. We have to face the fact that sooner or later I'm going to die and so are you, whether I die from breast cancer or some other cause."

"Okay you said it. Now, let's try not to think about that too much," Damian suggests. After a long silence, Damian turns to Magda and utters, "I can't imagine what my life would be like if you died. What would I do without you?"

## Circle of Life

As a psychotherapist who makes house calls, Fredda shares many intimate conversations with Carley, a 32-year-old woman with brain cancer. Carley is outgoing and enthusiastic, with a contagious smile. She wears a baseball cap to cover the patches of hair that have fallen out during her recent chemotherapy.

"You know," says Fredda, "I am someone who has been with people right through their illnesses and even their deaths." A puzzled look crosses Carley's face and then a wide smile, "Really? You do that? You would visit someone even if you thought she was dying?"

"Yes I would," Fredda confirms looking directly into Carley's eyes.

Over the next several visits, a variety of art activities and guided imagery visualizations seem to unlock Carley's previous reluctance to talk about her illness and her feelings about death. Carley entitles her first drawing *The Moods of Cancer* and explains how the colors and symbols represent her fears about hospitals, doctors, and dying a painful death. In one of her visualizations, she meets an inner guide and tells him "Get the grave ready." The guide speaks to Carley about the circle of life—how people are born, how they live, and how they die. For the first time, Carley verbalizes her hope for a peaceful death and wonders what heaven will be like.

## At the Hospice

Since moving into hospice several weeks ago, Chad, a successful business executive, has slowed down the pace of his hectic life and contentedly spends his days on the patio tending his potted strawberries and herb garden. Some days he sits for hours in a lawn chair admiring the plants and communing with nature. When his nephew Dirk offers to take Chad to lunch at their favorite trendy restaurant, Chad suggests, "Why don't you just bring in sandwiches?"

While they are enjoying their lunch, Chad talks about his newfound interest in gardening. Dirk comments, "You know, Uncle, you've changed. You used to be such a Type-A; I couldn't keep up with you. I like you better this way." Chad nods and smiles, acknowledging with pleasure his newly acquired appreciation of life in the slow lane.

Later, while sipping chamomile tea, Chad broaches the subject that he and his nephew have been delicately avoiding all afternoon, "You know, Dirk, I don't have long to live."

"Of course, I know that Uncle Chad, but I didn't think you wanted to talk about it," Dirk admits. Daring to go further, he adds, "What is it like to know you are dying? Are you afraid?"

"Well, I'm not as afraid as I thought I would be, but it is a bit unnerving just waiting and not knowing when death will come," Chad replies.

"I'm going to miss you, Uncle Chad," Dirk acknowledges. "You have been an amazing inspiration to me all my life. I'm so lucky to have had you as my role model."

## AIDS Support Group

Nikolas confides to members of his AIDS support group that he is afraid of dying. "My worst fantasy is being alone, in pain, and losing control," he explains.

"I felt afraid too," acknowledges Milos, "until I was at my partner's bedside. I sat with him, held his hand, moisturized his lips with lip balm and told him it was okay to leave. It all felt very natural."

Lily describes the changes in her brother's breathing and the way he could smile and squeeze her hand, even when she thought he was unconscious. "He seemed to know when I was there. Even the hospice nurses could see it."

"I'm so relieved that we are talking about this," says Nikolas, his eyes welling up with tears. "I have never spoken to anyone about death before. I have no idea of what to expect. I hope I don't have to die alone."

The eight members of the group pledge their willingness to be "on call" and available for one another, no matter what, to be sure that no one is alone at the end. The following week, the group leader loans Nikolas the book *A Gentle Death*. When he returns it to her, Nikolas has tied a gold bow around the book. "I never knew that anybody could talk about death so beautifully," Nikolas reflects. "I'm not as afraid anymore. I think it will be OK."

Talking about dying isn't most people's idea of acceptable social conversation. Yet talking openly about death can be a relief to you, your loved one, as well as your family and friends. The discussion can provide opportunities to say what needs to be said now and prepare you for saying your final goodbye.

## How to Talk to the Dying

- Be honest and gentle.
- Find out how much the dying person knows and how much she wants to know.
- Be curious about what she thinks will happen next.
- Reassure her that she has your support.

## Phrases You Might Use

- What do you think lies ahead?
- What are your spiritual beliefs about end of life?
- What are your fears?
- What do you believe happens after death?

## KEEPING HOPE ALIVE

As your dear one approaches the end of her life, you reassure her that acknowledging death does not mean you have given up hope. Maintaining realistic hope, however, does mean that what you wish for changes over time.

## If We Could Go to Rome

Betsy confides to Fredda that she is having a hard time believing that her sister, Heather, is dying. Although the chemo is no longer working, hospice has been in place for weeks, and Heather is deteriorating rapidly, Betsy continues to talk about their plans to visit Rome. On one of her home visits, Fredda finds the two women sitting amidst maps and tour books, as Betsy talks about all the wonderful places they will see—the Vatican, the Trevi Fountain, and the Colosseum.

"Now, don't you worry," Betsy promises Heather, "You'll be much better soon, and we'll be taking our trip by summer."

Heather looks at her twin sister in disbelief. The reality of how she feels is not consistent with the scenario Betsy describes. Noting the frustration in both of them, Fredda talks to Betsy alone.

Fredda suggests a shift in the way Betsy speaks to her dying sister, "Why not say, *'If* we could go to Rome' instead of *'when?'* " Initially, Betsy reacts with outrage and tears and, at last, a nod of understanding. Yes, they will hold on to hopes and dreams, and they will talk in realistic terms. Over the next few days Betsy's anxiety level decreases and she becomes less frantic in her conversation. Heather becomes less agitated too. She is soothed by Betsy's calmer presence and the twins laugh and giggle as they imagine their escapades *if* they could travel to romantic Rome.

## Dreams of the Future

Torrey is treated for a malignant melanoma on her back and is told by the doctor, "We got it all." After 16 years of good health, follow-up tests reveal that Torry's melanoma has metastasized to her liver. The prognosis is not good. When her daughter, Cassidy, moves up her wedding date, Torrey is elated and fully partakes in the celebration.

Three weeks later, Torrey's condition dramatically worsens and she is admitted to the hospital. Cassidy is constantly at her mother's side. Wanting to talk to Torrey about death, Cassidy finds the right moment to ask, "Mom, what do you think lies ahead?"

"I think I'm going to go right on living," Torrey replies earnestly. This response shocks Cassidy. Nonetheless, they spend hours talking, as they always have, and speculating about the future. Torrey imagines a life filled with grandchildren. "Wouldn't that be beautiful?" she says longingly.

"I hope I have a daughter and that I can be as wonderful a mother as you have been, Mom," Cassidy says wanting to let her mother know how much she adores her. Torrey dies early the next morning.

Two years after Torrey's death, Cassidy gives birth to a baby girl and proudly names her Torrey to honor her valiant mother.

## What Can We Hope For?

Dr. Morris holds Pei Pei's hand as he breaks the news to the couple, "These are not the results we were hoping for. Your latest CT scan shows that the chemo is no longer working, Pei Pei. The cancer has spread."

Fighting back his tears, Cleavon, Pei Pei's husband, clears his throat and asks, "Are you saying there is nothing more you can do?"

When Dr. Morris confirms that they have run out of treatment options, Pei Pei protests, "I've tried to keep a positive attitude. I've done everything you suggested. What's next? No more cures? No more treatments? What can we hope for now?"

"I will continue to be your doctor and manage your pain," reassures her physician displaying genuine compassion. "Now that you won't be experiencing side effects from the chemo, you'll be a lot more comfortable. And as your death approaches, we'll deal with symptoms as they arise. In the meantime, I suggest that you continue with your yoga classes and stay active. Live your life as fully as you can."

Cleavon suggests, "Maybe this would be a good time for your cousins to come in to town for a visit. Or if you want, I can take a few days off from work and we'll drive up the coast, just the two of us."

"I don't know what I want right now," Pei Pei responds. "Just promise me I won't be alone at the end."

"I'll be there. I promise," pledges Cleavon, "and for now, I agree with Dr. Morris, let's focus on making every precious moment count."

### Church in the Forest

After four and a half months in hospice, Kevin, now blind from complications of diabetes, remains a spiritual man who finds meditation and prayer of great value. At the same time, he often feels agitated and anxious about his pending death.

Kevin tells the hospice social worker about his dream. In the dream, he walks along a path in a forest feeling peaceful and at ease and enjoying the beauty of nature. When he crosses a stream, he comes upon a church and upon entering finds that the pastor is a squirrel and the congregants are all animals. At the end of his sermon, the pastor presents Kevin with a walnut. When he cracks it open, Kevin discovers a beautiful tiger's eye stone inside and immediately senses the energy of this stone moving through him like a healing light.

Kevin expresses his desire to own one of these stones. The next week when the social worker comes to visit, she finds that Kevin's friend has brought him a tiger's eye which he keeps close by, on his bedside table. "Whenever I feel anxious, I reach for it," Kevin confides. "Holding the stone makes me feel that I will die in peace."

> Talking about the end of life with your loved one does not mean that you have given up hope. Hope is not only about defying death. Whereas in the past you might have hoped for a cure, you may now change what you hope for—that her death will be pain-free, that she will be surrounded by loving ones, that there will be opportunities to say goodbye and complete unfinished business.

### How to Talk About Hope

- Create a wish list with your dear one about unfulfilled dreams.
- Explore ways to make her dreams come true in the time remaining.
- Avoid pessimistic statements that imply you have lost all hope.
- Tap into resources that have helped in previous stressful times.
- Maintain a balance between realistic expectations and hope.

## TALKING ABOUT GRIEF

After your beloved dies, it is natural to want to talk about her death. Rather than keep your feelings to yourself, seek the companionship of others who will be empathetic and willing to listen.

### What Is It Like?

"It was an incredible series of coincidences," relays Tava, describing her father's death to her friend Darolyn. "We were all there keeping vigil around his bed and we began to sing. For hours Dad had been completely unresponsive and then suddenly at the sound of our voices he sat up, looked around the room, waved his hand and said, 'Goodbye everyone.' He never regained consciousness and died within two hours. It was like a movie."

Tava gives an ironic smile as she recalls how just that morning her daughter Chaya, who was away in college, had called to say that she had a 3-day weekend with nothing planned. The minute her grandfather died, Chaya immediately booked her ticket and was on the next flight back to Los Angeles.

The attentive look on Darolyn's face encourages Tava to continue. "We were in a dilemma about attending a flute recital that my youngest daughter, Shoshana, was scheduled to perform that evening. But, knowing how Dad appreciated good music, we decided to continue with our plans. As Shoshana hit the highest notes, I turned to my family and said 'On those notes, Dad's soul is rising up to heaven.' We applauded loudly and let the tears flow freely. It was a perfect tribute."

"What's it like, now?" Darolyn inquires. "You have such great memories."

"Now that time has passed and everyone has gone back to their everyday lives, I'm just sad," says Tava. "It really feels good to talk about Dad's death. It helps relieve some of the ache. Thanks."

## You Have No Idea

"People tell me that they know what I'm going through, but they have no idea," Babs tells her friend Evelyn. "No one can ever know how close Sean and I were. Life is hell without him."

"When you talk about Sean's death, you look like you are in physical pain," observes Evelyn.

Nodding in assent, Babs describes, "The only analogy I can think of is that it's like I've had open-heart surgery, but no one remembered to invite the anesthesiologist. And I feel so angry. How could this happen to us when Sean was so young?"

When Evelyn inquires if being angry does any good, Babs replies, "Well, it certainly feels good to get it out. Without someone to talk to, I think I'd go crazy."

"Well, I'm here," Evelyn offers. "I don't know what to say to make things better, but I'm here."

## Grief Blog

Antonio's death has shattered his twin sister, Tonita. For 25 years, the twins were inseparable, and Tonita feels that she has lost her best friend and confidant. She is reluctant to display her grief in front of her parents, fearing that it will only increase their sorrow.

While searching for grief sites on the Internet, Tonita discovers numerous blogs memorializing people who have died. Inspired by these tributes, she creates her own blog *In Memory of Antonio*. Tonita designs a scrapbook page featuring visuals of her brother's favorite things: fudge walnut brownies, his motorcycle, and his German shepherd, Galileo. She adds a photo of the two of them together with Antonio's arm placed protectively around Tonita's shoulders. Beneath the picture, she writes a letter to Antonio expressing how much she misses him.

Visitors to the web page offer their condolences and embellish the blog with their own reminiscences of how Antonio touched their lives. A virtual dialogue develops between Tonita and Antonio's friends that comforts her in her grief.

## Group Support

"I have nightmares all the time. I keep reliving my wife's last moments in the hospital," explains Thad to the members of his OUR HOUSE Grief Support Group. "Other times, I dream that she comes back and is right here with me telling me that she didn't die after all. Either way, I don't sleep much."

"And everyone expects me to be back to my old self," shares Maya. "How do you explain to others what it feels like to have your whole world rocked?"

"I feel so misunderstood," Sue chimes in. "This is probably the only safe place I have to really say how I am feeling without the fear of being rejected."

In the heartfelt conversations that follow, the group members share their anger, frustrations, and memories. Week after week, they provide encouragement and support and affirm how grateful they are to have each other.

> You may be reluctant to express your grief to others for fear that no one will understand or want to hear about your sadness. While not everyone is open to talking about grief, others will be empathetic. A grief conversation can be healing for both of you.

### Talking About Grief

- Seek out those who are able to listen.
- Be candid about your feelings.
- Continue to talk about your grief whenever you need to.

Although conversations about end of life are not easy, ultimately you will benefit from developing an open dialogue. As you and your loved one journey toward the end of life and as you seek comfort in your grief, continue to speak about all that you are experiencing.

CHAPTER 3

---

# The "H" Word

*"Good morning, Honey. Your color looks good today."*
*"Yeah, mortician green."*

Norine and Harold

You have been told that your loved one has 6 months or less to live. Aggressive measures to prolong his life are no longer considered beneficial. Now what will you do? How you will spend this last precious time together? How will you help him live as fully and comfortably as possible?

Hospice care is designed to alleviate your dear one's suffering, manage his pain, and enhance the quality of his life. By choosing hospice, the emphasis will be on your loved one's comfort and dignity, not on treating his disease. What a relief it will be to have the medical team come to you. You will no longer make exhausting trips to the emergency room (ER), have him hooked up to medical equipment, and endure endless diagnostic tests. By opting for hospice care, you choose serenity over frenzy.

Hospice care can be provided in various settings, depending on what is right for you and your dear one. Home hospice allows him to remain in his familiar surroundings and be included in the day-to-day activities of the household as well as family gatherings and celebrations. The hospice service will provide the necessary equipment he needs for his daily comfort and care.

On the other hand, if being at home is not the right choice for your situation, hospice care can also be provided in free-standing hospice centers, hospitals, nursing homes, and other long-term care facilities. Regardless of location, hospice means that full attention can be turned toward caring for your loved one in a peaceful, nurturing environment.

# HAROLD

We are at the hospital where Harold, my 84-year-old husband, has been admitted. Over the course of 15 years, he has had coronary artery disease necessitating open-heart surgery, narrowing of the aortic heart valve, and congestive heart failure. Now he has pneumonia.

As one of the doctors is discussing Harold's condition with me, he slips in the word "hospice." When I hear that word I feel light-headed and cold. My heart pounds so loud that I am sure others can hear it, and I can't catch my breath. Even though I don't know what hospice means, I visualize emaciated AIDS patients attached to IVs lying in crowded facilities. What does this have to do with Harold? Maybe I heard wrong?

Hospice is mentioned again. I glance at Harold. He is hooked up to an oxygen tube, a catheter, and wired to electrocardiogram (EKG) and blood pressure machines. Yes, he looks helpless and wan, but I balk at the possibility that my lifetime companion of almost 55 years won't recover and return home well enough to resume our previous rich life together.

There *will* be more movie-going. There *will* be more trying new restaurants with friends. There *will* be more fun-filled family celebrations. There *will* be more laughing at in-jokes known only to the two of us.

Harold has been admitted into the ER three times in less than a month. We are both fed up with the routine that seems to lead nowhere except readmittance. He certainly doesn't feel any better. Each time different doctors ask the same questions. They poke and probe and order the same blood work, EKGs, and X-rays. One time he stays overnight. Another time they send him home after several hours. This last time he is admitted into the hospital's Cardiac Care Unit where he has been for almost 2 weeks while the doctors try to control what has been finally identified as a staph-based pneumonia. By now neither Harold nor I want any more hospitalizations. Reluctantly, we ask for a hospice representative to visit us in Harold's hospital room to explain what hospice means.

Despite his weakened condition, and as difficult as it might be for him to hear it, I want Harold to listen to the information and participate in any decisions we make. This is the most crucial turning point for our family, and all immediate family members need to be included. My two adult daughters and my daughter-in-law join us for a discussion with the hospice representative. My son in New York listens via cell phone, held up in front of Rachel, an upbeat nurse, who enlightens us.

She says, "The first criterion for entering the hospice program is that the patient has a terminal condition. Hospice care preserves the patient's dignity and offers comfort to him and the family during his final days." The words "final days" make me sick to my stomach.

Here's what else she tells us:

- Hospice occurs when a patient has less than 6 months to live.
- Medicare generally picks up the tab for hospice, but patients must forego curative and aggressive treatments.
- If the patient and family are dissatisfied with hospice, they can withdraw from the program.
- If a patient improves, he can leave the program.
- Hospice care can take place in different settings: in a hospital equipped with a special hospice unit, in a long-term care facility, in an independently owned hospice, or at home, the most common site.

I had assumed that Harold would be going to a special part of the hospital or to a long-term care facility. I am relieved to know that hospice care can occur at home, so choosing a location is easy. The only place for Harold to spend his last days is in our modest home that we built together over 50 years ago. Of course, I have no clue what home hospice means, yet I know that home is where he belongs and that it is what he deserves as a loving devoted husband and father. Home is a unanimous decision, and Harold looks happy.

When word gets out that we are bringing Harold home, Linda, a concerned niece, phones and asks me, "Are you sure you can handle all this?"

I hesitate. "I think so," trying to be optimistic, but my mind races at the thought of unknown possibilities.

On Valentine's Day, 2006, Harold comes home. The hospice arranges for a private ambulance, and they wheel him in on a gurney. They place him on an electric hospital bed that has been delivered hours before by a medical supply truck that delivers other equipment as well:

- A commode
- A wheelchair
- An electric oxygen concentrator
- A large backup oxygen tank in case of a power failure
- Five small portable oxygen tanks in case we leave the house

A bright red sign posted outside the front door warns visitors not to smoke because oxygen is in use and alerts the fire department that in case of a nearby fire, they need to evacuate him. I shudder: What have I taken on here? As excited as I am to have Harold back at home with me, seeing all that equipment and that scary sign is surreal. The responsibility is enormous, but there is no turning back. I can't return Harold to the hospital like a wrong-fitting garment. He is home. It is a done deal.

Harold looks so gray and vulnerable lying in his hospital bed. Can this be the same handsome six-foot energetic man I fell in love with in 1950? Yet despite his fragile exterior, his green eyes still look at me with the same intense love as always, and that look still warms me. We are about to take the greatest test of our love for one another.

Harold is so thrilled to be home, he keeps kissing my hand. Nonetheless, he is disoriented because the hospital bed and other equipment takes up so much space that we have to place it in a different part of the house rather than in the bedroom. I too am elated to have him home after 2 weeks of running back and forth to the hospital to visit him. At last I no longer need to experience growing panic as I approach his hospital room several times a day never knowing what I'll find.

There are so many positive aspects to his being home in hospice. We no longer have to travel to the medical center for services. What a relief! Because Harold has become frail, I can no longer drop him off and meet him in a particular location. I have to assist him in and out of the car and then escort him to the doctor's office. Hospice relieves me of those responsibilities. They not only provide all the equipment he needs but also bring all services to us at home:

- A doctor, nurse, and social worker make routine visits.
- Through weekly visits the nurse monitors small problems, relays the information to the doctor, who prescribes medications to reduce sleeplessness, ease agitation, increase appetite, and alleviate pain.
- If lab work needs to be done, the phlebotomist makes house calls.
- They can provide a volunteer to relieve me of duty for an hour or two a week.
- If physical therapy is needed, they will supply a physical therapist for a limited number of home sessions.
- They can supply an aide to give baths and change clothing and linens once or twice a week.
- If requested, a chaplain will call.
- We have 24/7 access by phone to a hospice advice nurse who answers questions, helps solve problems, and deals with concerns about Harold's change in status.
- In an emergency, we will no longer call 911. We will call the hospice number, and they will send a staff person.

Susan Romo, our appointed hospice nurse, arrives to evaluate Harold's condition and report to the hospice doctor, who will examine him on a subsequent day. She describes her role as being the eyes and ears of the doctor. What is so unexpected is how much time she spends with us. Visits to the doctor or a nurse practitioner at the medical center last only minutes; Susan is with us for hours on that initial intake. I can tell Harold feels comfortable with her. The twinkle in his eye returns, and he is flirtatious with her.

Nurse Susan puts me at ease as well, and we all have some good laughs despite the circumstances. After consulting with the doctor over the phone, she orders numerous medications that differ from his usual ones. When I look them over, I feel great trepidation, especially when I see the pill containers for hyoscyamine (to stop excess salivation that accumulates when dying), nitroglycerine (to ease severe chest pain), and morphine (to moderate severe pain and ease breathing). It is the morphine that especially scares me.

I also feel uncertain about being strong enough to take care of Harold: getting him in and out of bed, walking him to the bathroom, and changing his clothes and bedding. I hire Donna, a professional caregiver, selected from a list of agencies provided by the hospital.

Even with Donna on duty, I won't let her be in charge of the medications. I am paranoid about reading and rereading the dosages and placing the correct pills in the appropriate section of the pill box. I prepare all meals as well, because Harold is a very fussy eater and not open to trying anything new. I often tease him that despite Baskin-Robbins offering 31 ice cream flavors, he always chooses vanilla.

Harold soon becomes fairly skilled using the walker, and he can hold on to the bars in the stall shower for daily bathing. I can easily supervise that. He sits and slowly dries himself. He can put on his clothes and take care of his own toileting needs as well. I feel I no longer need a hired caregiver. No sense paying for someone to watch television with him. Besides, he doesn't enjoy having a "stranger" in his home telling him what to do. While having Donna on duty has been expensive, at first it was worth the respite it gave me at night while I regathered my forces. But, looking ahead, I need to conserve my dollars in the event that I will have to rehire someone as Harold's physical condition declines, so I let Donna go.

Many years ago when I purchased my first computer, the salesman used the term "steep learning curve" to describe the initial apprehension we feel when we begin learning a new skill. When a loved one enters hospice, there is also a steep learning curve for the family caregiver who is in charge of unfamiliar procedures. I have to become proficient in using the oxygen concentrator, correctly inserting the nose cannula (the tube leading from the oxygen source to the nose), ensuring that his medications are correct and given at the prescribed times, adjusting the bed so that he has an appropriate position, and following him in his walker to make sure his balance is stable. I am fearful and unsure of myself. If you do something wrong with a computer, it can crash but can be repaired or replaced. If I make mistakes in caring for Harold, he can terminally crash. What a terrifying assignment!

On subsequent visits, Nurse Susan updates a notebook of all of Harold's vital statistics. The notebook contains a copy of his Advance Health Care Directive that names me as his healthcare agent in case he can't make his own decisions. I sometimes use it against him in a good-natured way during the hospice year. For example, sometimes at noon or later, he would grumblingly ask, "Why do I have to get up so early for breakfast?"

I'd answer, "Because you signed a paper that said I was in charge of you!" Then we'd both kind of laugh, me more heartily than he, and he'd get out of bed protesting all the while.

The notebook also contains a signed Do Not Resuscitate document. That is pretty dramatic, and numerous times I go over it with Harold. I ask, "If you get worse, no more machines; no heroic measures, right?"

He double checks that point with me. "You agree, don't you?"

"Yes," I assure him, "That's what I would want for myself, too."

I initiate that discussion many times while he is in hospice because I want to make sure that he comprehends what is going to happen. For both of us, Do Not Resuscitate is hard to accept—like a bad dream, only we are awake.

The hospice doctor, Dr. Parmis Pouya, makes her first house call. Harold instantly warms to her, especially because she is attractive and seems so young. Once more, it is not a perfunctory visit. She spends more than an hour with us. Between Dr. Pouya and Nurse Susan, I start to relax a little. They are our team, and we will go through this crossing together. They treat Harold with honesty and dignity. When he asks Susan how he is doing after her weekly examinations, she never deceives him. She says, "Well you're in good shape for the shape that you're in."

The goal of the hospice doctor and nurse is to calm our fears and enhance our quality of life as long as it lasts. Warm and caring, they hug and kiss us like family members. These loving professionals guide us on our journey. With Pouya and Romo by my side, living so close to death for all those months is not just made acceptable, but it creates a beautiful memory for the entire family. There is elation in the satisfaction of knowing that we will escort Harold all the way to life's exit door.

## DOES HOSPICE MEAN GIVING UP HOPE?

"Oh no, you don't want your mother to go into hospice care," warns Myra's aunt. "Hospice is where they put you to sleep." This uninformed comment exasperates Myra, because she knows it is not true. Myra's mother, Olga, struggling with terminal esophageal cancer, is tired of chasing cures that exhaust her and prove to be futile. Mother and daughter agree that with hospice, Olga will be tenderly cared for and her final days will be as comfortable as possible.

Myra fixes up the sun room with a rocking chair, colorful paintings, and Olga's favorite afghan. The two women spend hours looking through old photo albums and reminiscing. Seeing her mother so compassionately cared for by the hospice team, Myra enthusiastically informs her aunt, "If I had known, I would have encouraged Mom to ask for hospice even sooner. I would recommend the hospice route for anyone with a terminal illness. I know for myself, if I came to that stage, I would insist on it."

## FREE TO DO THE MOTHERING AND THE LOVING

When Clarice's daughter, Carley, is too ill to keep her appointment with the oncologist, Clarice goes by herself. The physician calmly explains, "Now is the time for you to look into hospice care. It's important that Carley get to know these people and they get to know her. The sooner she starts, the more comfort she will receive." The meaning of the physician's words only hits Clarice when she reaches the parking lot and realizes that this time the doctor didn't offer a new medicine or new treatment. He used the word hospice. Clarice cries uncontrollably in her car.

The next day at Fredda's office, Clarice relates how she and her husband had a heart-to-heart conversation about the possibility of Carley's death and made the decision to call hospice. Clarice sighs with relief, "It will be so much easier to have the doctor and nurse come to the house."

"We can move our family sessions to your home as well," Fredda reassures Clarice.

After home hospice care begins, Clarice expresses to Fredda that she now feels more secure having the hospice team on board. "This leaves me free to do the mothering and the loving," reflects Clarice.

## SARAH HOUSE

Tucked away in Santa Barbara, California, is Sarah House, a beautiful one-story tile-roofed Spanish style home with palm trees that has become a social model for end-of-life care. Sarah House is staffed by nurses' aides who diversify their duties by cooking and cleaning, as well as by acting as primary caregivers. The staff personifies affection, love, compassion, and genuine concern.

Director Debbie McQuade caters to the special interests of the residents. One afternoon, local Hawaiian musicians perform in the spacious living room. Because Keiki is unable to leave her bed, the musicians enter her room and perform for her privately. She is thrilled and sings along with them the Hawaiian songs that she learned as a child. As she lies dying in the days that follow, the staff hears Keiki crooning the melodies.

Chester has no family and the staff knows very little about him. When McQuade unexpectedly learns from the doctor that Chester loves vanilla pudding, she immediately asks a staff member to run out and buy the ingredients. Chester is delighted that the hospice personnel cared enough to prepare his favorite dessert.

Even if the word hospice sets off alarms in your head, don't run away. Be assured that the hospice experience is intended to be positive and healing. Once your decision has been made, the sooner the care begins, the greater the benefit.

## SUGGESTIONS FOR CHOOSING HOSPICE

- Ask friends, family, doctor, hospital social worker, or discharge planner for suggestions of agencies used by others and check references.
- Include your loved one and appropriate family members and friends in the decision making whenever possible.
- Interview the hospice staff.
- Inquire about costs, insurance benefits, and services provided.

- If your loved receives hospice care at home:
  - Who is available to take a shift as a caregiver?
  - How will the family's routine be enhanced or disturbed?
  - Will you need to make physical changes in the home—install a ramp, move the bed, or install support bars?

## BENEFITS OF HOSPICE

- He will be cared for by compassionate staff, focused on comfort care and living well.
- He will receive physical, emotional, psychological, and spiritual support.
- He will not be hooked up to monitoring machines that beep and flash.
- You will have the opportunity to participate in a sacred shared experience as death is treated as a natural part of life.
- Your hospice team will be available to answer questions and teach you what to expect next.
- You will be provided with follow-up support after your dear one's death.
- If you choose to have hospice at home
  - Benefits for your loved one:
    - He will be in a familiar environment, surrounded by close family and friends.
    - He will enjoy the comforts of home—with familiar sights, sounds, and smells.
    - He will be on his own schedule and eat, sleep, watch TV, or listen to music, have visitors when he desires.
    - He will be included in family life and can still be a part of day-to-day living.
    - He will no longer have to endure the stress of traveling back and forth to the medical center.
    - He will die in the comforts of home.
  - Benefits for the family and friends:
    - You will instantly have a team to help you so that you don't feel so alone and overwhelmed.
    - You will have qualified professionals who take time to instruct you on how to competently provide care.
    - Your confidence will increase and you will become more at ease as your caregiving skills improve.

- You will no longer have to go back and forth to the medical center, which saves you time and energy.
- You will be able to hold, touch, and be close to your loved one whenever you want and not be subject to visiting hours and institutional rules.

## HOSPICE PROVIDES COMFORT AND DIGNITY IN YOUR LOVED ONE'S FINAL DAYS

Hospice is a gift to you and the one you love who is dying. Hospice helps everyone understand what to expect and sets the stage for a gentle death. Your loved one can enjoy the company of family and friends in an atmosphere that promotes physical, emotional, psychological, and spiritual comfort. He will be surrounded by the TLC (Tender Loving Care) that most would describe as the ideal condition at the end of life.

# CHAPTER 4

## Caregiver Challenges

*Doctor: Did you take those pills I gave you to improve your memory?*
*Patient: What pills?*

ahajokes.com

Enormous life changes, both positive and negative, may occur in your relationship when the person you love becomes seriously ill. Being her caregiver can be exceedingly rewarding. The intimacy and selflessness involved is one of the most precious gifts you can give to her and to yourself. Family and friends often express amazement at the great sense of satisfaction and gratification that caregiving provides. Yet with all its rewards, caretaking has its challenges.

Witnessing your dear one's physical and/or mental decline can be extremely painful as you recognize that the person you love is no longer the person she used to be. Roles and responsibilities shift, and adapting to these changes requires dedication, patience, and understanding from both of you. At times you may feel frustrated or even develop negative reactions toward your loved one as a result of all your new-found extra responsibilities. This does not mean that you love her any less but may be a sign that you need to evaluate the toll that caregiving is taking on you. You may need to incorporate a little more self-care into your routine or ask for help from your family, friends, and community.

Others may not grasp the challenges you face. Most of them don't have a clue as to the demands that have been placed upon you and the adjustments you have to adapt to on a daily basis. Sometimes just when you think you have resolved a situation, a new challenge arises. For example, you may express dissatisfaction with having a hired caregiver in your home, when just last week that was the very thing you wished for. Or maybe you experience internal conflict when you begin to feel relief at having hired someone to assist you, and then your loved one develops an aversion to that person or doesn't want to have anyone but YOU providing their care. Yet another scenario might unfold if your dear one's affinity toward a hired caregiver removes you from the primary caregiving position, and you find yourself feeling left out. Caregiving can be an emotional seesaw.

In the midst of caring for the person you love, it is important for you to take care of yourself. Self-care is sometimes the hardest caregiving of all. Perhaps you believe that your own needs should be of lowest priority, especially now. However, remember that in order to help others, you must first fill your cup; put on your own oxygen mask in flight before assisting someone else. As cancer survivor/activist Audrey Lorde states, "Self-care is not about self-indulgence, it's about self-preservation."

## CHALLENGE # 1: ADAPTING TO ROLE CHANGES

### Two Peas in a Pod

Jakob and Jordana are soul mates and seldom apart. The catering company they established together 10 years ago is enormously successful with an elite clientele. They appreciate each others' talents and easily divide up the responsibilities at home and at work. Their lives change dramatically when Jakob is diagnosed with metastatic colon cancer.

As Jakob's treatments progress, he no longer has the stamina to work the long hours required by their busy schedule, and Jordana has to take over the supervision of the kitchen, a task that traditionally belonged to her husband. One evening after Jakob uncharacteristically loses his temper in response to a mistake made by one of the servers, Jordana expresses her frustration, "You have never spoken to an employee in that manner. It's embarrassing."

"I'm sorry I got so angry over nothing," Jakob apologizes. "I feel irritable all the time lately, and I know I'm not handling my share of the workload. I hate what cancer is doing to our lives."

After a wrenching conversation about Jakob's deteriorating physical and emotional condition, the couple agrees to make some necessary adjustments. Jakob stops working and Jordana hires an assistant. Where once they were two peas in a pod, they are no longer together 24 hours a day. Jakob now sleeps in a hospital bed in the living room; decisions are no longer made mutually, and Jordana assumes the role of caretaker in addition to her responsibilities at work.

Jordana never knows what to expect when she arrives at home laden with morsels of appetizers and desserts that she has set aside from the party she catered. Sometimes Jakob is angry and jealous. At other times, he listens enthusiastically as Jordana vividly describes the details of the event.

"Our lives are so different now," comments Jordana as she snuggles next to Jakob in his hospital bed.

Wistfully Jakob adds, "I wish we could go back to the way things were. We were such a great team."

"We still are," lovingly reassures Jordana.

## Turn About Is Fair Play

Maman raises both children and grandchildren and at the same time establishes and runs a successful Persian restaurant featuring succulent dishes from her native Iran. When she reaches 92, Maman loses her sight as the result of her chronic diabetes. Her grandchildren, who adore and respect her, take over the running of the restaurant and set up a schedule so that she has full-time care. On weekends and evenings when there are no professional caregivers on duty, Maman's devoted grandchildren take turns being with her, bathing her, and changing her diapers. They perform these intimate acts with the same love that she has given them throughout their lives.

## Adapting to Role Changes

- Adapting to your new role will require flexibility and compromise.
- Make decisions together for as long as possible.
- Ask for assistance in learning new skills as you take on new responsibilities.

*Your relationship will change as you become the caregiver and she the recipient.*

---

## CHALLENGE # 2: ADJUSTING TO COGNITIVE CHANGES

### Where Is the Old You?

Ben can hardly bear to witness the changes in his beautiful wife, Dyan, a successful actress recently diagnosed with vascular dementia. The rhythm of their conversation is entirely different. Dyan doesn't get Ben's jokes anymore; she frequently smiles but laughs in the wrong places. When Ben tells her a story, Dyan is attentive, but when it is time to respond her comments aren't logical. Ben misses their political conversations, their making plans together, and their flirtatious banter. He longs for the old Dyan.

### Who Is the Widow?

Marian, a widowed octogenarian who lives in a nursing care facility, calls her daughter in a panic, "You know I haven't heard from your father recently."

Calmly Marian's daughter says, "That's because he's dead, Mother."

"How did his widow take it?" Marian asks.

"Mother, you are the widow."

"Oh," Marian comments and changes the subject.

### The Door Doctor

Seventy-year-old Sylvia refuses to go for her follow-up visit to the orthopedist who is treating her wrist fracture. "I'm NOT going to the Door Doctor," she tells her daughter, Darlene, adamantly. "I won't go to the Door Doctor."

Darlene assumes that her mother's dementia has caused her to forget the physician's real name. After much coaxing by Darlene, Sylvia reluctantly gets into the car.

At the office, the orthopedist completes a thorough exam but makes no conversation. Only when he has his hand on the doorknob to leave the room, does he turn back to Sylvia and Darlene and say, "You are doing well. Your wrist is healing nicely. I'll see you again in a month."

As Darlene helps her mother slip into her jacket she says with a smile on her face, "You were right, Ma. He is the Door Doctor. He doesn't even talk to you until he's practically out the door."

### Abuelita

Cristina happily anticipates her visit to her aged grandmother, Abuelita. When her grandmother does not show any signs of recognizing her, Cristina asks, "Don't you know who I am, Abuelita?"

Abuelita answers, "*Ay, mi hijita*, you look just like my granddaughter, Cristina."

"But, *Abuelita*, I am your granddaughter," Cristina replies as she lovingly kisses the back of her grandmother's hand.

### Throwing His Weight Around

Oskar had been a weight lifter in Austria before emigrating to the United States. He and his diminutive wife, Hedy, made a lasting impression. He, with his bull-shaped build, was as meek as a lamb. She, petite and lively, was the feisty one. All of that changes when Oskar develops early-onset Alzheimer's. Slowly, his sweetness gives way to belligerence. He becomes verbally abusive to Hedy and knocks the dishes off the table when she presents him with foods he suddenly dislikes. Despite safety locks on the door, he escapes from the house and wanders the streets of St. Louis, causing Hedy and her adult children great distress until some kind stranger calls authorities to escort him home.

The next day, the children get together and decide that Oskar needs to be placed in an Alzheimer's care facility. Even there, he is still defiant; he refuses to eat his meals unless Hedy is there to feed him; he takes off all his clothes, runs down the hall and threatens staff and other patients. Oskar's family is devastated seeing their formerly easy-going Papa behaving in such an erratic hostile manner.

### Adjusting to Cognitive Changes

- Recognize that her cognitive decline may result in unpredictable behavior.
- Be patient and understanding when what she says seems illogical.
- Be forgiving about memory loss and her repetitive conversation.

*Anticipate that your loved one may no longer be the same person she once was.*

## CHALLENGE # 3: DEALING WITH DIFFERING POINTS OF VIEW

### Keeping Ed's Secret

When Ed is diagnosed with AIDS, he keeps his illness as a secret from everyone except his sister Georgia. Ed makes Georgia promise not to tell anyone, not even their parents. Georgia believes the family has a right to know and begs Ed to tell them. When Ed refuses, Georgia is in a quandary. She loves her brother and she loves her family. Ultimately, she honors his wishes.

Georgia deals with doctors, Ed's deteriorating condition, and his inquisitive friends all on her own. Conflicted, Georgia turns to her therapist and asks, "Just because my brother is dying, do I have to let him have his way? I hate going along with his secrets. It's making me crazy."

### The Guest List

Kenneth and his wife Iryana go forward with their plans for a party to celebrate their 25th wedding anniversary even though Kenneth is enrolled in hospice. When Iryana reviews the guest list with Kenneth, he objects to a few names that have been included. Kenneth becomes hostile and threatens that if certain guests are going to be there, he isn't going to attend.

Iryana becomes furious. It makes no sense to her. She complains to her best friend, Malina, "Kenneth has turned into a rebellious old coot. I'd like to ignore what he wants. I'm tired of treating him as if he were as fragile as porcelain."

"Maybe you should make the party for immediate family only," Malina suggests. "That way you can avoid upsetting Kenneth and it will be easier on you in the long run."

"I know you're right," Iryana agrees with mixed feelings. "I want Kenneth's final days to be as happy as possible. And besides, I don't want to feel guilty later."

## Please Understand Me

When Marla is diagnosed with breast cancer, her daughter, Willow, assumes that she will follow the doctor's recommendation to have a mastectomy followed by chemotherapy treatments. But Marla refuses. Having come of age in the 1970s, Marla has lived her life as a free thinker. She is against the drastic surgery and injecting toxic chemicals into her body. Marla opts for alternative treatments and remains healthy for the next 7 years.

When her cancer advances, Marla invites Willow to come to Santa Fe for an extended visit. Willow arranges for a 1-month leave of absence from work and flies in to town to care for her mother. Grateful for her daughter's support, Marla's energy level gradually returns. The day before Willow is to go back home, Marla announces that she has read on the internet about a revolutionary new cure available in Germany, has booked her flight, and intends to leave the following week.

Outraged, Willow demands, "You are planning to travel half way around the world to get an unproven treatment from some quack? Mom, I've struggled with your alternative lifestyle decisions.throughout my life, but this is the last straw. How can I watch you pursue some outlandish scheme that will cost a fortune and do no good?"

"My darling daughter," implores Marla, "I know you don't agree with me, but I must pursue every possibility. Please understand me."

## Dealing With Differing Points of View

- Take time to listen to what your loved one has to say before overreacting.

- Determine whether or not the issue is worth fighting about.
- Find a confidant to help you cope with your dilemmas.

*Try to understand your loved one's point of view when conflicts arise.*

---

## CHALLENGE # 4: COPING WITH GUILT

### I'm So Sorry!

Orson, who has esophageal cancer and emphysema, has become so irritable that he gives his wife, Taryn, a difficult time when she tries to bathe him and change his linens. "What's the point?" he asks. "I'm going to die anyway," he goads her.

Orson has been repeating these statements for days and this morning, a worn-out Taryn explodes in reaction to his self-pity. "We're all going to die. I'm just trying to make you more comfortable. If you want, you can just die in your dirty pajamas and unmade bed." Taryn stalks out of the room.

An hour later as she hears Orson coughing uncontrollably, Taryn's guilt makes her sick to her stomach. She rushes into his room and when his coughing subsides, apologizes, "I'm sorry I overreacted. You are the person I love most in this world. I should treat you with more tenderness," she reproaches herself. "I know that if the circumstances were reversed, no matter how demanding I would be, you would never be so impatient."

### There Is No Tomorrow

Bertrand, a retired policeman, moves to Quebec to live with his son, Henri, and his daughter-in-law, Aurore, when he can no longer live independently because of his Parkinson's disease. When Henri comes home from work each evening, he pours himself a glass of Cabernet and sits with his father talking about the latest world news. Lately, Henri notices that Bertrand has difficulty swallowing and requires assistance from Aurore at mealtime.

One night, Henri tells his father, "Pappi, the company is sending me to France for two weeks. Aurore will take good care of you, and I'll call you every night to see how you are."

Henri keeps his word and calls home each evening. Eleven days into his trip, Henri is surprised when Aurore answers the phone and advises him that Bertrand is having increased difficulty speaking and swallowing. "Even liquids catch in his throat. Maybe you should come home early," suggests Aurore. "I think Pappi needs you."

Knowing that the business deal is almost settled, Henri replies, "I'll be in France just a few more days. Tell Pappi I'll call him tomorrow."

By the time Henri arrives home Pappi has slipped into a coma. Heartbroken, Henri laments, "Aurore, you were right. I should have come home sooner. I thought we had more time."

## In Sickness and in Health

Doug and Diana meet on a singles chat line and discover that they are kindred spirits. Before they marry, Diana reveals to Doug that she has a variety of serious medical problems. The couple savors every moment of their marriage, realizing that due to Diana's poor health, their relationship is on borrowed time. After 4 years, Diana's condition takes a dramatic turn for the worse.

Although Doug believes that his highest calling is to be of service to his wife, he is overwhelmed working all day and caring for his wife at night. As Diana's medication costs escalate, Doug is depleted financially as well as physically. When Diana's sister offers to have Diana live with her and take over all the caregiving, Doug confesses, "Diana, I love you dearly, but I can't do this anymore. Your needs are too much for me to handle."

Reluctant to leave her beloved husband, Diana moves to Texas where her sister takes over her care. Doug is tormented with guilt. In their phone conversations, Doug detects resentment in Diana's voice, and he feels that he has not fulfilled his promise to care for his wife in sickness and in health.

## Coping With Guilt

- Recognize that it is natural to find something you wish you could have said or done differently.
- Be realistic in assessing your physical, financial, and emotional limitations.
- Imagine giving advice to a friend who is a caretaker—would you judge them as harshly as you judge yourself?

*Be gentle with yourself. You are doing the best you can under very difficult circumstances.*

## CHALLENGE # 5: HIRING A PROFESSIONAL CAREGIVER

### Having Someone There

Maureen is a single mom whose only child, Ian, has been diagnosed with muscular dystrophy. When he approaches his teenage years, Ian requires increased physical assistance as his muscles weaken, and he has difficulty getting up from a lying or sitting position. Fortunately, Maureen is a physical therapist, and she can attend to many of Ian's needs. But as he loses mobility, he requires more care. Maureen begins having frequent headaches and lower back pain. Her usually good nature begins to take on an edge as Ian's condition worsens and her exhaustion grows. She has trouble falling asleep and frequently awakens during the night feeling frightened and alone.

After several emotional outbursts followed by hours of uncontrollable crying, Maureen decides that she has no choice but to hire a caregiver to relieve some of her stress. Initially, Maureen is overcome with guilt, believing that she should be able to competently care for her son by herself. It doesn't take her long to recognize the benefits of having a caregiver take over some of the responsibilities. Maureen now sleeps through the night and her disposition improves.

### I Wasn't There

Beverly is terminally ill with pancreatic cancer. Her partner, Yoko, decides to sleep in the den because Beverly's restlessness keeps her awake. Hearing Beverly call her name early one morning, Yoko goes into the room and finds Beverly on the floor. Beverly has slipped and fallen while trying to get out of bed by herself. Although she is not seriously hurt, the look of helplessness in her eyes breaks Yoko's heart. Yoko feels guilty for not staying in the same room with Beverly and ensuring her safety. The next day the two women have a frank discussion and decide to hire a nighttime caregiver.

When Beverly's mom, Reiki, learns about her daughter's fall, the tone of Reiki's voice reveals her disapproval of Yoko's caregiving skills. "If you had been in the room, this never would have happened," Reiki admonishes. "I want Yoko to come and live with me where she can be properly taken care of."

Yoko feels remorseful and confused about what to do. But Beverly makes the decision for them. "There's no way I could be at my mom's house," she reassures Yoko. With the help of a hired caregiver, Yoko continues to care for Beverly at home until her death.

### Family Decision

Jamal insists that he wants no one except family in the house caring for his wife, Ashifa, whose stroke has left her paralyzed on the left side. Pleased to be useful, Ashifa's sister, Fahdi, creates a schedule of 4-hour shifts, so that Ashifa is never alone. For three and a half months Ashifa receives tender loving care from generous relatives. Although he is grateful for the family's support, Jamal becomes irritated at the constant comings and goings every few hours. Fahdi is exhausted from running back and forth from work, to her own home, and arriving just in time to prepare Ashifa for the night.

Through her weekly home visits with Ashifa, Fredda gets to know the extended family as well. Jamal takes Fredda up on her offer to conduct a family meeting, which is held on a Sunday afternoon in Ashifa and Jamal's living room. Fredda encourages each family member to talk about the joys and frustrations of caregiving. Fahdi confesses that she fears that she has taken on more than she can handle; Jamal expresses his great love for his wife and his concerns that her care is wearing down the family. At last, there is a consensus that Jamal will hire caregivers. With the support of the hired caregivers the family relaxes and enjoys their remaining time with Ashifa.

**When you hire a caregiver:**
- Check references.
- Discuss your particular needs and expectations.
- Help the caregiver understand who your loved one is outside of her illness, as well as her likes and dislikes.
- Consider finding a new caregiver if you observe improper behavior or she is not a good match for your household.

*Most care providers are kind, compassionate, caring individuals who are there to complement your caregiving.*

## CHALLENGE # 6: RESPONDING TO INSENSITIVE HEALTHCARE PROFESSIONALS

Healthcare professionals may disappoint you when you look to them for reassurance and guidance. When they say something insensitive, you get angry. When they placate you, you lose faith. While you may be intimidated by the status of doctors and other professionals, remember that you have the right to ask for a clear understanding of your loved one's condition.

### Preserving Dignity
When the physician finds remnants of fallen-out hair on the dressing gown of his terminally ill post-chemo patient, he brushes off the strands

and says, "Well, you won't be needing this anymore." The woman and her visitor are bowled over by the doctor's thoughtlessness. The visitor follows the doctor out the door and dresses him down for his unfeeling hurtful remark to her dying friend.

Suggested response: *We're trying to let her know that she is still beautiful. Please don't say anything to damage her self-esteem.*

### Glucose Level

Ginny's mom, Peggy, is in the hospital with a variety of problems including heart disease, kidney failure, and diabetes. The doctor who is new to her case wants to discharge Peggy, but Ginny, who has been caring for her mom for decades, asks what Mom's glucose level is. When the doctor tells Ginny, she balks. She knows that number is too high for Mom to be released.

The doctor replies, "That's the problem with giving the family information. All of a sudden, they're the doctor."

Suggested response: *I am not trying to be the doctor. However I am safeguarding my mother's welfare. I know from experience that when her glucose is this elevated, my mother always ends up right back in the hospital. Is there anything further you can do?*

### Addiction Question

When the excruciating pain from her advanced cancer brings Cara to tears, her distraught sister pleads for more medication. The nurse answers, "Do you want your sister to become addicted?"

Suggested response: *I want my sister to be free of pain. In these final months of her life, I'm not worried about her becoming addicted to prescription medication.*

### Unnecessary Tests

When the doctor recommends an additional CT scan for terminally ill 89-year-old Melissa, her perplexed husband refuses to give consent.

Suggested response: *Quality of life is more important to us than additional test results. I don't see any point in putting Melissa through any unnecessary discomfort.*

### Death Rattle

The doctor announces to the parents, in front of their comatose terminally ill son, "I think I can hear the death rattle now." The dismayed mother wonders if doctors read their own literature about unconscious patients being able to hear.

Suggested response: *Please don't speak as if my son isn't in the room. I have heard that patients can hear even when they are unconscious.*

## Impatient Patient

The Marconi family registers a complaint with the charge nurse after their mother tells them that the nurse's aide responded to her call bell with the comment, "Oh, it's you again. Don't you know you're not the only patient I have to care for?"

Suggested response: *I know how demanding my mother can be, however, she is a sick elderly woman, so please ask your staff to treat her with respect and not scold her.*

## Missing the Point

Tears well up in Seymour's eyes as he complains to the doctor that his wife's brain cancer has greatly diminished her ability to carry on a lucid conversation. The doctor replies: "Well that is normal. Be glad that she is not in pain."

Suggested response: *Doctor, you are missing the point. This may be normal but I can't be happy watching my beloved deteriorate before my eyes.*

## Misleading Response

Sven is in a weakened condition after battling cancer for over 2 years. His wife, Tesuka, pushes him into the physician's office in his wheelchair. Sven is wasting away. Tesuka is hoping for validation from the physician when she asks, "What can we expect now?" To Tesuka's surprise, the doctor turns to her husband and says, "Everything's going to be fine, Sven. You'll be up and around in no time and enjoying life with your grandson." Tesuka's face turns ashen. Does this doctor not see the changes that she observes? Has she gone crazy?

Suggested response: *Sven and I know that he is dying. Why won't you talk about it with us?*

## Liver Transplant

In the hospital room, Kobe's doctor reassures Kobe and his wife, Magdalena, "You're a perfect candidate for a liver transplant. You're going to be fine."

When they step outside the door into the hallway, Magdalena asks the physician, "Is there even one-tenth of one percent chance that he will survive the transplant?"

Solemnly the doctor responds, "No, there isn't."

Suggested response: *If there is no chance of survival, why aren't you telling Kobe the truth?*

---

## CHALLENGE # 7: FOCUSING ON SELF-CARE: THE ULTIMATE CHALLENGE

### Respite Care for Norine

After a while I become resentful of the physical and emotional daily demands of caring for Harold. Hospice entitles me to respite care, but in order to take advantage of this opportunity, Harold would have to be moved to a local convalescent home. I am well aware that moving him to a facility where he would be in unfamiliar surroundings with unknown staff and chronically ill patients might darken his up-to-now sunny disposition. I am certain Harold would become fearful, and I foresee a setback in his condition if I were to change his environment.

Our daughter, Andrea, comes up with an alternative. Although she lives in another state and has a husband and teenage children to care for, Andrea offers to stay with Harold for two nights. Harold is excited to see her and to his delight, she fusses over him. Meanwhile, I book an appointment for a massage and check into a nearby luxury hotel, where I indulge in complete relaxation and pampering including room service for supper. I call Andrea to see how Harold is doing and learn that father and daughter are going out to dinner at his favorite Italian restaurant.

The next day, I have a lovely uninterrupted breakfast in the hotel, go shopping, and at lunchtime meet with a close friend. It has been a rejuvenating 36 hours, and I am ready to return to the routine. Meanwhile, Harold has relished the private time with his daughter and the refreshing of their relationship.

### Caring for His Own Health

Luis has been so absorbed with caring for his wife Marisol, who has multiple sclerosis, that he has not paid attention to his own health. He has overlooked the toll it takes to install a hoist in the bedroom, carry equipment to and from the car, help Marisol transfer from car to wheelchair to bed, monitor her medications and nutrition, and even assist her with catheterization.

One day while driving home from a wedding, Luis overreacts to a car that cuts in front of him and only then does he realize how much rage he has inside. He becomes exceedingly tense and short of breath and later makes an appointment with his doctor. After extensive tests, Luis' physician advises him that he will have to be admitted to the hospital for an angioplasty. But Luis insists: "There's no way I can be hospitalized. I need to be with Marisol." Only after the doctor explains that Luis' life is in danger if he does not have the procedure, does Luis understand how his all-encompassing focus on his wife's care has eclipsed his recognition of his own health needs.

When his circle of friends offers to assist him in caring for Marisol during his hospitalization, Luis gratefully accepts. He also takes his friends up on their offer to help him make changes in his home. They widen doorways, build ramps, and install a wheelchair accessible sink and shower making the daily tasks of caring for Marisol easier.

Luis expresses his appreciation to his friends, "I am so lucky for your support. You've helped me so much. If it weren't for you, I'd be sick in bed too."

### Taking the Afternoon Off

Jessica is the primary caretaker for her husband, Adam, who has been living with lung cancer for the last 14 months. Each day, Jessica drops her children off at school, runs the necessary errands, and arrives back home in time to assist Adam with his bathing and dressing and monitor his pain medication. The children have learned to turn to Mom for help with their homework; they have become accustomed to the fact that Dad can no longer be counted on to attend their sports events or take them on weekend excursions.

Lately, Jessica finds herself irritable and quicker to explode. She notices that she has gained weight and wonders what happened to her old exercise routine. She no longer seems to have time to talk on the phone, and consequently, her friends have stopped calling or inviting her to attend social functions. Without realizing it, Jessica has become isolated.

Adam recognizes that Jessica's life has become all work and no play. She has even declined an invitation to attend a baby shower at a neighbor's house. On the day of the shower, Adam urges Jessica, "Why not take the afternoon off, go to the party and enjoy yourself? The kids will be home and we can call you if we need you."

The 2 hours at the baby shower do Jessica a world of good. She laughs and feels like her old self, enjoying the companionship of her friends. A new acquaintance recommends a caregivers support group that meets weekly at Wilshire Hospital. Jessica returns home renewed, refreshed, and announces to Adam, "You were so right. I had a great time with the girls. I think it's good for me to get out once in a while."

## Focus on Self-Care

- Attend to your physical health.
- Care for your emotional, psychological, and spiritual well-being.
- Allow others to share in caregiving responsibilities.
- Set aside time for yourself on a regular basis.
- Consider joining a support group.

*Self-care will refresh and revitalize you.*

## Recognize Signs of Stress and Compassion Fatigue

- Loss of energy
- Lack of motivation
- A sense of worthlessness
- Loss of interest in doing things and going places
- Unintentional weight gain or loss
- Sleeplessness or over sleeping
- Emotional outbursts and unexpected crying

*Remember, compassion fatigue affects the strong and healthy not just the weak and fragile.*

## Put Yourself First

- Pay attention to your physical, psychological, emotional, and spiritual well-being.
- Get routine checkups from your doctor, dentist, and other health-care providers.
- Take care of your physical appearance—get a haircut, buy something nice to wear.
- Join a support group.
- Laugh and have some fun.
- Seek counseling through your church, temple, or community mental health center.
- Listen to music, write, or draw.
- Scream or cry in the shower.

- Go for a walk in nature or get some exercise.
- Participate in religious or spiritual practices that sustain you.

*Attending to your own needs will make you a better caregiver.*

### Friends are Your Lifeline

- Phone a friend who will be a good listener.
- Get together with a friend for a visit.
- Invite friends and neighbors over for tea or coffee; this may give both you and your loved one a lift.
- Ask a friend to sit with you while you pay your bills, put away your groceries, do the laundry, and so on. Remember that this does not mean that you are asking them to do these tasks for you, just for their company (although people may be more than willing to feel useful and needed!)
- Have a friend take a walk with you. It is an opportunity to get fresh air and a fresh perspective.

*Ask your friends to recognize what a toll this role is taking on you and to remember to give you a little extra TLC (Tender Loving Care).*

### Ask for What You Need

- From your loved one
  - Let her know what life is like for you now; every conversation doesn't have to be about her.
  - Have some fun together: play a board game, work on a puzzle, or snuggle.
  - Let her know when you need a short break, and tell her when she can expect you to return.
- From trusted family and friends
  - Ask someone to stay with your loved one for a while so that you can run an errand or take in a movie.
  - See if a neighbor will come over and play cards, read, or listen to music with her. Arrange for someone to take the children out or care for them in another room while you get some alone time.
  - Let people know that you would appreciate a meal being delivered—let them create a schedule and take turns.

*Be creative in asking for what you need (assuming you know what you need).*

## Find Ways to Get Away Without Leaving Town

- Go to a movie.
- Take a walk in a park.
- Go to the beach and take off your shoes!
- Get a massage.
- Go out for a meal.
- Take a class: exercise, yoga, drumming, art, music.
- Don't rush home.

*Taking a mini-vacation can be very satisfying.*

The responsibility of caring for your loved one is all encompassing. You had no idea that being a caregiver would elicit so many reactions: exhausted; inspired; overwhelmed; grateful. You have taken on a heroic role. You are giving your loved one a priceless gift. As you face the challenges of being a caregiver, remember to take care of yourself, and don't forget that there are still opportunities to celebrate life together.

# CHAPTER 5

# Celebrating Life

*Fernando loves birthdays, especially his own.*
*Being on hospice does not damper his enthusiasm for celebrating.*
*When he tells his wife that he wants to throw himself a birthday*
*party, she queries,*
*"A birthday party? This year? What are you going to serve, nutri-*
*tional supplements?"*

Support group member

How can you celebrate life when your loved one has lost her hair, wrestles with extreme pain, and has limited mobility? Facing the end of your dear one's life doesn't mean that you must sit around waiting for death to happen. On the contrary, this is a time to take full advantage of every moment and celebrate in ways that are feasible and realistic.

Celebrations come in all sizes and shapes. Maybe you take your loved one out to a ballgame or have someone drive her through the old neighborhood. You and your loved one might linger over a cup of tea on the porch with a close friend, reminisce with pictures and stories, or you might add color and fragrance to your loved one's surroundings by giving her a small bouquet, just the right size to fit on her nightstand. She also might enjoy cuddling with the cat in her lap, listening to music, inhaling the aroma of fresh ground coffee, rejoicing to sounds of children playing outdoors or other small pleasures.

Perhaps you plan a large-scale event such as a birthday party or invite friends for a long-awaited reunion. It may bolster her spirits to gather with friends and family who will let your dear one know how important she is in their lives. Fulfilling life-long dreams, even a modified version, may become her priority. You may be surprised at what is possible. In the midst of preparing for death, seize the opportunity to make the most of each day.

## HAROLD'S BIRTHDAY

Anticipating happy occasions gives everyone a lift. That's why I want to plan a birthday party for Harold to give him extra impetus to continue living.

As soon as Harold enters home hospice, neighbors, friends, and family visit him, usually laden with food. I thank them and say that if Harold makes it to his 85th birthday on May 27, we are going to have a celebration and they will be included. I want to recognize their contribution in acknowledging his life.

Before I realize, my guest list has grown to over 100, and there is no way our home can accommodate that many people. Nearby, Glendale has a lovely park, so I book it well in advance and keep my fingers crossed that Harold will survive that long.

As we get closer to the date, I order 115 Italian sandwiches and assign side dishes to our guests. When I explain the situation to the middle-aged woman who takes my order at the Italian Deli, she glances over to a fragile Harold resting in a chair, gives me a knowing look, and says I don't have to pay in advance. I can pay when I pick up the order and even cancel as late as the night before. I am touched by her consideration.

Prior to the event, an ex-son-in-law, who has remained very bonded with Harold, calls to ask if he can hire a belly dancer for the picnic as a birthday surprise. I give him the go-ahead.

On the morning of the picnic, our daughter Andrea arrives early with our two teenaged grandsons, Zach and Avi. Harold is still in bed, and when they enter the bedroom, he bursts into tears.

He discloses, "I'm not going to be able to go through with this. I won't be able to handle it."

I promise, "If it's too much for you, I'll bring you home early." That satisfies him, and I help him dress.

I consider two different consequences of the birthday picnic and share my thoughts with the children. I tell them about my promise to Harold that if the event is too much for him, I will bring him home early. Then I confide what I perceive to be a second alternative—that he might die at the picnic from the emotional stress. I figured that if that were to happen—what a way to go! Hearing this, the children groan, "Oh, Mom." However, in my wildest dreams I never anticipated the third alternative.

Harold is the last one to arrive in the park where friends and family have festooned the area with balloons and set up a gorgeous table completely covered with side dishes of stuffed grape leaves, hummus, crudités, exotic vegetable salads, and colorful fresh fruit plates alongside platters of piled-high hero sandwiches.

Each guest greets Harold with hugs and kisses, and he becomes emotionally drained. He slumps into a chair, eyes red-rimmed from weeping, looking pitiful—more dead than alive. Then suddenly, the sound of Middle Eastern music throbs on a boom box, and over a microphone our granddaughter, Leila, announces that her father and his new wife have a special present for Papa.

All at once, a gorgeous lithe 21-year-old, clad in a scanty royal blue belly dancing costume adorned with jingling gold coins, dances across the grounds. We begin to nervously giggle. Sensuously, she makes her way over to Harold, beckoning to him with her outstretched arms and undulating hips. She dances closer, still motioning to him. Transfixed, Harold slowly rises from his chair. He begins emulating her gyrations in perfect rhythm with the music. We laugh in surprise and delight. The more he dances, the more energized he becomes.

He abandons his cane as a support and holds it high overhead, making Fred Astaire-like moves. He revels in being the center of attention, and his transformation stuns us. Before our eyes, Harold changes from a decrepit old man to a virile one. We too are transformed. As Harold dances with this nymph, the occasion shifts from a living memorial to "poor dying Harold" into hand-clapping laughter-filled revelry. The joyfulness is so raucous that neighbors look out their windows from buildings surrounding the park.

This is a consequence that I have never imagined. We are unprepared for the magic of the music and the beautiful young woman who lures Harold from his chair to participate in a life-affirming dance.

Fortunately, our other granddaughter, Isa, videotapes the event and records this wondrous scene of a triumphant dancing Harold. Literally, he is having the time of his life. On camera, Isa also captures a private exchange as Harold looks at me across the grounds and mouths, "I love you."

A week later, one of our son Mark's music colleagues views the video and after seeing Harold's restoration proclaims, "Ah, the power of music."

No way! Ah, the power of a beautiful young body magnetically pulling Harold out of his chair. This is a testimony to testosterone. There is life in the old boy yet!

That energy endures. We are the last ones to leave the park, and when we reach home, Andrea asks where we keep the plunger because there is stoppage in the guest bathroom. "Let me fix it," insists Harold and, to our amazement, he does. We conclude that perhaps the belly dancer should make weekly house calls instead of the social worker.

## DEATH ON THE DOORSTEP

Charlene and Liam excitedly mention to the doctor that Liam will be officiating at their daughter's wedding 10 months from now. The doctor slowly shakes his head "no." Both Charlene and Liam understand the implications of this nonverbal communication. The doctor does not expect Liam to live that long.

"How do I cope with the feelings of marrying our daughter and burying my husband?" Charlene reels with this dilemma, "How will I do this?"

The bride- and groom-to-be frantically contact the Irish branch of the family requesting that they make arrangements to fly in immediately. Two weeks later, the wedding takes place under the rose adorned gazebo in the bride's backyard. Liam takes his daughter's arm and proudly escorts her down the aisle. He then turns to face the bride and groom and, in his official role as Judge Liam, unites the couple in marriage.

After the ceremony, Charlene whispers to her sister, "This is amazing. Here we are celebrating life, with death on the doorstep."

## TISSUES ON THE CEILING

Seven-year-old Matthew, in the last stages of cancer, has been moved to a separate room in the family's small apartment. His parents keep water and tissues on his bed stand. Only after he dies and his body has been removed, does his mother notice that Matthew has wadded up the tissues, soaked them with water, and thrown them up above his bed so that they stick to the ceiling. Despite the cancer destroying his body, Matthew was still a playful little boy.

## MILDRED'S BATH

While Mildred is at home in the last stages of cancer, she spends her days listening to opera, occasionally eating a small amount of her favorite foods, singing, joking, and drinking brandy. One day, while waiting for the hospice aide to arrive and bathe her, Mildred looks at her daughter with a twinkle in her eye and says, "It ain't over 'til the bath lady comes."

## TAJ MAHAL

The large beautifully framed color photo shows Danny, a good-looking man in his early fifties, wearing jeans, dark shirt, and running shoes, posed on bent knee in front of the pearlescent breathtaking Taj Mahal in Agra, India. Although Danny is in fragile health with a heart condition, he has made the decision to journey to a family wedding in Asia.

En route from California, Danny and his partner, Bruce, stop for a few days in Paris. Danny frequently experiences shortness of breath, and it becomes increasingly difficult for him to climb stairs and handle his luggage. The men discuss whether or not they should return home, but Danny is determined to proceed on their exciting journey.

Once they arrive in Agra, they explore and take in all the spectacular tourist sights. Danny has a magical elephant ride, and they purchase a large woven rug for their dining room. After spending a picture-perfect day at the Taj Mahal, they board a train bound for Varanasi, the Holy City of Temples, located on the left bank of the Ganges River, where people purify themselves and scatter ashes of loved ones in the water. Danny jokes, "I want a one-way ticket to Varanasi." This statement becomes prophetic, for during their overnight train ride, he calls out to Bruce, "I can't breathe." The porter immediately summons a physician on board. By the time the doctor reaches Danny, he has stopped breathing. Moments later the doctor pronounces Danny dead.

Back at home, each time Bruce shows the photo of Danny at the Taj Mahal, he comments wistfully, "I'm so grateful that we were able to make this one last trip."

## PLENTY OF CHOCOLATE

Nina has a large circle of friends from all walks of life who adore her because she is so caring, nonjudgmental, and respectful. After being diagnosed with ovarian cancer, now advanced to Stage IV, Nina plans two Gratitude Luncheons to express her appreciation to her friends. She dictates the menu to her daughters: grapefruit salad, gazpacho, and dessert. Nina adds, "Make sure there is plenty of chocolate—at the luncheons and at the funeral."

"How lucky I am to have friends like you and I want to celebrate you," the invitation reads. Upon arriving at Nina's home, guests find candy dishes filled with chocolate and two dozen roses of myriad shapes, colors, and fragrances heaped on a table. When all guests are present, each selects a rose, reveals why she has chosen that particular color, explains how she knows Nina, and what she loves about her. The women tell funny stories about Nina that bring laughter. They tell sentimental stories that bring tears. One by one the guests place their selected roses into a large glass bowl in the center of the table until the centerpiece becomes a bouquet of living memories. The Gratitude Luncheon both gastronomically satisfies and emotionally enriches everyone.

Nina's health deteriorates rapidly after this first celebration, so much so that she cannot have the second party. After she dies, her daughters fulfill their promise to their beloved Mom. At the funeral, they set out two large crystal punch bowls of chocolate kisses and above the bowls place a calligraphy sign: "Make Sure There Is Plenty of Chocolate!"

## THE SMALL STUFF

Ava's friends greatly admire her zest for life and love of joking. Even in her final months, Ava retains her sense of humor. One morning, her husband, Mort, surprises her and with breakfast he serves a tabloid newspaper screaming, "HILLARY NAMES BIGFOOT AS HER RUNNING MATE!" They have a joyous laugh over the absurdity of the idea and delight in this moment of simple pleasure. A mere reference to the headline over the next few weeks becomes a running gag.

Ava appreciates life more than ever now, knowing her days are numbered. The beauty of a sunrise thrills her. When a neighbor visits to introduce his puppy to Ava and the little dog jumps onto her bed and can't stop licking her face, she loves it. Whether listening to her favorite Joni Mitchell recordings or laughing heartily at a classic film on television, Ava epitomizes living one day at a time with as much gusto as possible. Despite her intense pain and breathing difficulties, Ava celebrates the small stuff.

## FREEING THE ARTIST WITHIN

Seventy-year-old Dora resides in an Assisted Living Facility. Although she has end-stage renal failure, she admits to Miriam, her social worker, that she has always wanted to be an artist. Miriam asks, "Why not now?"

At their next appointment, Miriam presents Dora with sketch pads, crayons, and pencils and encourages her to start experimenting with her materials.

Dora plunges into her artwork and creates an abstract piece she calls "Perspective." The drawing reflects her deepest feelings. Dora achieves her life's dream of becoming an artist.

## THEIR FINAL ACT

For several years, Zoe and her loving husband Paul are aware of Zoe's poor prognosis due to the progression of ovarian cancer. Thus, they attempt to celebrate life as frequently as they can. They discover a clubhouse in the nearby foothills that becomes their healing center. In this rustic setting, Zoe and Paul, both award-winning actors, spend weekends with 20 or more of their friends from the theater. They walk in the woods by day and gather in the evenings to play improv games and participate in music and song.

Two months before Zoe's death, she and Paul stage a reprise of an old show highlighting their clever repartee. The chemistry between them is still evident to the full house of friends and fans. This becomes their Final Act.

## RACE FOR THE CURE

Participants attending the Susan B. Komen Race for the Cure are treated to a fashion show before the race begins. Despite her weakened condition from chemotherapy, Caridad joins other breast cancer survivors on the fashion runway. As she walks across the stage to thunderous applause, Caridad exclaims, "This is the first time I've felt pretty since I was diagnosed."

Later, during the race, Sharon Schlesinger, an affiliate volunteer proclaims, "Hundreds of participants run in pink shirts. Some are long-term survivors who provide hope to the women who are in the midst of treatment with no hair and no eyebrows, and to those who are just starting their breast cancer journey. All are proud to be alive. This is a sisterhood linked by the thread of appreciating life."

## HEALING CIRCLE

Everyone asks for Samantha to wait on them when they shop in her trendy women's boutique in Chagrin Falls. Since her cancer treatments, Samantha only works part time, but her incomparable flair for style and accessorizing remain unchanged. Even the scarves she wears to cover her bald head make a fashion statement.

When metastases are discovered throughout her body, the doctors advise hospice care. Although nothing more can be done to cure the cancer, surgery is scheduled to relieve the pain caused by a tumor pressing on a nerve in her neck.

Three days before the surgery, Fredda leads a healing circle in the cozy living room of Samantha's best friend. The glow of candles enhances the mood as Samantha snuggles into a wing-back chair and 15 guests settle in around her.

Fredda leads the participants in a guided meditation:

*Find a comfortable position and begin to focus on your breath as you prepare for a journey of healing.*

*Imagine yourself in a clearing in the forest. Take in the beauty and serenity of the environment. As you look around with your inner eyes, see Samantha standing before you. Notice what she is wearing, how she is moving, and the expression on her face.*

*Have a conversation with Samantha or find a way to communicate without words. Look deeply into each others' eyes. Are there memories you want to share? Or feelings you wish to express? Take your time.*

*Now imagine finding a healing symbol that represents the sacredness of this visit and share it with Samantha.*

After Fredda guides them out of the meditation, guests use oil pastels to draw or write a message to Samantha. The artwork reflects images and words of love, encouragement, and appreciation. Fredda assembles the pages into *Samantha's Book of Healing*.

Treasuring the book Samantha says, "I have received the gift of love that will help me heal. No matter what the outcome, my soul is full."

## BRIGHT RED NAIL POLISH

As Monsy lies on top of the log cabin quilt next to her dying friend Julianna, she senses this is likely to be her final visit. The two old friends fall silent, each soberly contemplating the future.

Monsy suddenly suggests, "Let me paint your toe nails bright red!" Julianna chuckles and tells her where she keeps her nail polish. Just as they did when they were teenagers, Monsy applies the gleaming ruby red enamel to Julianna's toes. This playful act brightens Julianna's feet, lifts the spirits of both women, and renews the gaiety they have shared through life.

## THE SERENADE

The four women are brought together by their love of folk music. When Eudora is diagnosed with breast cancer, the women spend as much time with her as possible. Throughout Eudora's 5-year struggle with the disease, she has brief respites and when she is able, she joins with her friends and their guitars to sing and play music again.

After Eudora's cancer spreads to her brain, she loses her ability to speak. One afternoon, Eudora's friends make a surprise visit to serenade her. While she sits on the living room sofa, the women begin playing and singing. The acoustics in the room make the women sound better than ever before. When they sing "Tumbalalaika," one of Eudora's favorite songs, her face lights up and her eyes radiate love and happiness. It is an exquisite moment.

A few weeks later Eudora's friends reunite at her funeral to play guitars and sing "Tumbalalaika" one last time.

## FINAL GIFTS

Ethel, whose husband Sid died 15 years ago, reclines in her bed on freshly laundered sheets with the delicate scent of lavender filling the room. At noon, her four children, their spouses, and her three granddaughters arrive to celebrate what would have been Ethel and Sid's 68th wedding anniversary. Ethel's granddaughter, Elana, concerned that Ethel might not have the stamina to get through the afternoon, asks the hospice nurse whether this is a good idea.

"I consider it essential," asserts the hospice nurse. "Ethel has a vital spirit and has been looking forward to this for days."

The family enjoys a light meal together, complete with a toast to Ethel and Sid. After dessert, Ethel announces to her kin, "I have had a wonderful life. This morning I called my friends all over the country to say goodbye, and now I would like a few minutes alone with each of you."

Ethel exchanges a private conversation with each member of the family and then lovingly presents her heirs with a memento: a piece of jewelry, a scarf, a book, a vase, a piece of artwork. One grandchild receives the painting of horses that her grandparents displayed in their den over the mantle. Another receives her grandmother's pearl earrings. Ethel gives her crystal water pitcher and eight engraved glasses to Elana. "I'll use them every Passover, Grandma," promises Elana. "You and Grandpa Sid will always be with us in spirit."

## CELEBRATING LIFE HAS THE POWER TO

- Rekindle diminishing spirits.
- Honor the life of your loved one.
- Allow your dear one to engage in living.
- Add quality and meaning to life.

*Celebrate Life in the Midst of Preparing for Death.*

As your dear one faces the end of her life, each moment is precious. Large or small, doing something special will lift her spirits and let her know how important she is. Celebrate life while your loved one can still hear your voice, see your face, and receive your hugs. Cherish these extraordinary moments before it is time to say goodbye.

# CHAPTER 6

## Preparing to Say Goodbye

*As the aroma of meatballs browning in garlic and olive oil for a*
*simmering spaghetti sauce wafts into the bedroom where Luigi*
*lay dying, the odor rallies him into consciousness. He gathers*
*all his strength, grabs his walker and pushes his way into the*
*kitchen. Luigi dips a piece of bread into the spaghetti sauce, but*
*his wife Maria hits his hand with a wooden spoon.*
*"Luigi, no! That's for after."*

Internet joke

As impossible as it is to fathom, here you are, facing life's final chapter.
How can it already be time to say goodbye to your loved one? How will
you make the most of this time? And how will you say goodbye to him in
a way that is tender, honest, and meaningful?

Saying goodbye can be one of the most precious and important parts
of your relationship as you take time to:

- Convey your deep love for him.
- Express how he has enriched your life.
- Reminisce about the joyous times you have shared.
- Let your loved one know what you will miss about him.
- Address unfinished business.
- Acknowledge the importance of his life and how he has made a
  difference.

Saying goodbye is familiar; you practice it daily: a kiss goodnight, a
"have a good day" at the end of a phone call, a farewell when you leave
someone's home or a party. Of course, at those times, you anticipate
that you will see the person again. What if this is the final goodbye?
Acknowledging that this may be the last time you will see or speak to the

person you love pays homage to the value and significance of the relationship you share.

What do you imagine you would say? You might begin with, "When I think about your dying it breaks my heart. I have so much I want to tell you," or "Every time I leave you, I worry that we may not see each other again."

Those words can be followed by a conversation that includes tributes to your dear one and to your relationship. You might even use the words that you would say at his memorial.

You may be hesitant to express your thoughts and feelings because you think that you have plenty of time and don't want to rush things. You may fear that your words will be taken the wrong way, and you don't want to upset your loved one. But if you keep waiting for the ideal circumstances, you may postpone these tender moments of goodbye until it is too late.

And, what if your dear one doesn't die after you have that meaningful conversation? Nothing will have been lost. Chances are you will not regret having a heartfelt talk. Sharing laughter, tears, and loving goodbyes will enrich the last days, weeks, or months that you have together.

## Thank You for Taking Such Good Care of Me

A few months before he dies, Harold begins saying, "I know I've said it before, and I'm sorry to repeat myself, but thank you for taking such good care of me."

I cannot respond appropriately to this. "You're welcome" seems inane.

Often he follows up with, "Are you going to miss me?" I freeze inside and all I can say is, "Sure, and I promise not to date for the first two weekends." We both laugh half-heartedly. What a pathetic answer! I can't tell him what is truly in my heart. I don't want to break down in front of him and make feel him sadder.

One week before he dies, as I am joining him in bed, Harold says, "Give me a kiss, a real kiss." I do and choke up afterward.

Five days before his death, he makes me promise to tell the children how much he loves them and how much he adores his grandchildren. I make him laugh when I ask, "Any messages for me?"

Actually, I need no reassurance. At least a dozen times a day he tells me he loves me. He regularly expresses gratitude for a wonderful life together and how much his family means to him. We have always been close but by tending to him with such vigilance during this final year, I feel we are bound together tighter than ever.

Then, 48 hours before death, he craves a pastrami sandwich on rye bread with pickles and a chocolate phosphate soda. He wants me to take him to his favorite delicatessen for what turns out to be his last supper. He rejoices in every bite.

I have fulfilled Harold's last wish and it is ironic that his last meal takes place in a crowded plate-clattering setting with impatient waitresses. Harold seems oblivious to the environment and to the sympathetic looks of other customers noting this feeble man whom I carefully steer at a snail's pace into and out of the deli. A feeling of doom overcomes me as I see us reflected in the eyes of others.

## Imagining the Future

During their married life, Nadine and Fred spend weekends going out to dinner and the theater or to see the latest foreign films. Especially as Fred becomes more fragile, Nadine often notices the large numbers of single women going out together in twos, threes, or larger groups. With resignation, she realizes that these must be widows and that someday she will probably join their sisterhood.

One evening after returning home from the theater, Nadine asks Fred, "Did you notice all the old ladies in the row in front of us? I keep thinking how one day I'll be one of them. I'm going to really miss holding hands with you."

Fred answers, "And even though I usually snore through the movies, I'm going to miss keeping you company."

Nadine recalls, "Remember the ticket taker who called us lovers? How did he know?"

With assurance Fred responds, "He could tell."

## Take Care of My Daughter

Gretchen's cancer progresses to a point when no recovery is possible, and her best friend Regan regularly visits her, despite having to travel overnight from her hometown.

On her next to last visit, the two women talk about Gretchen's fear of dying. Gretchen also describes her painful decision to not undergo another round of chemotherapy, because it has only a 30% chance of being effective. "Besides," she comments ruefully, "I can't stand the thought of having a moon face and being all swollen again. The only reason I might have considered it would be to have more time with Libby. I would give anything to see her through her teenage years. But the odds are against me." Gretchen declines further treatment.

On Regan's last visit, Gretchen is bedridden. Regan brings in a tape recorder so that Gretchen may create messages to leave for her daughter and husband. The dying woman begins, "These are my goodbye messages to the two of you, the most important people in my life. You have brought me joy and given me reason to fight to live."

Gretchen tells Libby, "I am blessed to be your mother. I'm so proud of how you have pitched in to help me. You are turning into such a fine young woman and have given me a preview of what a fine wife and mother you will become."

To her husband she says, "You are my soul mate and have been with me on every step of this torturous journey. You are the love of my life, and I dread leaving you. I'll carry your love with me. Please don't forget me."

Gretchen asks Regan to promise that she will maintain a relationship with Libby. "She'll need a strong female role model in her life to guide her." Regan pledges to look after Libby.

## Message to Classmates

Pat Dolci, who has been dodging cancer for several years, flies in from the Bay Area to attend her 50th high school reunion. Although she has been in and out of chemotherapy, Pat rallies her strength and has a wonderful time reconnecting with her old friends. Shortly afterward Pat undergoes another round of chemo, this time unsuccessfully. She sends a note to her classmates.

*Well, the message from me to all of you who have been and are special in my life I want you to know I'm into another phase of the cancer dance. The term "battle" just does not fit for me somehow.*

*I suppose it's like two steps forward and one step back. Cha, Cha, Cha. The latest and most brutal chemotherapies didn't quite complete the job we had hoped for. Any further chemo will do more harm to the body than good. The doctor has advised me to discontinue chemotherapy.*

*Having been on chemo eight of the eleven years I've been doing this "dance," there doesn't seem to be a fresh solution. A bit scary, yes. But just another "blip on the screen 'o life."*

*.... Since the greater concern is the effect of fluid build-up in the lungs you can find me tethered to a fifty foot tube that's hooked onto an oxygen tank.*

*Now, all of this sounds a bit morbid/sad/final but right now, I'm not in the middle of any of those emotional feelings. (Check with me later though.)*

## Chat Line

Beatrice, Kathleen, and Alverta meet in an online chat room for terminally ill patients. Each of them has been diagnosed with a different form of cancer. Feeling free to raise even the most taboo subjects, today they are chatting about funerals.

Kathleen: I love Irish music. I want my grandson to dance a traditional Irish step dance in front of my casket at the Rosary.

Alverta: I'll ask my friend from church to play the saxophone. I can see him now, wailing on that mean sax as people enter the service.

Beatrice: I'm not that conventional. I'm going to leave my ashes to my friend Barbara and ask her to take them to Bali for a traditional ceremony.

Kathleen: You gonna leave her money for the airfare?

Beatrice: LOL... laugh out loud!

## Goodbye to a Friend

Kidding has always been part of Greg and Walter's relationship. Three days before Walter's death, Greg visits his long-time friend who is hooked up to wires and tubes and is unable to speak.

Greg chides, "Walter I've got you just where I want you. Remember in golf when you lied about your stroke? And remember when you cheated in cards? Well Walter, you're paying for it now."

A mute Walter's eyes begin to dance. Greg has uttered the perfect sentiments, recalling their past moments of enjoyment. Walter's death journey has been spiced up by levity and nostalgia. With humor, Greg has conveyed his love of Walter; he has overcome his quandary about how to speak to his dying friend.

## Goodbye Darling

"You start saying goodbye a long time before death," observes Joan regarding her husband Clark's struggle with Alzheimer's. For 6 years, he lives in a nearby board and care facility that Joan visits daily. When Clark's cognitive abilities decline dramatically, the staff moves him into hospice care.

"I can see him deteriorating cell by cell," Joan admits to the nurses tearfully.

Even when Clark is comatose and Joan is unsure of whether or not he senses her presence, she remains faithful to her schedule. She hugs and kisses him after each visit and says, "Goodbye, darling. You are the love of my life." Although Clark can no longer respond, in her heart Joan believes he can hear her.

## Refusing to Say Goodbye

Becoming a cancer specialist has been Hiyoshi's goal since he began his medical training. He and his wife, Fujita, also an oncology resident, are devastated by the diagnosis of his late-stage pancreatic cancer. Ordinarily self-assured, Hiyoshi becomes unhinged at the prospect that his life is going to be cut short.

He explodes at Fujita, "Just when I'm on the verge of fulfilling my dream of becoming an oncologist, cancer strikes out at me. What a cruel trick fate has played."

Fujita agrees, "You have worked so hard and have such a promising career. We should be planning our future not saying goodbye."

"I'm not ready to say goodbye," Hiyoshi insists, "Don't mention that again. No one is going to deny me my future."

Recognizing that Hiyoshi will never acquiesce and say goodbye, Fujita writes her farewell in an email that she never sends.

## Please Forgive Me

Lance, carrying a giant teddy bear, flowers, and a pink iPod, arrives at his ex-wife's home to visit his terminally ill daughter, Ashley. Lying in a hospital bed and hooked up to oxygen, Ashley brightens when her dad enters the living room.

"Daddy, I'm so happy to see you." Lance kisses Ashley's cheek and holds her hand.

"I'm so happy to see you too, Baby Doll."

Ashley tells Lance that her friends have been visiting, "But nothing means as much to me as having you here, Daddy."

"I know I haven't been the best father." Lance chokes up as he continues, "I feel so guilty because I wasn't here for your surgery, but I'm going to make up for it now. There were so many times that I thought I was too busy working to be with you. I don't know how I let that happen. Please forgive me."

Ashley's eyes fill with tears and she says, "That's OK, Daddy. You're here now and that's what matters."

Lance places his hand on Ashley's pale cheek and strokes his daughter's forehead.

## CREATING A LEGACY

Creating an oral, written, or multimedia biography honors the life of your beloved. It allows him to share significant stories and transmit history and values to you and to future generations.

### A DVD Legacy

Sean films every major event in their lives, so it is a natural for him to use his camcorder to document Jason's final days. Jason bares his soul to the camera so that when Chase, aged 6, and Dana, aged 4, are older they will have a legacy of who their Papa was.

Standing in front of the performing arts center, Jason plays a few notes on his clarinet and says to his son, "Chase, playing 'It's a Small World After All' for you makes all my years of practice worthwhile. Your laughter brightens my life every day."

At the ocean, Jason builds a sandcastle for Dana and waits for the tide to reclaim the beach. "Nothing is permanent, Dana, but that doesn't mean we can't enjoy each moment. I love you to the top of the sky and higher."

One Sunday after church services Sean has an idea. He asks Jason to hold Dana's hand and walk from the back of the church to the altar. "I'll show it to her on her wedding day," Sean promises. "Dana will know that her Papa walked her down the aisle."

### Life Journeys: Video Biographies of the Terminally Ill

Guatemalan-born Manuel, age 43, explains to the videographer that in his culture many believe that if you talk about death you will make it happen sooner. He has advanced cancer, and that's why he hires LIFE JOURNEYS to secretly videotape farewell messages to his family and friends that are to be played after his death.

Manuel selects photos from his picture albums and talks in front of the camera about the happy times recorded in the pictures. Manuel conveys his love to his wife, children, and friends. He tells his wife that he hopes she will be able to get an education to help support the family. He asks his friends to step in and help the family as much as they can after he is gone.

Instead of waiting for the tape to be played after he dies, Manuel decides to show it to them right away. The family becomes very emotional as they watch the video.

His daughter Patricia says, "Papa, *no quiero que te mueras.*" (I don't want you to die).

Stroking her hair, Manuel consoles his daughter. "*Ay mijita. Asi es la vida. Tampoco, yo no quiero irme, pero cuando me llama nuestro Diosito no hay nada mas que hacer.*" (Oh, my daughter. This is life. I don't want to go either, but when our God calls me, there is nothing more to do.)

## Letters to a Granddaughter

Granny Margo is dying from advanced adrenal cancer and fears that she will not live long enough to attend her granddaughter Tara's First Holy Communion. As she thinks ahead to all the rites of passage that she will miss, she is filled with heartbreaking sadness.

A church member, Nellie, suggests that Margo write a series of letters to Tara to be opened on major future occasions. Margo responds with great enthusiasm and asks Nellie to purchase fancy stationery and ribbon for the letters Margo intends to write. Energized by this plan to be a part of Tara's future, Margo uses her best calligraphy pen to address four envelopes:

> *To my precious Tara on her First Holy Communion*
> *To my brilliant granddaughter Tara on your graduation*
> *To Tara, the most beautiful bride in the world*
> *To Tara on the blessed birth of your first child*

Over the next several days, Margo pours her heartfelt sentiments into these letters for Tara and signs each one: *From Granny with Love.* Margo seals each message in an envelope and ornaments it with a matching ribbon and entrusts these letters to Tara's mother.

Gratified with the knowledge that she will be included in Tara's future celebrations, Margo feels that she can rest in peace.

## Recipe for Life

"Use your best china, and don't let the marshmallows burn on top of the yams," advises Shayestah as she delights in the photo of her beautifully set Thanksgiving table in the old house on Gibson Street.

Although her grandchildren have heard the stories over and over again, they delight at sitting on Nana Shayestah's bed and listening to her recount how the holidays were celebrated before they were born.

"What about the time Daddy ate so many olives, he hid the pits in his pockets?" teases Aaron.

Jay-Jay chimes in, "How about when Scooter was a puppy and he ate all the pumpkin pie while it was cooling on the baking rack?"

"Look, there's the picture of Aunt Lilia dressed up as a pilgrim!" laughs Bonnie, mimicking her aunt's facial expression.

"Nana, can I have your secret recipe for mushroom stuffing?" begs Jesse, the oldest granddaughter soon to be married and thinking about the day when she will host Thanksgiving dinner herself.

By the end of the afternoon, Shayestah is tired, but her heart is full. "I'm one happy grandma, kids. You can remember this day with your Nana forever."

## PRACTICAL MATTERS

### Things to Remember

Daisy, living with non-Hodgkin's lymphoma, worries about her daughters Pam, age 10, and Kimmie, age 8, and how her husband, Perry, will care for them after she dies. Daisy makes a master list of THINGS TO REMEMBER for her distraught husband. Daily, she reviews the ever-growing list, anxious that Perry understand the complexities of the girls' schedules: music lessons, Girl Scouts, ballet, soccer, school and homework.

Daisy reminds Perry to register the girls for summer camp. "You must submit the application no later than three months in advance," she warns. Perry, unwillingly contemplating life without Daisy, merely nods.

"And when Kimmie leaves for school, be sure to part her hair on the left," Daisy adds. "As for Pepe," she says, pointing to the Tortoise Instructions section on her list, "he must have two cups of romaine lettuce chopped into small pieces every day with two or three different fresh fruit toppings or he'll get sick." Overwhelmed at the thought of having to care for a sick tortoise on top of everything else, Perry barely maintains his composure. "OK, I get it," he impatiently answers.

Daisy takes Perry's hand and apologizes, "I'm sorry to leave you with all these responsibilities, darling." Perry squeezes Daisy's hand as they share a moment of quiet sadness.

### Nuts and Bolts

Charlotte tenses up when her husband Brant announces the night before surgery to remove his brain tumor, "There's something important we need to discuss."

Brant, who has always been the take-charge person in their marriage of 22 years asks, "Do you know how to do everything? Are you sure you remember where I put the deed to the house and when the mortgage payments are due?"

Charlotte assures Brant that she remembers where all the important papers are located.

"And who will you call if something in the house needs repairs?"

"Vilius, the handyman, of course," she replies.

Brant continues, "And in case I don't survive the surgery, what will you do with my car?"

Charlotte reminds him that they have discussed this before. She promises to give the car to their nephew, Glen.

"One last item," he adds. "Who will kiss you goodnight?"

As you plan ahead for all the responsibilities you will have to assume after your loved one dies, consider making a list of practical information to keep on hand. This should include name, account number and passwords for bank accounts, credit cards, investments, safe deposit boxes, insurance papers, trust, will, and deed to the house. You might also want to have the names and contact information for your attorney, financial advisor, and home repair specialists. Be sure to inquire about location of heirlooms, photographs, recipes, and other personal memorabilia.

## END-OF-LIFE DECISIONS

### Life Support

Irv and Elsie, both in their eighties, have been married almost 60 years when Elsie is diagnosed with amyloidosis, a progressive incurable disease affecting her respiratory system. For 105 days, Elsie lies unconscious, hooked up to a ventilator. Irv labors under the hope that his wife will eventually recover and insists on keeping her on the ventilator, even though their daughter Florence argues that her mom would be against it.

At last Florence acquiesces and honors her father's decision. In a private moment with her mother, Florence whispers, "Mom, please forgive me; you know how much I love you. And please forgive Daddy. He's just not ready to let you go. But you don't have to hang on anymore." Florence leans over and gives her mother a goodbye kiss.

## Five Wishes

Molly's emphysema has worsened; she constantly feels out of breath and requires oxygen around the clock. As she is admitted to the hospital once again to drain fluid from her lungs, Molly makes it known to her son Steve and to the doctors that this is the last time she intends to have this procedure done. "I'm tired of all this," Molly informs them. "I want to know my rights."

Dr. Edmonds asks Molly if she has ever put in writing her wishes for end-of-life care. When she says no, her doctor suggests that Molly and Steve learn more about making advance directives, completing Physician Orders for Life-Sustaining Treatment, and completing the Aging with Dignity Five Wishes living will that details her preferences and wishes.

Before leaving the hospital, Steve helps his mother complete the forms, and Molly feels relieved. "This really helps," she exclaims. "I feel like we have covered all the things I worried about." (See Resources for information about specific forms.)

## Aye for an Eye

Kasim is a 42-year-old officer in the U.S. Navy when he has a stroke while on duty in Cota, Spain. Navy medics are pessimistic about Kasim's chances for recovery. When notified, his wife Shireen immediately flies from North Dakota to the Naval Base hospital in Spain.

On her plane ride, Shireen sits next to a woman whose 10-year-old son, Geraldo, is visually impaired. His English is much better than his mother's and he translates for her. Shireen is impressed by Geraldo's spunkiness and intelligence, and she learns that he has been waiting for a cornea transplant for almost 5 years.

By the time Shireen reaches her husband's bedside, Kasim's condition has worsened, yet he is still conscious. Inspired by her encounter with Geraldo and his mother, Shireen tells her husband about these remarkable people. Cautiously, she talks about how this gifted child is handicapped without eyesight. Kasim is touched by her story.

After a conversation about the seriousness of his condition, Shireen nervously asks Kasim if he would consider signing an eye donation form so that after his death he might give the gift of sight to someone else, perhaps even a child like Geraldo. Warming to the idea of such a gift, Kasim gives his consent.

## SPIRITUAL ISSUES

### Spiritual Advisor

When Harry tells the hospice social worker, "I find my spirituality in nature," she arranges for Harry to meet Michael, a spiritual advisor with a background in shamanic studies.

Harry and Michael become acquainted the next day. Seated in his wheelchair in his heavily wooded backyard, Harry requests that before he dies he would like Michael to create a ceremony that will honor his connection with nature. That weekend, beneath the fragrant pine trees, Michael wraps a Navajo blanket around Harry's shoulders. Standing above him, Michael chants a Native American blessing and together they recite a prayer that Michael has created for the occasion. The two men acknowledge the sanctity of all living creatures and pay homage to the earth, the sun, and the sky. Michael ends the ritual by blessing Harry, his ancestors, and future generations.

Michael wheels a fatigued, but content, Harry back into the house. Harry feels satisfied that he has ritually honored his spiritual beliefs.

### Threshold Choir

The Threshold Choir travels throughout the city, singing to those who are dying. Today, the six-woman chorus arrives at a small group home, tastefully decorated with Oriental rugs and handsome oil paintings. Although Jacqueline, in her late nineties, has been unresponsive for the last several weeks, a staff member wheels her into the living room in a reclining chair.

The choir begins with "Brahms' Lullaby" followed by "Fourteen Angels" from the Humperdinck opera, *Hansel and Gretel*. As Jacqueline listens, her face lights up with a look of great joy and peace. For the first time in weeks, she speaks, "Thank you. Thank you very much."

When the singers enter Gustavo's room, he pulls the sheets up over his head. As the choir intones the opening words of a Welsh lullaby,

"Sleep my child and peace attend thee," unexpectedly from under the sheets, Gustavo's resonant bass voice joins with theirs on the phrase "All through the night." Still hidden, Gustavo continues harmonizing until the song ends.

## Where is God?

Rabbi Norm walks into the hospital room to visit his congregant Scot, who is dying of cancer. Scot, surrounded by his worried family, complains about the pain he is in.

Typical of their teacher/student relationship, Scot questions Rabbi Norm about God's existence. "Where is God now, Rabbi?" Scot asks bitterly.

As Scot's daughter-in-law, Rifka, picks up a washcloth to cool Scot's flushed face, Rabbi Norm points to Rifka and says, "That's where God is, Scot, right there."

## Near-Death Experience

Lourdes' daughter takes her to the doctor for a follow-up appointment after her recent stroke. As she lies on the examining table, Lourdes drifts off and sees herself walking toward a bright light where a pretty lady is waiting to take her hand. Lourdes asks, "Where are you taking me?"

The pretty lady answers, "I am taking you to the Mother of all good Mothers." Lourdes is ready to take the pretty lady's hand and go with her, when she feels herself being pulled back and wakes up to the sound of the doctor's voice, "Wake up, Lourdes, wake up."

Lourdes later reassuringly tells her daughter that since her experience with the pretty lady she is no longer afraid of death.

## Final Symbol

For many years, Fredda considers Marielle her mentor and spiritual teacher. Through guided imagery journeys, Marielle assists Fredda in exploring her spiritual path. At the conclusion of each guided journey, Marielle suggests, "Before you leave, you will find an important symbol or message that represents your experience."

Now it is Fredda's turn to give to Marielle who is at home receiving hospice care with very few moments of consciousness each day. At her mentor's bedside, Fredda sits very near and speaks softly. Occasionally, Marielle opens her eyes and tries to say something. Clearly it is too much effort to speak and Fredda tells her that words aren't necessary. They are communicating on a deeper level.

Fredda thanks Marielle for allowing her to be her pupil, her colleague, and her friend. With a full heart, she says "Goodbye, Marielle. I am leaving now. My heart and thoughts will be with you always."

On Fredda's drive home, zigzag bolts of light with a reddish aura appear in the western sky. "Thank you, Marielle," she whispers aloud, "for giving me this final symbol of our sacred time together."

### You Made the World a Better Place

Madison and Cambrien enjoy the crisp autumn air as they sit by Lake Wallenpaupak in the Pocono Mountains exchanging ideas about the meaning of life. The two women have been together for over 20 years, devoted to each other and to their Buddhist philosophy. Now that Madison is in the last stages of ovarian cancer, Cambrien is her sole caregiver.

"My belief in the teachings of Buddha give me the strength to face the pain," Madison tells her partner. "I can handle the discomfort because I know that this life is merely temporal. My soul will return someday in another form."

"But this life counts, too, Maddy. Look at all the good you have done." Cambrien reminds Madison of all the time she has devoted as a volunteer holding AIDS babies in the neonatal intensive care unit (NICU). And how, as a social worker, she developed a project on Skid Row assisting the homeless in obtaining food and shelter and teaching job-preparation classes. When Cambrien praises these acts of charity, Madison reacts in her usual modest fashion saying, "It was the work I was here to do."

"You've made this world a better place," Cambrien reminds her partner, "and your love has touched many beings on this earth."

### ANTICIPATORY GRIEF

Your grieving process began the moment you started contemplating your loved one's death. Now as you prepare to say goodbye and imagine what life will be like after he dies, you are flooded with a myriad of emotions including sadness, anger, guilt, helplessness, and anxiety.

### The Bridge

Colleen feels exhausted. She is pressed for time. The groceries, the cleaners, and the bank have been taken care of, but she still needs to pick up another prescription for her terminally ill, bedridden husband, Rudolfo.

Colleen is grateful that a kindly neighbor came over to visit with Rudolfo while she gets out for a couple of hours.

As she drives over a bridge toward home, Colleen flashes forward to the day when she will be driving home from errands and the house will be empty. Rudolfo will be gone. Colleen bursts into tears, and then feels guilty for having such thoughts.

## Brotherly Love

Brothers George and Mel are tightly bonded throughout their lives. They go to boarding school together and during World War II, although they enter different branches of the military service, they remain in close contact. Mel becomes a journalist and regularly writes letters to his brother describing his adventures that he knows George will enjoy vicariously.

Thirty years later, when George is diagnosed with lung cancer, Mel and his wife fly to take care of George in his Nevada home. Mel tries to be supportive when George discloses that he has refused chemotherapy, which he believes is worse than death. He says he is ready to die and puts his affairs in order. During the 3 months the two brothers spend together, they reminisce about old times and George reflects on the full life he has had.

Mel feels good about taking this time to be with George. Nonetheless, each night when he unwinds in the shower under the spray of the hot water, he clenches his fists and yells profanities.

Later, Mel sits down at his computer and expresses his outrage: "George, it infuriates me that you are leaving me. How can I live the rest of my life without you? Who will appreciate my ironic commentary on the world? Who will be my big brother? My life will never be the same."

## Split Personality

Although he is dying, Lina and her father both pretend that Dad is going to successfully overcome his cancer. When Dad professes, "I'm going to live!" Lina goes along with the pretense.

She never breaks down in front of her father nor alludes to the possibility of his dying. But when she leaves his room, her grief is heavy and she cries uncontrollably.

"I feel like I have a split personality," Lina reveals to her counselor. "I wish I could get real and talk to my dad about the fact that he is dying, but he won't let me go there."

## A Mother Watching Her Daughter Die

As her 48-year-old daughter, Sydney, lay dying from a rare form of cancer, Yvonne Cannon chronicles the horrific images she witnesses. Yvonne expresses her anticipatory grief in her poem "Villanelle".

My daughter was falling faster every day
Every day, every hour I practiced hope,
tried to practice what she wanted every way.

She'd laid her violin in its case.
Could no longer bow the chords,
arpeggios falling faster every day.

Her husband filled a porcelain vase
she'd made with fragrant roses,
tried to practice what we wanted every way.

He hung her portrait she'd painted on a better day.
I rubbed her feet and hands with scented lotion,
my daughter falling faster every day.

The radiologist told me just the other day,
"Enjoy her while you have her." Knowing
then I'd lose her though I'd practiced every way.

I practiced loss, every hour, every day.
It is hard to practice coping.
My daughter's spirit was falling faster every day
Though I tried to practice what she wanted me to say.

*When This You See*
Cannon, Y. San Francisco: Browser Books Publishing, 2006

As you say goodbye to the one you love, you straddle two worlds. You strive to focus on the present moment and the love that you share, while simultaneously you grieve for what will be in the future. At times you want to pretend that your loved one's death is not approaching and avoid acknowledging it to yourself or to him. But saying goodbye is essential.

Say goodbye to your beloved in a way that is meaningful to you. Take time to share what is on your mind and in your heart as you approach the final moments of his life.

# CHAPTER 7

## Final Moments

*"You should just accept that death is part of life,"*
*a friend tells Jonna.*
*"Death is part of life?" Jonna asks.*
*"Maybe other people's death is part of my life.*
*My death? Not a part of my life.*
*It's the end of my life."*

from *Jonna's Body, Please Hold*

Your beloved is dying. Not someday, not at some far-off time in the future, but now. As the end of her life draws near, you are probably wondering where you will be when death happens and whether or not you wish to be present.

Being with your dear one as she dies is an intimate act of love. These sacred moments, enhanced by tender words, music, and human connection, can be healing, giving you peace of mind knowing that you have accompanied your loved one as far as possible.

Yet being there may not be the right choice for you. No matter what your friends, family, or others with good intentions suggest, this is a very personal decision. What does your heart tell you? Will you sit vigil at her bedside? Will you be somewhere nearby but not in the same room? Have you already said goodbye and prefer not to be there when she takes her final breath? What if you have a change of heart at the last moment?

Remember that the exact time of your loved one's death is not predictable. You may fully intend to be there and then inadvertently miss the moment of her death. You may have no intention of being present and then although she appears to be doing well, or even improving, she dies in front of you quite unexpectedly.

Whether you plan to be present or not, there are several ways for you to take an active role at the end of your dear one's life. You can prepare an environment of beauty, order, and peace. You can attend to your loved one's physical comfort. And you can prepare yourself by knowing what to expect.

Create an Environment of Beauty, Order, and Peace
Play music that your dear one enjoys. Speak softly. If it pleases her, open the windows and allow sunlight. Or if the room is too bright, she may prefer that you dim the lights. Place favorite objects nearby that she can see or touch. Small bunches of fresh flowers may be easier to appreciate than large bouquets or plants. Keep medications and medical equipment out of sight. Consider limiting the number of visitors in the room at any given time.

Attend to Physical Comfort
Before you implement any of the following changes, consult with her medical team for Do's and Don'ts. Place pillows around your loved one to support her head, body, and limbs. Sit very near with the bed railing down. Use gentle touch. Hold, rock, or cradle her.

Anticipate Physical Changes
Your loved one may exhibit some or all of the following signs: increased time asleep; confusion; changes in body temperature—from warm to cold; changes in breathing—less rhythmic, slower, more congestion; restlessness and/or inability to be aroused; loss of bladder or bowel control; glassy-looking eyes that may be only partly open or staring; changes in coloring—hands and feet purplish, face yellow; loss of control of facial muscles, jaw, and tongue.

---

## BEING THERE

### Nurturing Papa

Harold rings a bell on the nightstand. "It hurts to breathe," he says in strained tones as we reach his bedroom. We put on the oxygen mask and Nurse Romo shows us how to administer morphine drops in his cheek. He falls asleep.

Amy calls her sister Andy, who asks if this is an emergency and if she should leave Las Vegas now, around midnight, or wait until morning to make the precarious drive through the desert. Nurse Romo matter-of-factly answers, "Well, he's dying."

"He's dying" cuts through me like a knife. Despite Harold's having been in hospice care for a year, one is never prepared for those words, no matter what.

Amy leaves the room to call her brother and her husband, and fully clothed I climb into bed with Harold alone for the last time. He has fallen the day before and hurt his back, so I hesitate to put my arms around him. Instead I lie on my side and squeeze his hand, and for the first time in over 55 years, he doesn't squeeze back.

His breathing sounds labored, and I stroke his arm and softly tell him how much I love him and that there has never been anyone else for me. I review some of the wonderful times we have had together, recalling specific memories. I don't know how long I lie there with him. I doze off and am awakened by the arrival of our son Mark, who sits at the foot of the bed and begins gently massaging his father's feet.

Andrea arrives with her sons, Avi and Zach, and each one goes in to have a private moment with Papa. They return to the living room, and Mark is once again alone with Harold. When I step back into the room, Mark says that he thinks his Dad has taken his last breath, that he has opened his eyes, closed them, and has stopped breathing.

Harold has left us. I am content that his very last breath has been taken while his son nurtures him. It seems fitting—the next generation is now in charge.

## A Toast to His Life

Frankie's mother, grandmother, aunt, and two sisters surround him with love in his last hours as he dies of AIDS. Frankie sleeps most of the time now with very few moments of consciousness.

His mother, Sofia, remains with her son as the other women go into the kitchen to fix breakfast. When she hears Frankie gurgle, Sofia recognizes that this is the end. She tenderly caresses her firstborn, alone with him as she was 24 years ago at the moment of his birth. Tears stream down Sofia's face as she whispers, "Rest in peace, my beautiful boy."

Sofia lingers for a few moments before calling the rest of the family back into the room. She ties a ribbon around Frankie's head to hold his jaw in place. This creates a serious expression on Frankie's face and makes him look like he has a toothache.

After the women kiss Frankie goodbye, they return to the kitchen, crying and laughing as they reminisce about his life. They pop open a bottle of champagne and make a toast to wish Frankie Godspeed on his journey. One of the sisters returns to the room to be with Frankie's body. She notices that his serious expression has changed to a smile and excitedly calls the others back into the room. The family stays with Frankie's body for a few hours before calling the mortuary. Although they are sad to bid Frankie farewell, they are bolstered by their belief that Frankie's spirit will be reborn.

## Thank You for Waiting

Stan, who has been keeping vigil at his father's bedside, calls his sister, Tammy, at 6 a.m. and tells her to come to the hospital immediately. Tammy thinks that this means that their father, Miles, has died, so she and her boyfriend take their time dressing and even stop for coffee. Forty-five minutes after the phone call, the couple reluctantly enters the hospital room. Tammy doesn't know how she is going to react when she sees her father's dead body.

As she enters the room, Stan screams at Tammy, "Where have you been? You've been late your entire life, but now?"

To Tammy's surprise, her dad is still alive and gives his daughter a weak smile.

"Thank you for waiting, Daddy," whispers Tammy as she puts her face close to his. Barely able to move, Miles reaches up and taps his cheek with his pointer finger. Tammy gives her dad a light kiss on the spot. He points again, and she repeats the action. After the third repetition, Tammy asks, "Enough?" Miles nods and closes his eyes. "Looks like you're tired, Dad," Tammy continues. "It's okay. Sleep."

Stan gives his father a gentle hug, says, "Goodbye, Dad, I love you," and walks into the hallway. Although he has been with his dad for days, he realizes that he cannot stay present to witness his father's final breaths.

## Pajama Party

Estelle's breast cancer metastasizes to her brain, and at times she doesn't recognize her daughter, Valerie. "She thinks I am my aunt," Valerie admits to her husband, "and I go along with it because it makes her so happy to see her sister who lives out of town."

After palliative radiation treatments, Estelle becomes more lucid and asks her daughter, "Who is going to be your mother after I die?" to which Valerie replies, "You will be my mother forever, Mom."

Realizing that Estelle's time is short, Valerie takes a leave of absence from work and promises her mom that she will not leave her. Valerie's 14-year-old daughter, Adrianna, receives permission from her school to postpone her final exams so that she can be with her grandmother as well.

The first evening, Adrianna, wearing her pink flannel pajamas, enters her grandmother's bedroom and announces, "Grammy, we're going to have a pajama party."

"It's going to be so much fun," replies a smiling Estelle. "I love you Pussycat."

The three generations of women stay together for the next week. They play Estelle's favorite operas. They reassure her how much they love her and that it is okay to let go. Estelle's breathing gradually becomes slower, more shallow, and more irregular. The family surrounds Estelle as she takes her final breath. Through her tears, Adrianna cries, "If Grammy is watching, I know she is happy that we are all here."

## The Right Time

Selma has been unconscious for weeks, and her daughters take turns sitting with her. Tina and her sister hold Selma's hands and speak tenderly to their beloved mother. When Selma grimaces in pain, the hospice nurse plays a meditation CD. As she is gently guided through a body relaxation, Selma falls back into a deep sleep.

One day Tina telephones her sister from Mom's bedside: "Let's all meet here tonight at 6:30." At precisely 6:30, with Selma's daughters, sons-in-law, and three grandchildren surrounding her, Selma takes her last breath. Tina wonders if Mom overheard her conversation and was waiting for all the family.

## The Chapel Seats 300

Veronica's father, Del, is in home hospice care. Despite medication, he thrashes around and cries out in his sleep. Veronica and her mother, Trilby, feel helpless because they cannot alleviate Dad's suffering. When the hospice nurse advises them that Del's death is imminent, Veronica asks her mother if they have made burial arrangements. Mom says that they haven't gotten around to it, so Veronica takes action and uses the internet to shop for funeral homes in the area.

The next morning Veronica and her mother talk in the kitchen while Dad lies unconscious in his hospital bed in the next room. Veronica announces to her mom that all is ready: "The chapel can seat 300, there's plenty of parking, and it's located near the veteran's cemetery." After hearing the details, Trilby says, "I'm happy with the arrangements. This is what he would want." Moments later, Dad takes his last breath.

### Green Pick-Up Truck

Terminally ill Alfredo is agitated as death approaches. His nurse suggests that the family members give Alfredo permission to leave. The family complies, but Alfredo keeps asking, "Did you take care of it?"

His son, Ernesto, assures his father, "Yes, the house payments have been made and we will take care of Mom."

Yet Alfredo persists. "Is it done?"

Alfredo's grandson, Julio, remembers an important story his grandpa once told him. When Alfredo was a boy, the family had a green pick-up truck that they needed to sell. No matter how hard they tried, no one would buy it. This caused a financial hardship for the family. Julio suggests, "Do you think the green pick-up truck is the key to grandpa's agitation?"

The next time Alfredo asks, "Did you take care of it?" Ernesto answers, "Yes, Dad, we sold the green truck yesterday." A relieved Alfredo exclaims, "Oh, thank goodness." Four hours later Alfredo dies.

### The Vigil

While still in the hospital, Timothy tells his wife, Frances, "I'm ready to die and I want to be at home." Unsure of how to make this happen, Frances connects with the Sacred Dying Foundation, an organization that specializes in creating sacred spaces and vigils for the dying. Megory Anderson, the founder and executive director, works with Timothy's wife and three teenage children to prepare the bedroom for Timothy's homecoming. She suggests that the children look for objects of nature to fill the room. The daughter brings in a fragrant basket of leaves, twigs, and pine cones and arranges them in one corner. Timothy's eldest son creates a collage of fishing equipment and photos of the family engaged in this favorite pastime. The other son places a small waterfall on the nightstand. The outdoors has been brought inside, and Timothy responds positively to the smells, sights, and sounds of this serene environment.

Over the next few days, as Timothy drifts in and out of sleep, he listens to his favorite music, the hits of the 1960s. The iPod playlist includes "When a Man Loves a Woman," a song that has been meaningful to him and his wife throughout their lives. Whenever that song plays, Timothy smiles and his ordinarily erratic breathing becomes more rhythmic.

Extended family members visit, but Frances limits the number of people who can be with Timothy. Those who choose not to go into the room demonstrate their support by helping out in the kitchen. In Timothy's last hours, his wife and children encircle his bed and sing to him. They stroke his arms, his feet, and his head, and Anderson leads them in The Lord's Prayer. They give Timothy permission to let go, and he dies peacefully. Timothy's family stays with his body for several hours after his death because they believe that it takes time for the body and soul to separate.

## Cradling Nancy

Nancy peacefully lies in her hospice bed, a warm breeze wafting into the room through the open window. All the medical supplies and equipment have been moved out of the way or draped with an Indian print bedspread. Carla and Jessie cradle their younger sister in their arms and in a soothing voice, Carla reassures Nancy, "Everything is going to be okay, Baby. You can let go. Mama is waiting for you in heaven."

A moment later Jessie looks quizzically at Carla as Nancy seems to have stopped breathing. Jessie asks hesitantly, "Did Baby already take her last breath?"

Jessie and Carla watch Nancy closely for what seems like an eternity. At last Nancy inhales again, followed by a long, slow, final exhale. Disbelief shrouds the sisters, as the hospice nurse enters the room and confirms that their precious baby sister has died.

## Father's Advice

As his strength diminishes, Ray asks his wife Norma to have their daughters come over so that he can say goodbye to each of them. Norma calls the girls and says, "It's time."

With the family gathered around him, Ray counsels his youngest, "Brenda, even though it may be an economic hardship, please stay in school because having a teaching credential will allow you to be an independent woman."

"You will be a wonderful mother," he tells his daughter Martha, who is 6 months pregnant. "I'm so honored that you are going to name the baby after me."

Ray falls into a deep sleep. When death comes, Norma, Martha, and Brenda do not panic. They neither call 911 nor rush to call the mortuary. Instead they spend sacred quiet time with Ray's body, surrounding him with their love.

## One Last Tear

Rowena sits in the ICU at the bedside of her mother, Suri, who is unconscious and hooked up to life-support machines. Suri has never signed any

Advance Directives or Do Not Resuscitate instructions, so Rowena has to make terrifying decisions on her own.

The physician informs Rowena that Suri's Glasgow Coma Scale measurements show no motor, verbal, or eye-movement response. Although, as a science writer, Rowena understands that this means that her mother can never recover, she dreads making the decision to remove her from life support. Reluctantly, Rowena decides that if her mother's condition remains the same by morning, she will no longer artificially prolong her mother's life.

The next day, the doctor examines Suri and confirms that there has been no change in her condition. Rowena holds her mother's hand while the nurses disconnect the machines, and she stays at the bedside until Suri's heart stops beating. A few moments later, Rowena startles when she notices one tear slowly falling down Suri's cheek thinking that perhaps her mother is still alive and in pain. The nurse calms Rowena's fears and explains that the tear was a reflex response, a result of the body shutting down. Rowena sheds her own tears as she bids her mother a final goodbye.

## My Brother's Keeper

Yale responds to an ad placed in *The Advocate*, a major news source for the gay and lesbian community, requesting volunteers to be with AIDS patients who have been abandoned at the end of their lives. This is the 1980s when facts and fictions about AIDS are confused and fear reigns regarding the way in which AIDS is transmitted. Horrified that AIDS patients are being ignored and isolated, Yale volunteers to become an AIDS Buddy. He pledges to be with patients as they die and to comfort their loving ones.

As his first patient, Cesar, approaches death, he asks for a special favor. Cesar wants Yale to inform his grown sons that their father is gay and dying of AIDS. "I will call them for you, but you will have to tell them yourself," Yale insists.

Cesar anxiously anticipates his children's reaction, fearing that they will reject him. They do not. Instead, they immediately offer to visit. Yale models the care he gives Cesar, encouraging the sons to sit near their father, hold his hands, and place extra pillows around him for comfort and support. When Cesar becomes unresponsive, Yale assures the boys that their father can still hear them and suggests that they say their goodbyes and give Cesar permission to die. They are grateful that Yale sits with them through their father's death.

Summing up what he has learned from his experience Yale concludes, "When you take care of someone who is dying, your own mortality comes into view. You learn to be a better person, to walk more slowly, to fit into the rhythm of the dying." He explains, "We are our brothers' keepers."

## I Will Bathe My Husband

Haley is by her husband Spencer's side every moment of his hospitalization. Watching his body shut down in 3 short weeks is unreal. Eight members of the extended family are present, holding hands and saying a prayer, as Spencer takes his final breath. In her gentle manner, Spencer's favorite nurse, Phoebe, turns to Haley asking, "Would you like to wash his body?"

Haley nods solemnly and, taking their cues from Phoebe, the other family members quietly exit the room. With a basin of warm water and a wash cloth, Haley gently bathes Spencer's face, arms, and hands. She tenderly combs Spencer's hair as the tears stream down her face.

"Do I have to put him back in the hospital gown?" Haley whispers to the Phoebe.

"Anything you want," replies the nurse.

Together they dress Spencer in his favorite blue and green plaid cotton Pendleton and sweats. "Now he'll be comfortable," Haley reassures herself as she leans over and murmurs goodbye.

## One Final Wink

After battling ovarian cancer for 5 years, Zoe's condition worsens, and she requires hospitalization. Each night her husband Paul stays with her and creates a loving atmosphere. He turns the lights down low and reads to her. By being there all night, Paul insures that Zoe receives the attention she needs.

Paul adores Zoe and admires her spirit. She maintains a positive attitude even as she endures intense pain. On their final night together, they sing songs to relieve Zoe's fear and discomfort. After a few moments of silence, Zoe turns, winks at Paul, and is gone.

## How to Be Present in the Last Hours of Life

- Find your own way to be there.
- Recognize and honor your limitations.
- Approach gently, tell her you are here.
- Continue to speak to her—the sense of hearing is the last to remain.

- Speak directly to her "I see that you are resting comfortably" rather than saying to someone else, "she's resting comfortably."
- Use soothing, reassuring, and validating words.
- Speak in her first language or mother tongue.
- Include humor, smiles, and even laughter.
- Sing or hum songs from her childhood.
- Give permission to let go.

## WHEN YOU AREN'T THERE

### We Only Left for a Minute

Cathy and Florine spend every possible minute with their father, Rick, as they have from the time he was put on home hospice. They consider it a mission of love. Cathy is on a leave of absence from work, remembering how her father did the same when she was recuperating from back surgery 7 years earlier.

Florine calls every few hours to inquire how things are going and looks forward to spending time with her dad after work. One evening, she walks into the house, blows Rick a kiss and says, "I'm going to fix myself a little dinner, Dad. I'll be right back to tell you about my day." Florine putters around the kitchen for a few minutes and calls for Cathy to come in to visit with her. Seeing that their dad is resting comfortably, Cathy steps into the kitchen and the two sisters have a few minutes of alone time. They laugh together over how Florine arranges every slice of carrot around her salad bowl and Cathy puts the olives onto her fingertips like puppets. It is a welcome relief to be silly and playful for a few minutes.

Cathy precedes Florine into the bedroom and stops in her tracks. Florine drops her tray of food as the two sisters rush to their father's side, his mouth agape and his eyes wide open with a blank stare.

"He's gone," Cathy announces incredulously. "Why did we leave the room? Why did he have to die alone?"

"Maybe Dad was trying to spare us the pain of watching him die," Florine replies tearfully. "So he left to the sound of our laughter."

### Desert Home

For the last 3 months of his life, Charles lives in a small residential home in a remote part of the desert that accommodates only five Alzheimer's patients. He is mostly mute, uttering an occasional "yes" or "no." His wife Shira visits him daily, and when she goes home in the evening, her mind is at ease knowing that Charles is being lovingly cared for by the compassionate staff.

One evening, Shira receives a call from the director. She believes that the end is near, yet advises Shira to stay home because it is too dangerous to drive through the desert alone at night on unlit curving roads. This upsets Shira until she is reassured that Charles' favorite nurse, Ms. Ballas, is with him, holding his hand. "Have her tell him that I love him," requests Shira. "I will," the director assures her. "And I want you to know that Ms. Ballas has promised to stay with Charles until the end."

## Madilynn's Choice

The trauma of taking care of her father in the last weeks of his life 4 years ago causes Madilynn to decide not to be present with her sister, Carlotta, as she dies.

"How can you be so cruel and unfeeling towards your own sister on her deathbed?" demands Madilynn's brother. "She keeps calling your name."

Madilynn cries herself to sleep that night as she anguishes over the pressure her family has put upon her. However, when she awakens, she is confident that she has made the right decision. She knows that Carlotta would understand.

Carlotta dies the next morning encircled by everyone in the family except Madilynn who remains at home, honoring her sister's life by lighting a candle and saying a prayer.

## Death Is Not Convenient

After struggling for success in the entertainment business, Audrey finally has her chance to "make it." A television production company hires her to go on location in Borneo to tape a show for a series pilot.

While Audrey is preparing to leave, her husband Elliott receives a call that his mom is in the hospital. Although her condition doesn't sound dire, Audrey encourages Elliott to fly home to Vermont to be with her.

When Audrey lands in Borneo, she receives a text message from Elliott: "Mom's condition critical. Doctors don't think she will survive. Wish you were here." Audrey wrestles with her conscience. Should she give up her big opportunity and join Elliott? She consults with other cast who share their experiences. Most of them who stayed on the job when someone close was dying, later regretted their choice. They encourage Audrey to leave. By the time Audrey arrives in Vermont, Elliott's mother has died. Although she is saddened that she wasn't with her husband earlier, Audrey is pleased that she is able to support Elliot now and help with the plans for the funeral and reception.

## The Snow Storm

Diego and Lupe have a cozy mountain home in Taos, far from El Paso, where Diego's grandmother, Nana Consuela, is on hospice care. Lupe cherishes her husband's grandmother because she and Nana Consuela share the same sense of humor and they both adore Diego.

As much as they want to be there for Nana Consuela's passing, the couple determines that the prediction of a heavy snowstorm makes it unwise to travel. They agonize over not being able to hold Nana one more time and compromise by calling the family and having them hold up the phone to Nana Consuela's ear.

Although Nana is no longer able to speak, she smiles when she hears Diego and Lupe sing "Duérmete Niño," the lullaby she sang to Diego when he was a little boy.

> If you are not present at the time of your loved one's death, try to be easy on yourself. Remember that her last breath represents only one brief moment in your relationship. Remind yourself that you did what you were able to do, given the circumstances. And perhaps your loved one needed to die alone. You may want to write your loved one a letter or express in a journal how you wish you could have comforted her in her final moments.

## SPIRITUAL CONNECTIONS

### I Still Feel His Essence

In the final hours of his life, Ronnie lies peacefully in his bed as his friends keep vigil. Lit candles adorn the room and Gregorian chants play softly in the background, the fragrance of dozens of roses filling the air. As Ronnie's breathing slows, everyone gathers near, their eyes filled with tears, declaring their love and goodbye sentiments in hushed tones. Each breath is followed by a long pause and finally one last exhale. Ronnie's best friend, Jami, gently closes Ronnie's eyelids, kisses him on the forehead, and remains by his side. "I still feel his essence," she says.

An hour later, Jami solemnly opens all the doors and windows to allow Ronnie's spirit to leave.

**Last Rites**

Father Dominick, a hospital chaplain, makes weekly rounds to Roman Catholic patients who wish to take communion. He looks forward to his visits with Rosa, an elderly woman, whose heart condition has worsened over the last 6 weeks. When Father Dominick encounters Rosa's daughter, he asks if she thinks her mother would want him to administer Last Rites today. Rosa's frazzled daughter hesitates before suggesting, "Why not ask her, Father?"

Father Dominick enters Rosa's room and asks her if she is ready for the Last Rites. Rosa glares at him and screams, "No. Get away from me! I'm not ready to die!"

Father Dominick receives quite a different reaction several years later when he and his younger brother, Father Franco, visit their eldest brother, Angelo, as he lies dying in the hospital. Angelo's 11 children, their spouses, and all his nieces and nephews crowd the room. The grandchildren climb in and out of bed taking turns hugging Grandpa. Everyone quiets as the two Roman Catholic priests administer the Last Rites to their dying brother. With their thumbs they use holy oil to anoint the sign of the cross on Angelo's forehead and the palms of his hands to symbolize how he has touched the world and life. As a man of faith, Angelo gratefully receives the holy sacraments from his own two brothers.

**Spiritual Son**

When 69-year-old Bernadette falls into a coma after her recent stroke, the doctor advises the family, "Your mother has suffered severe brain damage. Her breathing has become irregular and you will need to make a decision soon whether or not to put her on a ventilator."

Bernadette's son, Russ, knowing his mother's wishes regarding life support, confers with his sister, and they decide to allow Mom to die naturally without artificially prolonging her life. During their bedside vigil, Russ suggests, "This is Mom's time. We're all here. Let's make this as spiritual as we can."

They begin to tell stories about Bernadette, remembering all the good things about her. Russ, who has adopted an Indian Spiritual Philosophy, reads aloud the sacred Hindu Vedas. Drawing his chair closer, Russ lowers the bed rails and whispers Hindu chants in Mom's ear.

A hospital staff member compliments the family, "I wish everyone could see the enlightened way you are dealing with your mother's death."

Russ and his sister stay with their mother as she dies. Despite their sadness, they are uplifted by the thought of someday going to India to scatter Bernadette's ashes in the sacred Yamuna River.

### Prayer Shawl Ministry

Every evening 93-year-old Leilani recites the rosary awaiting God's call. One day, Cora, Leilani's eldest daughter, presents her mother with a purple and orange prayer shawl, knitted by the Prayer Shawl Ministry. The accompanying card reads: "May the love we have knitted into this prayer shawl bring you blessings and warmth."

The unexpected gift becomes so meaningful to Leilani that for her burial, Cora insists that her mother's frail body be wrapped in the brightly colored shawl.

### Please Come Back Later

Xian, a soft-spoken gentle man, lives in a modest room on the second floor of the hospice. Today he does not acknowledge Fredda as she enters his room for their weekly therapy session. He lies quietly in his bed, a beautiful green and lavender tapestry draped across his legs and his long black hair shining against his pillow. Xian stares upward at a 45 degree angle, and after a few moments says, "Please come back later."

Fredda offers to return in half an hour, but as if he is not aware of her presence, Xian murmurs, "No, not now, I'm not ready." Xian raises his arm and points to the blank wall across the room, just below the ceiling.

"Who is it, Xian?" inquires Fredda. "Who is there?"

"My grandmother, and my aunt and my father," replies Xian, almost imperceptibly, with long pauses between each word. "They are here for me; they are inviting me." Fredda recognizes that Xian is no longer addressing her when he says, "Not now. Come back later. I will go with you later."

Xian drops his hand, closes his eyes and falls asleep. Fredda wishes him peace and rest and leaves the room.

When Fredda attends her "Music and Healing" group that evening, the facilitator has coincidentally chosen Chinese healing music for their meditation journey. Fredda visualizes what seems to be an important ceremonial event: a man reclines in an old wooden cart filled with beautiful blankets as nearby musicians play traditional Chinese melodies.

The next morning when Fredda calls the hospice to inquire, she is told by the nurse that Xian died at 8 p.m. the previous day. Fredda marvels at the synchronicity of the ceremonial images she experienced just at the moment of Xian's death.


Being present with your dying loved one can provide a tremendous sense of satisfaction for you as well as comfort and reassurance for her. Those who have had the privilege often find that accompanying their dear one to the end reinforces the sanctity of life. Whether or not you are present at the moment of death, by choice or by circumstance, there are still many ways to demonstrate your love and respect for your beloved. The funeral or memorial service will provide you with another opportunity to say goodbye with love.

# CHAPTER 8

## Funerals

*Larry La Prise, the man who wrote "The Hokey Pokey,"*
*died peacefully at age 93. The most traumatic part*
*for his family was getting him into the coffin.*
*They put his left leg in...and then the trouble started.*

Internet joke

In the midst of the emotional upheaval that has your head spinning, decisions about farewell rituals for your loved one will need to be finalized. A funeral provides the opportunity to say goodbye to him in the presence of community. As you begin to adjust to the reality that your dear one has died, you are surrounded by the support and love of others. If you decide to have a traditional service, prescribed religious and/or cultural customs will guide you as you make the arrangements. You may derive great comfort from hearing the familiar prayers, liturgy, and music. At the same time, you might want to create a unique customized ceremony, taking special care to put together a service like no other.

## PRE-NEED ARRANGEMENTS

### Twenty Years Ago

While planning a trip to Italy with Harold, I realize that if something should happen to us while we are away it would put unnecessary stress on emotions and pocketbooks of our children if we do not have our funeral plans in place. We have our wills and trusts, but no burial arrangements have been made.

When I mention this to Harold, he is reluctant yet says that if I set it up, he will go with me to sign on. I make the mortuary appointment and lure him by saying, "After we sign the papers, we will go out to celebrate by having a drink."

The entire transaction takes no more than an hour. We look at the space, sign the contract, and write a check. The big surprise is that we have no need to go out for a drink. We both feel exhilarated. At first, we can't figure out why we feel so good about the transaction, but then we realize that the emotional lift comes from taking care of life's business. We have removed an unnecessary burden from our children.

## Let's Take Care of It Now

Seven months after the death of their dad, the four siblings decide that they want to make their own funeral arrangements. Each of them is still reeling from having to go to a mortuary on the day of their father's death to conduct business when all they wanted was to be home with friends and family. So as not to leave their own families with the last-minute trauma of choosing a casket and a final resting place, they make an appointment with a memorial counselor on a Sunday afternoon.

They crack dark-humored jokes: "I wonder if they'll give us a fleet rate?" as they walk up to the mortuary office. Entering the building, they are flooded with emotions reminiscent of the last time they were here for dad's funeral. Sandy rushes ahead, wanting to get the whole thing over with. Deidre doesn't know if she can take another step forward and has to be guided by her husband. Mike and J.T. lag behind talking about last night's baseball game.

Once inside, everyone seems a bit hesitant. The memorial counselor puts them at ease, offering a comfortable place for them to sit at a large round table. An hour and a half later the decisions have been made. Deidre and her partner William want to be buried near a tree; Mike and his wife Susie insist on being buried near the waterfall. Sandy chooses the music she wants played and stipulates who will be allowed to speak; J.T. wants the "no frills" package, and leaves open the option for cremation.

Satisfied with the arrangements, the siblings go out for a hearty meal to break the tension.

## Second Line

Even though he has moved away from his Louisiana birthplace, Reno is convinced that he wants a Creole funeral after he passes and writes down instructions to that effect. He would like to have a traditional Louisiana marching band playing solemn music while carrying his body toward the gravesite. When the guests leave the cemetery, Reno envisions mourners parading in a Second Line holding open umbrellas, dancing, and waving white handkerchiefs behind the musicians. "When the Saints Go Marching In" and other upbeat tunes will transform the mood from sadness to joy.

## Deciding Not to Have a Funeral

Gloria and Christian are a gregarious couple, always entertaining people in their home and always on everyone's *must invite* list. With her lilting soprano voice and his basso tones, they entertain wherever they go, and they love costume parties. Once they show up as Lillian Russell and P.T. Barnum, and Christian performs rope tricks learned from his younger days when he traveled town to town as The Lone Ranger. They enliven every party.

When Christian dies of Parkinson's, it is shocking to learn that he has left strict instructions that he *absolutely* wants no funeral service; he adamantly does not believe in them. Accordingly, after his death, his children phone friends merely to inform them. Gloria tells her daughters that following her death, she wants no funeral service either. Friends find it difficult to accept that there will be no gathering to pay tribute to such unique people. Nonetheless, the daughters will respect and honor their parents' wishes.

## Kathryn in Charge

Kathryn, terminally ill with cancer, has completed numerous rounds of chemotherapy and wears a bandanna to cover her bald head. Recognizing that her death is inevitable, Kathryn convinces her husband Ivan that she wants to go to the cemetery and make arrangements for her final ceremony.

When they arrive at the mortuary, Ivan looks stricken but follows his wife's lead. Even the young memorial counselor has difficulty maintaining aplomb in spite of Kathryn's wit to lighten the mood. The moment comes when they must step into the Casket Room to select something appropriate. Kathryn recognizes how difficult this is for her husband and the memorial counselor. She advises, "I'm fine, but you two might want to bring some tissues!"

While funeral planning may seem like an intimidating task at any time, it is easier to arrange a funeral in advance. Making inquiries when the need is not imminent gives you plenty of time to think about your choices. Furthermore, having the plans in place will allow you to focus on your feelings at the end of life rather than on business. Even though you and your dear ones may be reluctant to address such matters, taking action provides peace of mind. If you are making your own funeral arrangements, think of it as a gift to your family and friends.

## Planning a Funeral in Advance

- Determine who should be included in the decision-making process and who should be informed after decisions are made.
- Consult with your church, temple, or trusted sources for recommendations of mortuaries and cemeteries or cremation societies.
- Choose the casket, coffin, or container for burial or cremation.
- If the body will be cremated, consider whether the cremated remains will be scattered, buried, preserved in an urn, housed in a columbarium, or made into memorial art.
- If the body is to be buried, select burial space—crypt, mausoleum, or plot.

*Planning and prepaying for a funeral can provide peace of mind now and spare the loving ones additional responsibilities after the death.*

---

## FUNERAL ARRANGEMENTS AT THE TIME OF NEED

### Going to the Mortuary

David takes Thelma's arm and supports her as they open the doors to the mortuary. They are greeted by a friendly young woman who guides them to a small, private room where they meet with the funeral director. Over the next few hours, David and Thelma plan every detail of the funeral service and burial for Thelma's mother who died yesterday.

They discuss the options regarding embalming and answer questions about whether there has been organ/tissue donation or an autopsy, any of which might affect the preparation of the body for viewing. Thelma will bring the clothing she would like her mother to be buried in, along with perfume, cosmetics, and a recent photograph so her mother's makeup and hair will look natural.

David, hesitant to enter the casket room, asks, "Can't we just pick one out from a picture?" The memorial counselor advises that it is best to see the actual replicas. David and Thelma decide on a mid-priced wooden casket, with white satin lining.

The flowers are an easy choice for Thelma, knowing her mother's preference for pink roses. They purchase a plot close to where other family members are buried. They will ask their six adult sons to be the pallbearers and two teenage nieces to be honorary pallbearers, walking behind the casket in the procession from the hearse to the graveside.

Through tears and bittersweet smiles, David and Thelma get into their car and on their drive home begin to write the obituary. "I think Mom will be happy with this," says Thelma with a sigh.

## Two Services

The Blakey brothers come to make arrangements for their mother's burial. A disagreement ensues about how she should be buried and who is going to pay. They become loud and destructive, and security escorts them from the building. Outside they continue their scuffle, slugging it out on the cemetery grounds and rolling on the grass like adolescents. After they cool down, the memorial counselor intervenes and comes up with a creative solution. The following week they hold two different funeral services for the same mother.

## Compassionate Staff

Nanette arrives at the funeral home to make arrangements for the burial of her partner, Ellen. She cries throughout the meeting, unable to fathom that Ellen has died after her valiant struggle with lupus. As she listens, Sylvia, the mortuary representative, reaches for a tissue to dry her own eyes. She apologizes profusely, thinking her tears are unprofessional. On the contrary, Nanette appreciates Sylvia's compassion.

Sylvia's openness actually puts Nanette at ease enough to ask, "When Ellen's body was brought here, she was wearing a necklace that I gave her when we first met. Is it possible for me to get the necklace back? I would really like to have it."

"Of course," Sylvia reassures Nanette. "The funeral director will have it for you on the day of Ellen's service."

> Going to the mortuary after his death involves making many important decisions at an already stressful time. Consider who to include and whose wishes will be honored. Memorial counselors are there to listen to your requests and guide you in creating a fitting ritual for your loved one.

## When You Meet With Mortuary Staff

- Prepare a list of questions and requests.
- Be mindful of financial resources and limitations.
- Feel free to express your emotions.
- Bring people with you who can support you.

## Questions You Will Need to Answer

- What pre-need arrangements have been made? (See pre-need guidelines above.)
- Will his body be embalmed?

- Will casket be open or closed?
- Will there be a viewing or visitation—private or public?
- What burial garments are preferred—shroud, favorite clothing, or traditional garments?
- What is the preference for makeup and hairstyle? (bring recent photograph)
- Will there be a graveside, church, and/or chapel service—public or private?
- Will you be sequestered in the family room or will you sit with the congregation?
- Who will officiate?
- Who will give the eulogy?
- Will there be additional invited speakers or opportunities for others to talk?
- Are flowers acceptable?
- Will objects be placed in or on the casket?
- Will there be a printed program with biographical information and who will be responsible for it?
- Will a photograph be displayed?
- Will there be military or fraternal organization tributes?
- What is the preferred music?
  - As people enter?
  - During the service—hymns, soloist?
  - As people exit?
- Will there be a procession from service to cemetery?
  - Will you ride in a limousine?
  - Will there be a police escort?
  - Will guests walk or drive cars to the interment site?
- Who will be the pallbearers and honorary pallbearers?
- Will there be a reception, and who will be invited?

*Be prepared for intense emotions to arise as you finalize the details of the arrangements.*

## CARING FOR THE BODY YOURSELF

### The Vigil

The family transforms their home for the vigil. In the center of the guest room stands the pine coffin Melanie's husband has hand-crafted for his mother-in-law's body. They place dry ice at the bottom of the coffin, cover it with fabric, and place flowers in Mother's hands. Burning candles set the scene. "Mother's face looks blissful," Melanie describes in an email to her cousin.

A dear friend comes daily to play the lyre and family members read spiritual passages. One day, when Melanie leaves to pick up her daughter and friends at the train station, Mother's precious cats enter the room and stand watch. Upon her return, she finds her 13-year-old son reading "Star Wars" to his grandma.

When the 3-day vigil ends, they place silk over Mother's face and sprinkle her with flower petals; the priest blesses the body before closing the casket, and each family member hammers in a nail. They take Mom's body from their home to the crematorium where they say their final goodbye.

> The decision to bathe, dress, and care for your dear one's body yourself is a privilege that may be unfamiliar to you. If he dies at home, you may want to groom his body before calling the funeral home. If his death occurs at the hospital, ask the staff for permission to assist in the ritual.

## Taking Care of the Body

- Determine if you want to participate in caring for his body after death.
- Do you want to wash and dress him?
- Do you want to keep his body at home for a wake or viewing?
- Consult with state laws regarding home funerals.

*Caring for your loved one's body is an intimate act of tenderness.*

## OBITUARIES

An obituary is the written announcement of your loved one's death. Similar to the eulogy that will be delivered at his service, take this opportunity to convey an account of the life he lived and publicly honor his memory. Perhaps your dear one wrote his own obituary in advance, or it may be up to you or a friend or family member to compose it. Don't be afraid to imbue this article with humor and personal references, if you are comfortable doing so. Let this tribute reflect the life he lived.

### Pepperoni Pizza

Harold Dresser: Sweetheart of a husband for almost 56 years to his beloved wife, Norine. Born on May 27, 1921, he died peacefully at home, February 2, 2007, surrounded by his loving family. He will be greatly missed by his son Mark (Carol) and daughters Andrea (Barry) and Amy (Julio). "I love my children, but I adore my grandchildren": Leila, Zachary, Isa, and Avi. He is also survived by his brother-in-law and close friend Mickey Shapiro as well as loyal nieces and nephews. An ardent film fan, after retirement he made his dreams come true by making countless movie and television appearances.

Services will be held on Monday 10 a.m. at Mt. Sinai Memorial Park. In lieu of flowers, donations can be made in his name to your favorite charity.

To honor the joys in Harold's life—kiss someone you love and eat a piece of pepperoni pizza.

### Online Obituaries

Throughout Camille's long battle with lung cancer, her husband keeps everyone informed of Camille's condition via their website and several social networking sites. The couple makes an agreement that Camille's online obituary is to be posted immediately after her death. When Camille dies, the news spreads electronically through the community within minutes.

### Generous of Heart and Spirit

Alexandra Gould died on May 9, 2008, as a result of Parkinson's disease. Alexandra was a loving, spirited person with a great sense of humor, forever young at heart. Born in Kansas City on April 7, 1925, to Sadra and Russell Rowen, she attended Lakewood High School and the University of Nebraska. In 1945, she married Philip Gould and raised four sons. After her children were grown, she went back to work teaching kindergarten until her retirement.

Generous of heart and spirit, Alexandra put others before herself. She was supremely intuitive and had great sympathy for those less fortunate than her. Deep kindness, compassion, and dedication characterized her life. She embraced life's challenges as well as its many rewards. She loved nature and found great solace in the wide-open skies of the Midwest.

Alexandra leaves behind her four sons and their lovely families: Jeffrey (Jody) of Flagstaff, Arizona; Mark (Fay) of Los Angeles, California; Patrick (Davina) of Deerfield, Illinois; and Joel of Kansas City, Missouri.

## Writing the Obituary

- Who will write it?
- Where will it appear?
- Possible information to include:
  - full name and nickname
  - age
  - city/country of residence
  - date and cause of death
  - survived by (partner, children, grandchildren, siblings, parents, other family, friends, or pets if appropriate)
  - predeceased by
  - life review
  - date and place of birth
  - education
  - employment
  - hobbies and interests
  - achievements
  - unique characteristics, humor, and stories
  - information about the service (if applicable)
  - requests regarding memorial tributes—flowers, charitable donations

*Let the obituary reflect the essence of who your loved one was in life.*

---

## VIEWING THE BODY

### Who Identifies the Body

Morrie and Jackie have been colleagues for decades at the state university when Morrie dies unexpectedly. His two daughters fly in from another state to make arrangements for the funeral. However, on the day of the ceremony, when the mortuary requires identification of the body before closing the casket, his daughters cannot bring themselves to do this. To relieve Morrie's daughters of this painful task, Jackie willingly looks at Morrie one last time and assures the mortuary that he is indeed the correct person in the coffin. The ceremony proceeds with a closed casket, according to Morrie's wishes.

### Unfinished Concerto

Yina, a child prodigy pianist, dies of leukemia at the age of 12. At the mortuary, the night before her funeral, Yina is laid out wearing the frilly pink dress she wore at her concert debut and holding a bouquet of red roses like those presented to her after the performance.

Floral wreaths sent by fans and family friends fill the room. Hundreds of mourners come to pay their respects and file past the casket for a last look at the beautiful Yina. Viewers then patiently wait in line to murmur their condolences to Yina's pale exhausted parents.

As they leave, visitors pause to sign the guest register. Mr. Leischin, Yina's first music teacher, writes the following personal note: "Yina's death is a tragic loss to our community and to the world of music."

### That's Not My Sister

Trina spent hours preparing herself to see her sister's body in the coffin at the viewing. Approaching the casket Trina shouts, "That's not my sister. Her hair is all wrong. She likes it pulled away from her face!" Trina grabs a brush from her purse and frantically attempts to restyle her sister's hair.

Viewing the body before burial or cremation is customary in many traditions and discouraged in others. Viewing your loved one's body may help you accept the reality that he has died. Difficult as it can be, you may find comfort in seeing him lying there in the coffin, at peace. On the other hand, it may be too emotionally upsetting for you and you may chose to forgo this practice.

### Viewing the Body

- If there will be a viewing—will it be public or private?
- Who will identify your loved one's body for the mortuary?
- Expect that his body will not look exactly as you remember him in life.
- Respect the decision of others who choose not to see the body.

*Viewing the body is up to individual choice and custom.*

## THE SERVICE

### Farewell My Darling

Zena's children guide her cautiously into the car as they depart for their father's funeral. Oblivious to the world around her, Zena startles when her son Gabriel coaxes her, "Mom, we're here at the cemetery. Lean on me. We're going in together."

Zena looks quizzically at the placard outside the mortuary and nearly collapses at the sight of her husband Jack's name. In stunned silence, she takes her seat in the front row of the chapel next to her sons. Zena turns around and looks desperately toward the gathering crowd searching for her beloved husband. She turns to Gabriel and asks, "Where's your dad? I want to see him."

Gabriel calmly asks his mother if she would like to step behind the curtain and see Jack's body in the casket. Although Zena had made the decision yesterday not to view Jack's body, she now feels an urgency to see him one last time. Accompanied by her son, Zena walks resolutely forward. She stands before the open casket, avowing, "I will love you forever, Jack."

## Oh My Papa

The Weinberg family sits in silence in the front row of the chapel. Soft music begins to play and Doreen recognizes it as their father's favorite cello concerto. As the doors open behind them, they hear the hushed voices of guests arriving and taking their seats. Doreen gets up to greet friends and family. Her younger sister, Marika, remains motionless until cousin Emma touches her shoulder and gives her a kiss. Marika turns to Emma and discloses, "I don't know exactly how I made it here this morning. My world has stopped, yet I saw my neighbors packing up their car to go to the beach. How can the rest of the world be going on as if nothing has happened?"

The music stops and the rabbi begins with the familiar prayers. Doreen gives the eulogy. What warms Marika's heart most are the personal remembrances by the grandchildren and the photo montage they created. The service concludes with the guests filing past the closed casket. As they exit to their cars, the sound of Eddie Fisher singing "Oh My Papa" fills the sanctuary.

At the graveside, a few chairs are set up in front of the burial plot. Looking around, Doreen realizes that now these chairs are here for her and Marika; with the death of their father, they have become the eldest generation. Marika tosses in a rose and a decorated envelope containing her final farewells to her dad as attendants lower the coffin into the ground. Friends and family take turns shoveling earth on the casket.

## Exodus

In planning her own ceremony, Ruth is adamant about the music. "Before the chapel service begins, I want you to play the theme from 'Exodus' over and over and over again." Six months later as funeral attendees enter the chapel, some think that the recording has stuck because all they hear is the musical passage from "Exodus." They chuckle when, during the eulogy, Ruth's daughter explains the reason for the repetitiveness of the "Exodus" theme song.

### Military Honors

James, who died while serving in Afghanistan, lies in his coffin in full dress uniform at the front of the church. His mother, Linda, discovered that James is entitled to a military burial. After the service, a procession of 50 cars follows behind the hearse to the cemetery.

At the gravesite, members of the armed forces perform the military funeral honors ceremony, including folding and presenting the U.S. burial flag to Linda, and the playing of "Taps." A volunteer group of seven veterans fire a 21-gun salute: each of the seven guns fired simultaneously three times. A bayonet, helmet, and cross are placed on the grave. The guests and family stand at attention as they lower James' casket into the ground.

### Service at Sea

Miyumi and her husband have purchased a burial plot for their ashes adjacent to plots of other family members. However, after they attend a burial at sea for their nephew, they decide that is what they want for themselves instead of interring their ashes in the ground. It makes sense to them because so often the two of them have gone on enjoyable fishing excursions together during their over fifty years of married life.

After Miyumi's husband dies, she makes the arrangements. A small group of family and a few close friends go out on a boat used exclusively for this purpose. The ocean air lifts their spirits; it is not a gloomy occasion. The captain places the ashes in a basket with a flower wreath on top. Then he says a prayer and lowers the basket into the sea and the flowers float up and drift away. Miyumi tells her daughter, Sachiko, "They're on their way to Hawaii."

### Theme Funerals

At Hollywood Forever Cemetery, in Hollywood, California, Chanell O'Farrill, Funeral Home Manager, describes personalized funerals. One family uses the theme of the deceased going on a journey and requests that everyone, even the deceased, be dressed in Hawaiian shirts. Another woman asks all her grandmother's friends to wear purple to the service, because that was her grandma's favorite color. An associate of a designer in the fashion industry arranges to bring in mannequins wearing the man's favorite suits. Elsewhere, a man who portrayed a television circus clown is buried with his famous round red nose.

Galen Goben, Grief Support Coordinator at Forest Lawn Parks and Mortuaries in California, describes mementos that are presented to the funeral-goers as they leave the service, for example, flower seeds at the funeral of an avid gardener and poker chips for a Las Vegas dealer. At some services, tokens of love are placed into the caskets: photos, candy, a flashlight, and teddy bears. At the funeral for the director of a facility for mentally challenged children, the children draw pictures and write messages on paper hearts that they place inside the casket.

Personalizing the funeral for your loved one allows you to place your unique stamp upon the ceremony. Being creative with the service does not take away the sanctity of the occasion. Individualizing the rituals allows the service to reflect your dear one's personality.

## EULOGIES

Writing and delivering the eulogy for your dear one may bring you great satisfaction. The eulogy can be sentimental or humorous, as long as it reflects his life accurately—everyone in attendance will know if you are painting a false picture of him. Consider inviting close family and friends to share recollections from the dais. If the person officiating at the service is giving the eulogy, make sure that he has an authentic understanding of your loved one's personality, what he accomplished in his life, and what was important to him.

### Harold—February 5, 2007

In 1951, when Harold told his mom, Annie, that we were getting married, she turned to me and said: "You're such a lucky girl!" Forty-five years later, a journalist reasserted that opinion when she wrote that Harold was a "sweetheart of a husband."

You may have been surprised to hear the "Buena Vista Social Club" music when you entered. Although we are sad, with Harold's approval, we wanted today's music to reflect Harold's life. When he and I first met at a dance in 1951 and he asked, "Do you like Latin Music?" that became more than just a clever pick-up line; it became a *leit motif* in our marriage of almost 56 years. In the early days of our courtship, we loved to go out dancing to Cuban music with his best friend Bernie Sternhill and his wife, Shirley. Decades later, while on a cruise ship, we even won first prize in a rhumba dance contest.

We had a very rich life together, full of adventures and laughter. Sometimes when I would become exasperated by him, he'd make a bad joke, and when I would respond with a moan or a giggle, he'd proudly say, "See I can still make you laugh." That laugher sustained us through the good times and bad.

Throughout his 85 years, Harold knew exactly what he wanted—whether it was cigars, See's candy (nuts and chews), vanilla ice cream, cheeseburgers and fries, or pepperoni pizza. He never wavered. In 1992, as nurses wheeled him in for an angiogram, he called out, "Long Live Pizza." After open heart surgery in Kaiser's Cardiac Care Section while still attached to a portable IV, he attended an "Eating Healthy Food" lecture. Harold had the very first question for the nutritionist: "Is it OK if we cheat once in a while?"

Harold was a contented man and left this world just as he chose—at home, in his own bed and surrounded by the love of his wife, children, and grandchildren. He was also bolstered by all the love and generous acts by extended family, friends, and neighbors. He almost seemed surprised by that, totally unaware of how many people he had touched with his kindness and gentility.

His family was his life. Only a few weeks ago, he turned to me with tears in his eyes and said, "We have such a wonderful family. After I'm gone, be sure to tell them that I loved my children, but I adored my grandchildren!"

Our children and grandchildren have lived up to his star billing. I never appreciated them so much as now in the way that they have participated in the making of difficult decisions as well as their providing outstanding physical and emotional sustenance. Harold and I have been blessed by them—and by all of you here today for your support and love given, especially throughout this past difficult year.

I also want to express our gratitude to the Kaiser Hospice staff and most particularly to Nurse Susan Romo who helped us traverse this painful yet inevitable journey.

Harold's mom was right, "I am such a lucky girl."

### The Environmentalist

Margaret Jean's friends have no doubts that she wanted a green burial on her land in a rural area of New Hampshire. They hold the service on a cool spring day amidst a grove of birch and dogwood trees. Margaret Jean's body is swaddled in her favorite blanket. "She's wrapped herself in that blanket every winter since I've known her," eulogizes best friend Talia. "We say goodbye to her au natural; no embalming, no pomp and circumstance." As others speak, they weave the story of Margaret Jean's life: her devotion to the environment, her political activism, and her appreciation of contemporary art.

## No Holds Barred

Over a 10-year span, Arthur has been sole caregiver for both his mother and father. He insists upon giving eulogies at both funerals and prepares by writing a few notes and then talking from his heart so that he can look directly at the audience. At his mother's service, Arthur describes his mom as "bigger than life and full of love." After the service, the neighbors tell him how proud his mom would have been to hear the kind words he has spoken and to learn that her son thought so highly of her.

Five years later, as he prepares his father's eulogy, Arthur believes it is dishonest to only talk about Dad's strengths. He is reminded of other funerals he has attended where the guests recognize that the words spoken from the dais have been false. Arthur shocks the guests when he reveals that during Dad's prostate cancer, the sicker he got the meaner he became. He tells a hushed audience that while growing up, Dad had been physically and verbally abusive. "But that's the way he was," Arthur states flatly. To balance these statements, Arthur concludes his eulogy by praising his father, "My dad never drank or missed a day of work. He served valiantly in World War II as a military photographer. My father was a good provider and, despite his faults, he did the best he could."

## Spaghetti Gravy

Galen Goben creates a personalized celebrant service after interviewing members of Annamaria's family and discovering that everyone raves about her homemade spaghetti gravy. For the eulogy, Goben builds an allegory around her signature dish. Each ingredient represents a specific aspect of Annamaria's life. The tomatoes form the foundation of the gravy and represent her birthplace and her marriage. The spices symbolize the holiday meals she hosted and how she enlivened the family. The meat provides basic nutrition, just as she supplied tuition for the education of her children and grandchildren. By creating this personalized metaphor, Goben honors Annamaria and captures the essence of this beloved matriarch of the family.

## RELIGIOUS AND ETHNIC CUSTOMS TO HONOR THE DEAD

Funeral rituals and customs that are deeply rooted in religious and cultural beliefs also have important psychological, sociological, and symbolic functions. While you may be familiar with your own religious and social customs, you might be interested in expanding your awareness of ways in which others pay tribute to their dead.

### Catholic Funeral Mass

Maureen, born in Ireland, spends 26 years as a social worker in an urban healthcare center. Her compassion is so great that patients and staff alike dub her "The Mother Theresa of Holy Angel Hospital." Her death, after a brief battle with cancer, jolts everyone.

The night before her funeral Mass, the family holds a wake at the funeral home. Many friends and family arrive, and they have to line up in the hallway before they can step into the flower-filled room to pay their final respects to Maureen.

Father O'Connor officiates the next day at a Roman Catholic Mass where bread and wine are consecrated and consumed in remembrance of Jesus' death. Standing next to a large picture of Maureen, Father O'Connor delivers a glowing eulogy about how extraordinary a person she was, moving the congregation to tears. Choral music, prayers, and the taking of Communion occur, as does the distribution of Holy Cards showing a picture of the Virgin Mary on the front and the dates of Maureen's birth and death on the reverse side. In the days ahead, Maureen's body will be cremated and Father O'Connor will carry her ashes to Ireland and bury them alongside other family members.

### Pentecostal Funeral

After Candy's mother dies, her three children plan an old-fashioned Pentecostal church service. They buy Mom a fancy church dress for burial and adorn her with rings and bracelets. They hold an open casket service in the church where grandfather had been the pastor and Candy played the piano and organ. Being back at church where she grew up brings Candy great comfort. She is warmed by the number of people in attendance and the accolades for her mom. Guests tell stories that surprise Candy; she learns for the first time that they called her mom the "The Songbird" in the rest home.

After the burial, the family holds a reception in an old house owned by the church. They partake in a repast including familiar nostalgia-inducing foods—black-eyed peas, fried chicken, greens, and sweet potato pie.

## Filipino Funeral

When Mino's father dies in the Philippines, he is unable to fly home for the services because the events of 9/11 have just occurred and he is told that he might have trouble returning to the United States. However, when his mother dies a few years later, he makes the trip and, because he is the eldest son, he is in charge of carrying out Filipino funerary traditions.

Mino, on a leave from work for the 10 days of the wake, ensures that his mother's body is never left alone. Her embalmed body lies in state in the family living room, dressed in evening wear, surrounded by yellow chrysanthemums. Neighbors, friends, and relatives come to pay their respects. Visitors play mah jongg in the kitchen and the proceeds are given to his family to defray the costs of the funeral. They drink ginger tea and serve alcohol to celebrate the death. After the wake, Mino's mom has a Roman Catholic funeral.

## A Traditional Jewish Custom

"Hevra (Chevra) Kadisha grants an extra sense of holiness to life," maintains Rabbi Regina L. Sandler-Phillips, who heads the Sacred Burial Fellowship at Park Slope Jewish Center in Brooklyn, New York.

The Hevra Kadisha consists of five core practices: 1) sh'mirah: vigil-keeping from the time of death until burial. Traditionally, one or more Jews watch over the body around the clock, often in 2-hour shifts, reciting Psalms; 2) rehitzah: washing of the body to remove dirt and foreign matter; 3) taharah: ritual purification of the body; 4) halbasha: dressing the body in shrouds (takhrikhim); and 5) hashkavah: placing the dead in the coffin (the actual laying out). Rabbi Sandler-Phillips often sings to the deceased vocalizing melodies in Yiddish, Hebrew, and Ladino (language of Spanish Jews). She likens the process to singing lullabies to babies and compares the Hevra Kadisha to childbirth. "What we're doing is like the swaddling and washing at the beginning of life."

## Muslim Style

Reza and his Iranian-Muslim family have made no pre-need death plans. Consequently, when Reza's father dies, Reza, as the eldest son, is in charge of washing and wrapping his father in a white shroud at a funeral home specializing in Muslim traditions. This custom must be carried out within 3 days of the death. In Reza's California community, there is no Muslim cemetery, but a special section has been created inside a local Christian cemetery that arranges for Muslims to be buried facing Mecca.

Graveside, a Muslim official recites prayers while the family weeps as they lower the coffin into the ground and the backhoe replaces the dug-up earth. Meanwhile, close friends and family serve dates and halvah. Rose water is available in case anyone faints during this open show of emotion. After the earth is restored, the marker set, and flower arrangements are placed on the grave, Reza invites everyone back to his home for a traditional Persian meal of kebabs, salad, rice, and sweets.

## Hindu

When Padmala makes arrangements for her husband Dhani's funeral, she has the body cremated according to Hindu traditions. Thirteen days later, friends and family come to Padmala's home to celebrate the departure of Dhani's soul. They display a picture of Dhani, burn oil candles day and night, and prepare Dhani's favorite foods: okra curry and Bisibelabath (hearty rice with vegetables and lentils). Dressed in white, Padmala and her daughters greet visitors when they come to pay their respects to the family.

### Additional Ethnic Customs You May Encounter

1. Armenian: From the time of death until the 40-day service, when the tablet or tombstone is unveiled, the community does not leave the family alone. Showing emotion is important at this service and loud weeping is encouraged.
2. Cambodian: The family prepares a basket filled with objects the deceased will need in the next life, such as new clothes, rice, medication, and cooking and eating utensils. Seven days after death, the family has a ceremony at home and dedicates the objects to the spirit of the deceased.
3. Chinese and Vietnamese Buddhists: In special small incinerators, they burn paper replicas of items believed to be needed in the next life while they are waiting to be reincarnated. Artifacts include cars, houses, microwave ovens, TVs, and clothing.
4. Ethiopian: Following burial, guests bring food for the 3 days when the family stays home in respect for the dead.
5. Hawaiian: Money enclosed in a white envelope is handed to a family representative who later announces the amount given by each guest.

6. Indian: During the 12 days of mourning, families accept food and flowers but not money.

7. Japanese: At the funeral service, the family accepts monetary offerings in white envelopes (*koden*), used to cover funeral expenses.

8. Jewish: A pitcher of water may be placed outside the front door where mourners wash their hands and symbolically wash away the sorrow of the cemetery.

9. Korean: Three days before the funeral, visitors pay their respects to the departed and make donations in white envelopes. On a special table, the family displays a black-and-white framed photo of the deceased, a floral arrangement, and burning incense.

10. Lao: Guests at the home ceremony bring fresh-fruit offerings or homemade food and an envelope with money to place on the family's home altar.

11. Mormon: Prior to the service, the family holds a viewing of the body in an open casket. Men and women who were devout during their lifetimes are laid out in white clothing. The service and burial are quiet and reverent. Mormons consider the funeral a celebration of life, not a final goodbye. They believe they will be reunited after death.

12. Native American: There are tribal variations. While most are buried in a horizontal position, medicine men are buried in a seated position. Tribal members prefer silence rather than words of condolence.

13. Samoan: Before closing the casket, the spouse or oldest child performs the last bath, pouring perfume over the body. During interment, they sing and throw flowers, especially rose petals.

14. Thai: The Buddhist Temple has a special room where people keep ashes in a pagoda-style container alongside a photo of the deceased.

15. Tibetan: For 49 days after the death, the family prepares a dough of barley mixed with honey, milk, butter, sugar, and dried fruits. Three times daily, a small part of this mixture is offered into a flame to feed the spirit of the deceased. After the 49th day, Tibetans believe that the spirit is reincarnated.

The above customs might help you understand some of the funeral rituals of cultures with which you are not familiar. While it is not intended as a complete listing, these examples will expand your cultural awareness.

### Understanding Ethnic Customs

- Remember that not everyone from the same heritage or background will want the same customs for their funeral.
- Show respect for those who unexpectedly return to long-abandoned traditions.
- Inquire about appropriateness of flowers and memorial tributes.
- Ask someone who is familiar with the traditions about requirements and restrictions for appropriate style and color of clothing and expected participation in rituals.

*Don't hesitate to attend an unfamiliar funeral service.*

Planning and attending a funeral can help you heal. Funerary rituals are designed to honor the memory of your loved one and bring comfort to you and other mourners. The eulogies and music will reflect your dear one's personality and remind you of the sacredness of his life. The offering of gifts—be they charitable donations, flowers, or food—symbolize the love and caring that others have for him. You will gain strength from the gathering of friends and family who have come to pay tribute to your loved one.

# CHAPTER 9

## Memorials

*Grave marker, Sunset Memorial Park, Coos Bay, Oregon:*

*L.D. MAC MC COY*
*Oct. 8, 1900 to Aug.12, 1981*
*"I'D RATHER BE IN RENO"*

You may choose to hold a memorial service for your loved one in place of, or in addition to, a funeral. The memorial celebration commemorates your dear one without her body present and may be held weeks or even months after her death. One advantage of a memorial is that you can take time for planning and schedule it when out-of-town friends and family can be present, on a significant date like her birthday, or when you are ready to place the headstone on her grave or scatter her ashes.

You may also wish to honor your beloved's memory by participating in a public memorial. Joining a large gathering of people who are all remembering the lives of dear ones can be a powerful and moving experience.

## PRIVATE MEMORIALS

### Anchors Aweigh

On a drizzly gray morning in December, ten months after Harold's death, 30 relatives gather at the cemetery to unveil the marker over Harold's grave, now covered by a white cloth. In accordance with Jewish tradition, this memorial ritual takes place within the first year after death.

We recite the mourner's prayer in Aramaic. Then our four grandchildren kneel down and each lifts up a corner of the cloth to reveal the shiny marker below. When I see Harold's name etched in the granite, I suddenly feel ill. Other family members become emotional, too, especially the grandchildren.

Most people don't know about Harold's experiences in the U.S. Navy during World War II and of its significance in his life. I describe a few incidents, then lighten the mood recalling, "While in the Navy, he also learned many things helpful to me—how to make a bed, sew, and iron." The grandchildren distribute song sheets and red, white, and blue pinwheels, and with Mark playing the bass fiddle at a brisk tempo, we sing "Anchor's Aweigh" and wave our pinwheels. Afterward, each person plants a pinwheel around the grave marker.

I explain that one of Harold's favorite songs is "Guantanamera." Mark accompanies us again while we sing this beautiful Cuban-rhythmed song that lifts our spirits. As if to cooperate with our mood, the sprinkling stops and the sun peeks through the rain clouds. We adjourn for lunch at Harold's favorite Italian restaurant where we toast him and delight in the closeness of family.

## Airplane Memorial

Frank, a former flight instructor, runs an airplane business. Planes are his passion. Before his death, Frank requests that he be cremated and that no formal ceremony be held.

For his memorial, his artist wife, June, creates an invitation to a potluck picnic using an old photo of Frank flying an airplane on the front panel. She draws smoke coming out the back of the plane like that of a skywriter that reads: REMEMBERING FRANK. Inside are the details of the event to be held in a large park near their home.

At the picnic, they have live music: bagpipes, Irish harp, flute and drum, and singing. Family, former employees, and tennis partners make speeches to honor Frank's memory. In a special tribute to Frank and his love of flying, June invites guests to make folded paper airplanes from colored paper, after which they have a contest to see who can fly them the furthest. June awards a prize to the winner. Everyone leaves satisfied that Frank would have loved the celebration.

After the event, the family divides Frank's ashes into three parts. They bury one third near the tennis court where he played for decades; his son flies a plane over Frank's hometown and spreads one third from the skies, and his daughter sprinkles the remainder in her garden.

## Take Me Out to the Ballgame

To honor the memory of Dr. Chris, a sports-loving anesthesiologist, attendees sing "Take Me Out to the Ballgame," ending his memorial service on an upbeat.

## Two Different Memorials

Selena and Catherine spend the last 2 weeks of their brother Isaac's life at his bedside in Lincoln Falls, Nebraska. After his death, the community of Friends gather for a Quaker memorial. Inside a bare meeting hall, Friends come to honor Isaac. After a long period of traditional silence, people stand and one by one offer serious reflections about Isaac's spirit.

Catherine, comforted by the presence of so many people who loved Isaac, is nonetheless anxious to return to her home in Pennsylvania at the end of the week. She holds a second memorial service several months later in her hometown church, in keeping with her personal belief system, which is very different from Isaac's. The church is filled with flowers, and during the eulogy people laugh and cry. The service concludes with the singing of "Let There Be Peace On Earth."

## Traveling the World

Ludy travels extensively after the death of his wife Jill; something he was unable to do during her long illness. "I'm going to travel the world and take Jill's ashes with me," he announces to his friends. Wanting to be as inconspicuous as possible, Ludy puts handfuls of Jill's ashes into small plastic baggies. He keeps one in his laptop case and places another into his jacket pocket. Ludy smiles wryly as he wonders how he will explain the bags to airport security if he is questioned. Fortunately, he encounters no obstacles and is able to sprinkle the ashes where he is certain Jill would be happy.

## A Souvenir

Margarita, with her dark sense of humor, loves the macabre. This serves her well in a successful career as a writer of horror books. Before she dies, Margarita's family encourages her to sell her collection of off-beat memorabilia that she has gathered over her lifetime, but she refuses and makes a suggestion that these bizarre objects be distributed at her memorial.

At the ceremony, Margarita's children place objects from their mother's collection on a table and invite friends and family to choose one object each to take home in remembrance of Margarita. The guests clutch replicas of bats, witches, skeletons, vampires, and coffins as they leave the celebration, laughing just as she had hoped.

## Gravestones

Sean O'Regan is the Vice President of Cemetery Services at Mount Auburn Memorial Park, Massachusetts, founded in 1831 as America's first landscape cemetery. Monuments at this cemetery contain symbols of what gave meaning to the lives of those who are buried there: a sailboat for a sailor, a stethoscope for a doctor, and scales of justice for a lawyer.

## Diamonds

Danielle loves jewelry and wants her daughter and granddaughters to have diamonds as a way to remember her after she dies. She learns that more than one diamond can be made from the carbon derived from human ashes. Excited about this discovery, in her will Danielle requests that her ashes be converted into gems for her female heirs. Her daughter and granddaughter are delighted with Danielle's heirloom idea.

## The Paddle Out

Fourteen surfers gather on the beach in Maui at sunset, surfboards under their arms and flower leis around their necks. They paddle out into the ocean to pay tribute to their beloved Sunnie who died last month. Neile chooses the spot where they maneuver their boards into a circular formation, hold hands, bow their heads, and pray silently. At Neile's signal, they toss their leis into the center of the circle. From a nearby boat, Sunnie's grandmother, Tutu, floats a Hawaiian funeral wreath toward the circle.

"It was so beautiful; I felt like Sunnie's spirit was there with us" says Neile, as she climbs back up onto the beach.

## Tea Party

Janay lies on her death bed with a heavy heart. Thirty years ago, as a free-spirited teenager, she had broken away from her family and refused to attend her mother's funeral. She confesses to the hospice chaplain her deep regrets at not having made amends and worries that her own soul will be tormented for eternity. When the chaplain suggests they have a memorial now, Janay balks, "Isn't it too late?"

Two days later, reconsidering the chaplain's advice, the idea comes to Janay to have a tea party in her mother's memory. Early on a Tuesday morning, Janay and the chaplain sip tea from china cups as Janay tells fond stories of the tea parties she shared with her mother when she was a little girl. The familiar aroma of her mom's favorite orange-spice tea brings nostalgic warmth to Janay.

## Into the Ocean

The Roya family members are pleased with their decision to scatter Mom's ashes in the ocean. "I like the idea. Mom loved to travel; this way she can float all over the world," says her daughter Soroya as they fling handfuls of ashes into the sea. Other family members strew Gerber daisies into the water. The myriad of colors, the sparkling ocean, and the sound of the sea gulls fills their senses with great peace and joy as they remember the woman who brought so much happiness into their lives.

## At Home With Us

"I want Grandma at home with us," insists Ruby. Since Grandmother lived with the family for 23 years prior to her death, her loving presence is still felt in every room of the house. At Ruby's suggestion, the family dismisses the idea of scattering Grandmother's ashes at sea and dedicates a nook in the living room to her memory instead. The urn, surrounded by candles and fresh flowers, serves as a daily connection to their adored grandmother.

## Into the Ganges

On the first anniversary of her husband's death and cremation, Padmala and her daughter travel to Benares, India, to distribute half of his ashes into the Ganges River, as is their Hindu custom. Later, the family spreads the other half of the ashes in the Pacific Ocean. At the same time, Padmala goes to her local temple, gives the priest a white shirt and a monetary offering, and donates five white foods: bags of rice, sugar, ghee (clarified butter), flour, and milk.

## Art From Ashes

Craig spends hours in his backyard enjoying the garden that he and Heath created together. Pausing in front of the latest addition to the garden, Craig admires the ceramic statue of a dolphin that contains a vial of Heath's ashes. Around his neck, Craig wears a necklace with a glass pendant containing a teaspoon of his beloved's ashes.

## Keepsake Urns

"After Lazlo was cremated, my son's best friend made a pottery urn for me to keep the ashes in," beams Rosalyn. Her adult daughters, Lindy and

Patty, are envious and want to have decorative containers for themselves to keep a small portion of the ashes in their homes, too.

Searching for anything they might use, their quest leads them to an art gallery. The curator of the gallery overhears their conversation and approaches them, "I worked for a funeral home for years and I have fifty cloisonné keepsake urns at home. If you don't find anything today, come back tomorrow."

The next morning, Rosalyn and her daughters meet again in the gallery and the girls take their time admiring the cloisonné urns. Patty chooses one with green vines; Lindy selects one with a brown and orange motif. "How amazing that this woman showed up just at the right time to help us," says Rosalyn. "Lazlo must have had a hand in this."

## Zucchini Bread

At Jane's memorial, held in a park used by her family on many celebratory occasions, her cousins distribute a program with a picture on the cover of Jane in her birding outfit. The booklet contains Jane's autobiography that describes her battle with cancer, and how it made her more appreciative of life. The family also includes a recipe of "Jane's Famous Zucchini Bread" recalling the hundreds of loaves she baked every Christmas as gifts for friends, colleagues, and clients.

## At the Theater

Although his day-job is waiting tables, Tony is an actor. After moving across country to Hollywood to pursue his career, he lands several roles of which he is very proud. His new group of actor friends becomes his family. After Tony's death from an AIDS-related infection, his body is taken back to Wisconsin and buried in the family plot.

In Hollywood, Tony's friends organize a fitting memorial service of their own at the local community theater on a Sunday morning 4 weeks after his death. The stage is bare except for a chair, a microphone, and a tape recorder so that his mother, who is too fragile to make the trip to California, can have a recording of the service. One after the other, participants come up to the microphone and speak about Tony. Some tell humorous stories; one recites lines from a play; one sings a song; and several play musical instruments.

Fredda, the leader of Tony's weekly AIDS support group, walks onto the stage, looks directly at the tape recorder and addresses her comments to Tony's mother: "I want you to know what an amazing man Tony was.

He was kind and sincere and concerned about everyone in the group. He always spoke with gratitude about the love and support he felt from his family. I will hold him in my heart forever."

## Planning the Memorial

- Design a unique service that captures the essence of your loved one.
- Consider having a "theme" for the celebration.
- Hold the service when it is convenient for you and out-of-town guests.
- If possible, select a location that was sacred or significant to the person who died.
- When the location is not easily accessible to all, make accommodations so that those who are physically challenged are still able to participate in some way.
- Give yourself plenty of time to make the plans.
- You might choose her birthday, date of the death, or another meaningful date.
- If the body has been cremated, determine if the cremains will be kept in an urn, transformed into art, scattered, or buried.
  - Consult local laws about where ashes may or may not be scattered or buried.
  - Consider that ashes may be divided.
  - Be aware that some traditions do not allow you to touch or be near the cremated remains.

*Create a celebration that the deceased would have enjoyed.*

---

## PUBLIC MEMORIALS

### November Ceremony

At Corpus Christie Church in Pacific Palisades, Msgr. Liam Kidney draws on his Irish background for an annual memorial celebration. Each November, he drapes the sixth pew from the front of the church with a white cloth and dedicates it to the memory of those members who died that year. Family and friends light candles and display memorabilia and photos on the covered pew. Two banners hang from tall pillars on each side of the altar with the names of the deceased for all to see.

Msgr. Kidney encourages his congregants to be responsible for keeping the memory of the deceased alive. He tells a story that he learned from his mother, "We Die Three Deaths." The first death is the physical death of the person. The second death is when the person is remembered at the service where his life is celebrated. The third death is when there is no one left to remember that person. The Monsignor reiterates, "That is why it is so important to keep telling the stories of the departed."

## OUR HOUSE Run for Hope

Early in the morning on the day of the Los Angeles Marathon, hundreds of group members and alumni from OUR HOUSE Grief Support Center gather to walk or run a mile in memory of someone dear to them who has died. Although tears flow freely, there is an air of excitement as participants gather to celebrate the life and the memory of their dear one. Each wears a T-shirt printed with a picture of his loved one and the phrase "I'm running in memory of...."

Everyone has a story to tell. "I am thinking about my dad today. I think he can see me and is proud of me," says 7-year-old Jamal, whose father himself was a runner. Jamal's little brother Jared, aged 4, points to the picture on his shirt and says, "My daddy died, too."

Among the adults participating in the Memory Walk is Eileen, whose son died from testicular cancer at age 24. She expresses her gratitude for being in the midst of others who know, only too well, the pain of grief, "Without all of you, I'm not sure how I would survive."

Stephen and his brother-in-law take their turns talking about their wife and sister who died suddenly in a car accident. "Everyone loved Suzanne. Her smile could light up a room."

In the midst of the heartache, there is a sense of hope and healing. Tears mix with laughter as the memories of loved ones are brought to life.

## AIDS Memorial Quilt

In the community room of a small seaside town, Martin and Barry walk silently amidst the rows of quilts laid out on the floor. Both eager and apprehensive, they search for the panel they embroidered with a yellow sun and rainbow so many years ago for their dear friend Jeff, who died of AIDS.

"It's over here, next to the stairs," Barry sits down on the top step and waits for Martin to join him. "Do you remember his laugh? Can't you just hear it?" They exchange memories and stories of times they spent not only with Jeff but also with so many friends whose lives ended too soon.

"I stopped counting at 150 deaths," recalls Martin, "and I stopped going to memorials and reading obituaries. It got to be too much then. But now it feels good to let myself remember and reconnect. Jeff will never be forgotten."

## Entertainment Industry Foundation Revlon Run/Walk for Women

"It's very emotional when you first go," says Sally referring to her annual participation in the Revlon Run/Walk. "You know that the majority of people have had cancer or are still dealing with it or are remembering someone who has died of some form of female cancer."

The runners begin the race, sprinting through a shower of confetti that falls from the skies. Sally, walking in memory of her sister and grandmother, joins a large group of walkers. Some come in groups, some come alone, and some pull children in wagons or push strollers. They all revel in the enthusiasm of the observers on the streets who cheer them on.

## AIDS Ride

At the opening ceremonies of the AIDS Ride, Don's family greets him wearing matching T-shirts sporting a picture of his brother Bram looking vibrant and very much alive. "I ride in honor of my little brother, Bram, who died of AIDS when he was only twenty eight," remarks Don. "He was an amazing man, with an engaging smile, sparkling eyes, and a great personality. I feel that he is riding alongside of me as if his spirit is here motivating me to complete the ride."

At the closing ceremonies, Don pledges his commitment to raise money for AIDS research by participating every year. "I will continue to ride so that others will not have to experience the terrible tragic loss that my family lived through."

## Japanese Lantern Floating

Lantern floating is a time-honored Japanese cultural rite designed to comfort the spirits of the deceased. The lanterns are said to ferry spirits from this world to the next. Fredda participates in this annual Memorial Day service sponsored by the Shinnyo-en Buddhist Community and the Na Lei Aloha Foundation in Honolulu Bay.

As someone featured in the documentary film describing this ceremony, *Where the Ocean Meets the Sky*, Fredda joins other invited guests to inscribe lanterns with personal messages. Participants speak in reverent tones or write in sacred silence their prayers for peace and free-dom from suffering and messages honoring the memories of those who have died.

One hour before sunset, 40,000 men, women, and children gather along the beach. As the pink sky fades into darkness, they set two thou-sand candle-lit lanterns afloat on the ocean.

At the conclusion of the ceremony, a teenage girl exclaims, "I could feel my grandma there with me in the light."

A father comments that he is uplifted by the ritual, "I come back every year to honor my son's memory and to let him know that he is not forgotten."

"I believe my husband can somehow hear my prayers and is com-forted," asserts a widow as her eyes follow her lantern moving toward the horizon.

Fredda experiences the most private moments of remembrance, and at the same time, she feels the power and presence of thousands of others from all countries, religions, and ethnicities who have gathered to honor their loved ones.

## Winter Candle Lighting Service

AJ arrives at the memorial park on a Tuesday evening in early December. Piped-in music fills the air as he finds a seat among the crowd, carry-ing the unlit candle given to him by one of the cemetery staff members. After an inspiring invocation, ushers move along the aisles, lighting the candle of the first person in each row. As each participant's candle is lit, he says aloud the name of the loved one he is remembering and lights the candle of the person next to him. Flames are shared in this manner until 1,000 candles shine. The ceremony concludes with the singing of "Silent Night."

At the reception that follows, AJ remarks, "It gives me a sense of hope. Grief is a very lonely experience. To be surrounded by a thousand people who know what you are going through, that's powerful."

## Jewish Cemetery Memorials

Every year on the Sunday between Rosh Hashanah and Yom Kippur, the Hersh family attends the *Kever Avot* (grave ancestors) service where hun-dreds of mourners come together as a community. The rabbi offers prayers and tells a story, and classical musicians perform. After the mourner's prayer the family members receive pebbles from Israel, which they place on their loved ones' graves as a memento of their visit.

## Chinese Ching Ming Ceremony

Each Spring, Chinese communities throughout the world observe Remembrance of Ancestors Day, also known as Grave Sweeping Day. In East Los Angeles, Mr. Wong, Mrs. Lee, and other members of the Chinese Historical Society sweep and weed the graves of their relatives. They make offerings of incense sticks and paper money for burning, and place yellow chrysanthemums at the gravesites. After the Buddhist priests pray for the dead, those present feast on a variety of foods, including suckling pig, fruit, and wine.

## Day of the Dead

Every year on November 1, All Saints Day, in Oaxaca, Mexico, the Garcia family visits the graves of their ancestors, pulling weeds and cleaning the headstones. On November 2, Dia de los Muertos (Day of the Dead/All Soul's Day), they prepare an altar in their home for the most recently deceased in their family displaying photos, memorabilia, and the decedent's favorite foods. They believe that on All Soul's Day the deceased returns for a visit. In the evening, the Garcias shoot off fireworks to guide the spirits home.

## Butterfly Release

Corinne stands among the crowd of hundreds of grieving adults and children as Paula Marie Jones, music therapist, sings "Somewhere Over the Rainbow," at the annual Buena Vista Hospice Care Butterfly Release. When Corinne hears the words "blue birds fly," she opens the glassine envelope she is holding and releases a gorgeous black and gold monarch butterfly. Those around her gradually open their envelopes and the crowd watches as 450 fluttering creatures hover and take wing.

To Corinne, the butterflies represent transition and transformation. Until this moment, she has been trapped in her memories of the pain her sister, Penelope, experienced at the end of her life. Corinne's sadness diminishes and her spirits are bolstered as she imagines the butterflies representing Penelope's spirit being set free from her pain-ridden body.

Public memorials are large, powerful ceremonies that unite you with others who are gathered together to honor and remember.

Some memorials commemorate those who have died from particular illnesses; some are related to specific ethnicities and religions. You do not need to have a personal connection in order to participate in a public memorial. Memorials in general give you a sense of *communitas*—solidarity and togetherness.

A memorial celebration honoring your loved one's memory may take place immediately after her death or many weeks, months or years later. Taking time to create a celebration of life that reflects her personality may be uplifting for you as well as for family and friends.

Participating in a public memorial is a way to rekindle your connection to the person who died and continue to honor her memory year after year.

# CHAPTER 10

# Grieving

*"You're STILL going to that support group of yours?"*
*"Well, he's still dead."*

Support group member

The person you love has died. Shock and disbelief turn your world upside down. It does not matter that he had been ill for a long time. It does not matter that he expressed that he was ready to die. It does not matter that the doctors or the hospice nurses prepared you for this moment. Witnessing the death of your loved one or receiving the news that he has died brings your life to a grinding halt.

The numbness you feel is natural, although nothing about it seems natural or normal. As though on autopilot, you go through the motions of daily living in a surreal world. Perhaps some days, upon awakening in the morning, you have a split second of forgetting that your beloved has died. Or throughout the day you automatically reach for the telephone and then reality hits: "Oh no, he is dead. I can't call him any more."

At times, excruciating raw pain surges through your body. You may sense a hollowness in your stomach as if someone has punched you in the gut, an ache in your heart as if it is breaking in two, a lump in your throat, or a weakness in your muscles. Chances are you have either lost your appetite and can't eat or you are eating too much. Your sleeping patterns have probably been affected as well—either you want to sleep all the time or you find yourself unable to fall or stay asleep.

Waves of emotion including sadness, loneliness, and yearning wash over you with an intensity that astounds you. The fluctuating nature of grief may leave you feeling angry one moment and guilty the next. At times you find yourself filled with anxiety and unable to sit still, or you feel lethargic, hopeless, and barely able to move. Sudden bursts of grief or uncontrollable bouts of crying may be triggered by predictable reminders of your dear one and sometimes by nothing at all. When you are completely overwhelmed by sorrow, you may experience periods of deep despair, asking yourself "How can I possibly go on living?" In those moments, life seems unbearable.

Even when life seems more manageable, you wonder if you are going crazy. You misplace your keys, forget important appointments, and your attention span is fleeting. Unable to concentrate, you find yourself reading the same words over and over again in a book or newspaper with little comprehension. You think you see or hear your dear one, and you startle at the sound of loud noises. You just don't feel like your old self, and you wonder if you will ever regain your equilibrium.

While it would be unrealistic to expect your grief journey to follow a steady upward progression toward wholeness, you will start to have easier times. Gradually, you will have some grief-free periods, be they measured in minutes, hours, or days. Little by little you will discover that your bursts of grief don't last as long and you don't have them as frequently.

Be gentle with yourself when you find yourself wondering "Am I grieving correctly?" "Why do I still feel so bad?" "Is it okay that I have times when I can laugh and not think about him at all?" Grief is not a problem to be solved. It is a process to be lived. Your sorrow will have its own timetable, and you don't have to do it alone. Connect with others—loving friends, family, support groups, a therapist, spiritual advisor, or religious counselor. Although the fabric of your life has been torn by the death of your dear one, it will mend. While you will not go back to being the person you were before he died, healing will take place.

## SHOCK AND DISBELIEF

The reality that your loved one has died is a shock to your body and your mind. His death is almost too overwhelming to comprehend. You think to yourself, "I can't believe that he is not here by my side, that he won't be home for dinner, or that I will no longer be able to hold him in my arms." A surreal sensation wraps you like a cocoon, insulating you from the outside world. The numbness you feel is nature's way of anesthetizing you for a while to the excruciating pain permeating your physical and emotional being.

### In a Bubble

Eddie doesn't recognize himself since his precious wife, Lorna, died within 3 months of her diagnosis of pancreatic cancer. Usually an organized, reliable bank executive and father, Eddie has lost his anchor. The children turn to their Aunt Lizzy to help them pack their lunches, change the hamster's cage, and do their homework. Eddie, barely able to motivate himself to get off the couch, feels numb most of the time. "I feel like my heart has been violently ripped out of my body," he tells Lizzy. He relies on her to remind him when it is time to take a shower, get dressed, and accompany her to pick up his children from school.

After extending his bereavement leave to 4 weeks, Eddie returns to work. He hasn't worn a suit since the day of Lorna's funeral, and he moves in slow motion as he puts his briefcase into the car. Recognizing that his reflexes are dulled, Eddie takes surface streets rather than the highway. The world looks surreal, and Eddie feels like he is in a bubble.

As Eddie walks into the bank, the tellers and loan officers nod and greet him with a few awkward words of condolence. Eddie barely acknowledges them, grateful that he can retreat behind the closed door of his office. Like a robot, Eddie takes his keys out of his pocket and places them on the table. As he hangs his gray plaid suit jacket on the coat stand, Eddie looks down and notices that he is wearing two different colored shoes, one brown and one black. He reaches for his cell phone to send a text message to Lorna, knowing how she would laugh at his blunder, and then he remembers that Lorna is not there to joke with any more. For over an hour, he stares blankly at the pile of papers waiting for his attention until he realizes that he is not ready to return to work. As Eddie leaves the bank, he mumbles to his secretary, "See you tomorrow."

## And Then I Remember

To the outside world, Simone appears to function fairly well considering that her partner Portia died only 6 weeks ago. She goes about her routine, walks and feeds the dog, and gets to work on time.

When Simone's cousin, Malia, stops by unexpectedly, she is dismayed to see Portia's belongings strewn around the apartment as if Portia were still alive. Two pairs of her shoes lie near the front door. Her pajamas still hang on the bathroom hook, and her wallet sits on the kitchen table. Trying to be helpful, Malia straightens the stacks of mail that have accumulated and reaches for Portia's wallet.

"Wait! Don't move that," Simone intervenes. "Portia likes her wallet on the table where she can find it; she keeps her keys there, too. Where are her keys? Have you seen Portia's keys? I'd better find them; she gets frantic when they aren't right here on the table."

Noticing Malia's horrified expression, Simone pauses and starts to cry, "I can't believe she's not here. I feel like I'm living in an alternate universe."

"It's so unreal," acknowledges Malia, leaving Portia's wallet untouched. "I can't imagine what it's like for you."

"Sometimes I sense Portia's presence so strongly," admits Simone. "I think I hear her walking up the stairs. And then I remember."

## SADNESS

Heartbreak and sorrow are your frequent companions as you grieve. Bouts of uncontrollable crying sweep over you unpredictably. And shedding tears is only one manifestation of your sadness. You feel lethargic, helpless, and experience a lack of interest in the world around you. When your sadness seems like a bottomless pit with no way out, you ask yourself, "Will I feel nothing but this sadness twenty-four hours a day forever?" While it may seem that way right now, your sadness will naturally ebb and flow as you ride the waves of grief.

### How Will We Get Through This?

After his father's funeral, Andrew plans to remain in Florida with his mother, Arlene, until the end of the week. Then he will fly back to Baltimore and be at work Monday morning. Each night Andrew is awakened by his mother's footsteps as she paces restlessly from her bedroom to the kitchen and back again. His heart aches as he listens to her muffled cries. In the early hours of the morning, Andrew enters the den and finds Arlene wrapped in his father's bathrobe, drinking hot chocolate and staring into space. Her puffy eyes and disheveled hair are a sharp contrast to her usual meticulous appearance. Andrew sits beside his mom as she wonders aloud, "I'm just so sad. I feel so empty. How will we get through this?"

Andrew decides to stay with his mother for a few extra days. He calls the office and tells his boss, "I can't find the strength to fly back home. Work can wait. Everything can wait. I just want to be here with Mom."

### Today Would Be Our Wedding Day

Unable to get out of bed, Leora sobs uncontrollably. Today, June 21, would have been their wedding day, had Sean not died 3 weeks ago from a rare tumor.

Throughout his diagnosis and treatment, Sean and Leora continued to plan the details for their wedding celebration. But the minister delivered Sean's eulogy instead of officiating over their wedding vows. And rather than adorning the wedding reception hall, the white and purple gladiolus stood tall and graceful beside his casket.

Sheila, who was to have been the maid-of-honor, feels helpless knowing there is nothing she can do to take away Leora's pain. "How can this be?" Leora blubbers, "We had everything figured out. It was supposed to be the best day of my life, but it is the worst." Sheila, at a loss for words, holds Leora as she weeps.

## Voice Message

Serena and her sister Kaycee take a break from shopping and stop for a latte. Serena leans in and says with concern in her voice, "Kaycee, I called you yesterday when you weren't home and the voice message came on. You still have Raffi's voice on there. That's really creepy, Kaycee. Your husband has been dead more than 6 months. It's time to replace his message."

"You don't get it, Serena," Kaycee explains. "I love hearing Raffi's voice. In fact, when I get home, the first thing I do is play his outgoing message. It makes the sadness of walking into my cold empty house seem less lonely—at least for the moment."

# ANGER

It is unfair that your dear one died. You have every right to be angry even though others may say to you "Oh, no, you shouldn't feel that way. You must focus on the good times." Remember that if you are angry it is not only permissible but important to express your feelings, as long as you do so in constructive ways such as punching a pillow or screaming in the shower.

## Losing Faith

Each Sunday, instead of going to church, Anahit and Vartan visit the grave of their 24-year-old daughter, Anoush. Vartan's belief in God has been superseded by a boiling anger. He deliberately rams his truck into a cement block wall. He yells at his employees and is irritable with Anahit. How could God take away his beloved child?

"Anahit was so young and brilliant. She would have been the first in our family to become a doctor," Vartan fumes, slamming the front door as they return from the cemetery. "Why me, God?"

Vartan wonders how he will ever enter the church again. The only thing that brings Vartan comfort is his strong belief that he, Anahit, and Anoush will all be reunited one day in heaven.

## Unexpected Debt

"May I please speak to Dov?" asks an unfamiliar voice on the phone. Dov's wife, Natalia, tells the caller that Dov, age 50, has recently died from complications following a stroke.

Unsympathetically, the caller demands, "Well, when can you make arrangements to pay the outstanding balance he still owes me?"

Appalled, Natalia doesn't know how to answer. She has no knowledge of her husband owing anyone money. However, in the days following Dov's funeral, she receives a number of threatening phone calls. Creditors demand immediate payment of neglected bills, and the bank sends her intimidating letters.

As a stay-at-home mom, Natalia has been busy taking care of their three small children; she let Dov manage all their finances. Now she discovers that he has refinanced the house and is behind on the mortgage payments. Although Natalia knew that Dov liked to gamble, she had no idea they were in such serious financial trouble.

"How could you leave us like this?" screams Natalia pounding on the bed, furious with Dov for leaving her and the children in such a vulnerable economic situation.

## Second Time Love

Gina meets Sal a few years after both their first mates die. She is in her mid-seventies and he is ten years older. They fall in love instantly and while they do not marry, Sal moves into Gina's home and they share a deep romantic love for 6 years. Although Sal loses mobility, this does not deter them from taking cruises together and generally enjoying a blissful life.

When Sal dies, his daughter, Olive, makes sure that Gina's name is mentioned only at the end of a long detailed obituary. She identifies Gina merely as her father's "partner of later years." The minister, recognizing this dismissiveness, surprises Olive at the service saying how important Gina had been in Sal's life and how happy she made him in his final years. Olive becomes enraged and 2 days later phones Gina demanding her father's possessions, including his golf cart and scooter.

Gina feels angry, hurt, resentful, and sad. She can't sleep, and she has lost her appetite. She doesn't know who she is any more. For 6 years, Gina loved Sal deeply and took care of him. Now instead of sympathy and condolences, she is made to feel like an intruder.

## Family Disintegration

After their parents die, Cherie and Adele discover that their brother, Aldo, has unscrupulously gotten their mom and dad to sign papers leaving their entire estate to Aldo and his wife. The sisters legally attempt to retrieve some of the money for themselves and their children but without success.

Cherie admits to the lawyer that Aldo's behavior has ruined the family. She can't even grieve for her parents because she is so angry with Aldo, "How do I deal with a brother who destroyed all the love in the family?"

Pouring all her emotion into a letter to Aldo, Cherie sits in her den that evening and writes, *I hate you for what you've done to our family. And all because of greed. The folks would be so ashamed of you. I'll never forgive you.*

Cherie throws the letter into the burning fireplace and with some satisfaction watches it turn into smoldering ashes.

## GUILT, REGRET, AND REMORSE

Chances are you feel guilty about something you said or did not say to your loved one; or maybe you regret something you did or did not do. Thoughts about what could have been different weigh on your conscience. You relive uncomfortable situations and wish "If only...."

### What Was I Thinking?

During her freshman year at college, Arielle learns that her father Lester's cancer has metastasized. Lester has been ill for as long as she can remember, and he has overcome battle after battle with his illness. Certain that he will triumph this time as well, Arielle calls her dad in the hospital and tells him that she will be home as soon as finals are over. The day before her last final, Arielle receives a call that her father has died.

After the funeral, Arielle admits to her sister, "I feel so guilty about not being with dad when he died. What was I thinking? If only I had come home sooner."

On Father's Day, Arielle returns to the cemetery and stands at Lester's grave. She thanks him for being such a wonderful father and asks him to forgive her for not being with him at the end of his life.

### We Never Talked About It

Best friends, Michelle and Jhana marry two brothers from their hometown and move in next door to each other. The women envision that they will be life-long friends and that someday their children will also be best friends and share life's joys together.

When they are in their mid-thirties, Michelle is diagnosed with leukemia. Unwavering in her devotion, Jhana drives Michelle to doctor's appointments and sits with her as she receives her infusions. The two friends talk about everything but never speak about Michelle's impending death.

After Michelle dies, Jhana laments, "Over the six months that Michelle went in and out of treatments, we both knew she was dying. She knew that I knew. I knew that she knew that I knew, but we never talked about it." Jhana, tormented with regret that she and her best friend kept up this charade, wishes she could turn back the clock.

On Michelle's birthday the following month, Jhana buys a greeting card decorated with lace and rhinestones and writes the sentiments she wishes she could have expressed when Michelle was alive.

### Letting Her Go

Six months after the death of his wife, Jean-Pierre sits in the back seat of the car driven by his brother Luc. He, Luc, and his sister-in-law, Josette, are on the way to a baseball game. When Josette asks Jean-Pierre how he is doing, he admits, "I feel like I killed Martine."

Irritated, Luc retorts, "Oh, that's ridiculous. There was nothing left to do for her. Now, come on, we're going to a game. You'll feel better after a couple of beers and a hot dog."

But Josette encourages Jean-Pierre to say what is on his mind.

"Just before she died, I told Martine that it was OK to let go," Jean-Pierre admits remorsefully. "But I didn't mean it. I wanted her to live. I'm afraid she thought I had given up on her."

"No husband could have been more devoted than you," Josette reminds Jean-Pierre. "But I know that the memories of that last day must play and replay in your mind. I think about her all the time, too."

## ANXIETY AND FEAR

You feel anxious and afraid. You fear you will not be able to take care of yourself now that your loved one has died. You ask yourself, "Who am I without him? Can I manage alone? Will anyone ever love me the way he loved me?" Expressing your fears will help you gain control over them and will diminish their power over you.

### Will You Help Me?

As the principal of the high school, Tyrone is a well-known and respected figure in their small community. He plans wisely for his retirement. Consequently, his pension, along with Jillian's modest income, allows them to live comfortably in the home they shared for 42 years. When Tyrone dies just prior to Jillian's 70th birthday, she feels fearful and doesn't know how she will face the future.

"What will I do without him?" Jillian tries to convey the enormity of her loss to her cousin Fay, also a widow. "Tyrone was my partner, my lover, my provider. He was the one who made me feel safe in the world."

Jillian's worries run the gamut, from being afraid to drive alone at night, to concern about the finances, to apprehension that there will be no one to take care of her if she becomes ill. Fay encourages Jillian to express herself openly and then asks, "What would Tyrone say? How would he soothe your fears?"

Jillian toys with Tyrone's wedding band that she wears on the middle finger of her left hand. "He would hold me close and tell me to slow down. Ty had so much faith in me. I've got to get a grip. I owe it to him. But, how will I get through this alone?"

"It will be hard," Fay acknowledges squeezing Jillian's hand. "But I'm here and I'll help you find your way."

## YEARNING

You experience deep longing and wistfulness as your heart aches for your loved one to be here. There is so much you want to share with him. How do you face that emptiness? Find ways to stay connected to him. Visit places that were special to you if that helps, or avoid them if that hurts too much. Talk to your beloved, write to him, or carry treasured objects that make you feel close to him.

### Joke's Over, You Can Come Back Now

Stan Mack, nonfiction cartoonist, writer, former art director of *The New York Times Sunday Magazine*, and creator of "Stan Mack's Real Life Funnies", has no idea where to pick up his life after his partner Janet dies of breast cancer. The silence in his apartment is deafening. He sleeps on a mattress on the floor, because he can no longer get into the bed they shared.

In his illustrated love story, *Janet & Me*, Stan describes himself as a string without a kite. In the poignant chapter entitled "Joke's Over, You Can Come Back Now," Stan writes: *I was numb and probably half insane. Janet's ashes now sat on a shelf in a pretty wooden box.... But I couldn't go near that box. Janet's ghost sat at her computer. Her drawer full of single earrings promised falsely that she'd be right back.*

Ten years later, Stan tells Fredda, "I just wanted my old life back. I was talking to her all the time in the apartment. Whether I was speaking to her or to the fates, there was a small part of me that felt if I say it, maybe it can happen; maybe she can come back."

### The Story of Our Love

"We both knew he was terminally ill, but we never expected him to die so quickly," Ayaki tells a new acquaintance from her widow's support group. "We had so many plans and dreams. Our love story was only starting to be written. He died when we were in the middle of a sentence; not at the end of a chapter; and certainly not at the end of a book."

### Environmental Champion

Marshall had a hard life, working two jobs in order to provide his children with the opportunities that he himself had missed. A child of the 1960s, he was a passionate champion of the environment until the day he died.

Marshall instilled in his son, Logan, a great respect for nature. His dream was that Logan become an attorney with a specialization in environmental law. Fifteen years after Marshall's death, Logan achieves this goal and aches to share his accomplishments with his dad.

Logan writes a letter and reads it aloud at his father's graveside:

*Dad, I got it. The offer came through. They are making me a partner in the firm. I did it for you, Dad. Law school, passing the bar, working myself to the bone to fulfill your dreams has paid off. I only wish you were here to celebrate with me. P.S. I continue to wear your watch to work every day. It helps me feel close to you.*

### The Relationship We Never Had

Rochelle envies her friends who share close relationships with their parents. Growing up with a single mother who was critical and domineering, Rochelle remained aloof from her mother, Iris, and moved out as soon as she graduated from high school.

Years of therapy and coming to terms with her anger and disappointment allows Rochelle to make peace with the fact that they would never have the mother/daughter relationship that Rochelle longs for. When Iris becomes ill, Rochelle dutifully runs errands and visits for short periods without resentment.

After Iris' death Rochelle writes to a friend, *I'm in the midst of taking in the fact of my mother's passing. Though we had a difficult relationship and part of me feels liberated from her presence, she gave me birth and I honor her for that. Grieving takes so many forms and though I don't feel sad, there is an empty space where she used to be.*

## RELIEF

Feeling relief that your loved one died can be confusing. You wonder, "How can I be relieved that he died? Does this imply that I didn't love him?" Of course, if your relationship was not a good one, you feel liberated that you no longer have to interact with him. But given that you had a loving relationship, it is still natural for you to feel grateful that your dear one is out of pain and no longer suffering. Worrying about and taking care of him was exhausting for you and not having those responsibilities *is* a relief. This does not mean that you loved him any less.

### How Do You Spell Relief?

Most people are surprised that Celeste doesn't fall apart after Quentin's death, but they don't know the full story. Celeste writes an email to her friend Madge in England.

> *Dear Madge,*
>
> *It's difficult to tell folks that I feel better now. You should see the way they look at me. But I do feel relief because I don't have to watch Quentin suffer anymore. Don't forget, by the time he passed away, I had been grieving for five whole years. I hope you won't think I'm horrible for saying this, but seeing him so helpless and miserable, I sometime prayed that he would die. Of course I loved him and I always will. I would give anything to have our old life back. But that can't be.*
>
> *I'm heading off to work now. Tonight I'm going to a movie I've been wanting to see . . . a chick flick. You know, the kind Quentin would never go to. I know I'll have a good time.*
>
> *More later,*
>
> *C.*

## HOPELESSNESS

You may find yourself wondering how you can go on living without the person you love. It seems impossible. Your grief surrounds you like a thick fog, and you have temporarily lost your confidence that life will again be worthwhile. When despair shrouds your ability to feel hope for the future, confiding in someone you trust may help.

## How Can I Go On?

Raul and Clementine love jigsaw puzzles. They assemble them throughout their 53 years of marriage. Some are framed hanging in their bedroom. Two half-completed puzzles sit on card tables in the den. When Clementine dies, Raul can neither find the motivation to return to his hobby nor put them away.

"Since Clementine died, I feel like a jigsaw puzzle myself," comments Raul to his friend Esteban. "It's like someone separated all the pieces, shook up the box, and I don't know how to put myself back together again."

Raul confides to Esteban that without his wife he is desperately lonely, "Clementine and Raul. Raul and Clementine. Our names went together like bread and butter. I feel like half my identity is gone."

The world doesn't make sense to Raul these days, and he sometimes feels like he can't go on living without Clementine. When he shares these sentiments, Esteban worries that Raul is talking about ending his own life.

"No, I would never do anything foolish," Raul assures his friend. "I have my kids and grand kids to live for. I could never do that to them. It's just that life seems so empty without Clementine."

## Another Cocktail

Terrence prepares himself another cocktail. It was not uncommon for him and his partner, Louis, to relax with a martini after a full day's work. But since Louis died, Terrence doesn't stop at one or two drinks before dinner. A bottle of wine with his meal or several beers while mindlessly watching television is now the norm.

Terrence feels isolated in his grief. Because he moved to town after Louis died, most people are unaware that Terrence is grieving and consequently don't offer him condolences or recognize his unhappiness. They see him as a private person who minds his own business.

When Terrence doesn't show up for work 2 days in a row, his administrative assistant, Richard, goes to his apartment. Stumbling to the door, Terrence is groggy and disoriented as he greets his co-worker. "What's going on here, Terrence?" inquires Richard.

"It's embarrassing to have you see me like this," Terrence gestures toward his messy living room. As they talk, Terrence reveals to Richard that since his partner died, life does not seem worth living without him. Terrence admits, "I've been drinking myself into oblivion every night."

Richard shares that although he has never experienced a death, he has had his own struggles with alcohol and drugs. "Let me take you to a meeting," Richard suggests, "It will help."

The next morning, Terrence reaches out for support and goes to his first Alcoholics Anonymous meeting. He haltingly announces, "Hello. My name is Terrence, and I'm an alcoholic."

Twenty members loudly respond, "Hello, Terrence." He feels cautiously optimistic that this environment will encourage him along a healthier path.

### I Took the Pills

Seven weeks after her son, Elliot, dies of a traumatic brain injury received in combat, Stella finds life unbearable. It was hard enough sitting at his bedside where he lay unconscious for all those months, but Elliot's death has left Stella despondent. She spends her days sitting immobilized on her couch, wanting to do nothing but sleep to escape from the reality of her situation. Day after day, Stella feels desperate to end this pain.

"You don't understand," Stella laments to her daughter, Yolanda. "I can't go on. My precious boy is gone."

The next evening, Yolanda barely recognizes her mother's voice on the phone, "I took a bottle of pills. I'm sick. You better come over."

In the emergency room they pump Stella's stomach and she is hospitalized for 72 hours. As conditions of her release, Stella promises Yolanda and the doctors that she will remain under the care of a psychiatrist and begin twice weekly counseling sessions with a grief therapist.

## GRIEF TRIGGERS

You can anticipate that your grief will be activated by predictable triggers such as holidays, significant dates, returning to a familiar location, or the marking of major life events. It will be helpful to make plans and backup plans for support at those times. On the other hand, you may be blindsided by sights, sounds, smells, and experiences that will catch you completely off guard. Both predictable and unexpected triggers may set off an intense grief reaction even years after your loved one's death.

### Birthday Toast

A reminder pops up on Clay's Blackberry to alert him that his wife Gabriella's 34th birthday is 1 week away. Clay ponders the best way to honor the date this year without Gabriella, since she died almost 8 months ago. He invites three couples to join him at El Morfi, Gabriella's favorite Argentinian restaurant, noted for their savory empanadas. Their friends are delighted because Gabriella loved birthdays, and they know that she would appreciate still being celebrated.

Feeling nostalgic before he leaves the house, Clay opens Gabriella's closet and inhales the fragrance of the perfume that lingers on her clothing. The aroma connects him with her essence. At the dinner, Clay orders a bottle of champagne, and after they toast the birthday girl, each friend relates a memorable Gabriella story.

## Going to the ATM

Tamar sits in her car in the bank parking lot with the checks to be deposited lying on the passenger seat. She tentatively enters the bank, hoping that she won't see anyone she knows because she doesn't want to have to retell the story of her daughter's death. Tamar instinctively avoids the ATM in the lobby, but when she approaches the tellers' windows and sees the long line, she returns to the machine.

Mustering her courage, Tamar punches in her password, the birth date of the daughter she has just buried. With this action, Tamar bursts into tears. The bank manager rushes over and, when he learns of her dilemma, offers to change her password. He is surprised when Tamar emphatically shouts, "No!"

The manager shrugs his shoulders and walks away.

## Earthquake of Emotions

When Chandra's mother dies, she has no time to grieve. She is too preoccupied with the pragmatic details of making funeral arrangements and helping her dad cope with living without his life partner of almost 60 years.

Four years later, when Chandra travels to India, the tour group visits a small community hospital jam-packed with children afflicted with polio. At the sight of the handicapped children in medieval-like contraptions to help them grow properly, Chandra feels like she is drowning, runs out of the hospital, and sobs uncontrollably for more than an hour.

When Chandra's tears subside, she realizes that seeing the polio-stricken children triggered vivid memories and stories about her mom, who had herself contracted polio as a young woman. This spontaneous release of emotion provides a catharsis for Chandra who no longer has to bury her grief.

## Photo Op

Anya joins a married couple, with whom she has been friends for over 40 years, to visit the Ronald Reagan Presidential Library. She walks ahead of them as they approach President Reagan's official plane, Air Force One. As Anya is about to step inside, a professional photographer asks if she would like her photo taken entering this historic airplane. She declines the offer, but after she enters, Anya looks back and sees her friends having their photo taken. Sadness overcomes her. She feels no desire to mark this occasion without Yitzhak by her side.

## Our Song

Pilar has been in and out of the car all morning running errands. Now, stuck in the middle of a traffic jam, she and other drivers look helplessly at one another. Pilar turns on the radio and starts to cry as she hears Al Green singing "Let's Stay Together," the song she and her late husband Jude called "Our Song." The sharp memory of Jude's death cuts into her, and she cannot control her sobs. Stalled motorists on each side of Pilar notice her distress and mouth, "Do you need help?" "Are you OK?" Pilar gestures that she needs no help. The only help she could use right now would be to feel Jude's arms around her, but that can never be.

## AS TIME PASSES

You may be wondering, how long your grief will last. There is no set timetable for grief. Some people think it takes a year. After all, within the first 12 months you will have experienced your first birthday, his first birthday, the first of each major holiday, the first of each important date on your personal calendar, and finally, the first marking of the day of his death. Yet grief does not end in a year. It would be unrealistic to assume that grief automatically subsides just because you have gotten through the firsts.

The second and succeeding years present new challenges. The reality that he will never be here for *any* of his birthdays awakens the profound recognition that death is forever. You will have to live the rest of your life without your beloved. In many ways that seems too great a task. At the same time, you have made it this far. You are beginning to reengage in life and experience moments of contentment and healing. You have glimpses of hope for the future.

## The Unveiling

The immediate family sits at the graveside for the unveiling of Lola's mother Rachel's gravestone. It feels like déjà vu as they all occupy the same chairs they sat in just a year ago. Lola, who had been pregnant at her mother's funeral, now holds her infant daughter in her arms. Her grief feels raw and overwhelms her with a flood of emotion.

Lola's father, Rudy, gives a touching tribute to his wife and speaks of how difficult the last 12 months have been. He surprises the family with his concluding words, "I believe that there is a time to mourn and a time to stop mourning. Now that a year has passed, my official mourning period has ended. I know that this is what Rachel would have wanted."

Lola doesn't sleep well that night and tells a friend the next day, "I am pleased that my dad is feeling so much better. But unlike him, my grief hasn't stopped just because we have come to a certain date on the calendar."

## Secret Affair

Ten months after Ella's husband Denzel dies, she gets ready to go on her first date. As she anticipates the evening, Ella doesn't know if she wants to go through with it. But friends and family remind her how lucky she is to be only 35 with time to start life over with someone new. Ella heeds their advice and goes on the date.

As she sits at the table with a man who is not Denzel, Ella self-consciously scans the restaurant to make sure she isn't spotted by anyone she knows. Certain that someone will notice her and surmise that she is having a secret affair, Ella's guilt is overwhelming. And then it hits her—she isn't having an affair. Denzel has died, and she is a widow.

## Cemetery Visits

Although Arpi had time to prepare herself for the death of her beloved husband Armen, she is devastated after his death. She visits his grave weekly. She must look at his marker and see his name to believe that this nightmare is real.

After 6 months pass, Arpi visits Armen's grave only every other week. After a year, she visits once a month and sometimes skips a month. She tells her daughter, "I don't need to go to the cemetery so often now to visit your father. I keep him safely in my heart."

## No One Remembered This Year

"On our first wedding anniversary after Pascal died, my son brought me flowers and my in-laws had me over for dinner," Hosanna tells her co-worker Diane, "But no one called this year, so tonight it's going to be just me and my memories."

Refusing Diane's offer to take her out for a drink to mark the occasion, Hosanna explains, "It has been eighteen months since Pascal's death and getting through this anniversary seems harder than last year."

"Really? I don't hear you crying as often lately. I thought you were a lot better," Diane tells Hosanna.

"The grief is different now," reflects Hosanna, grateful to have someone willing to listen. "I don't feel it constantly like I did in the beginning, so that's good, but the pain hasn't disappeared. I guess it's more like a volcano that erupts every once in a while, especially on days like his birthday and our anniversary."

Hosanna spends the evening writing a love letter to Pascal. Her tears flow freely as she soaks in a bubble bath, surrounded by the warm glow of jasmine-scented candles. Before going to sleep, Hosanna kisses the wedding photo she keeps on her nightstand and whispers, "Good night, my love. I miss you."

## CONTINUING CONNECTIONS

Maintaining a bond with your dear one after his death means allowing the love you shared to continue as you hold him in your memory and in your heart.

### Sleeping on Papa's Side

Lelia and her grandfather, Papa Harold, have been very close for 25 years and on the evening of his death, she insists on sleeping on his side of the bed next to me. "Papa is here with me," Leila smiles as she places both hands over her heart. She adds, "Sleeping in his bed makes me feel more connected to him."

I learn from Leila. I now sleep on Harold's side of the bed. It's much easier to do that than experience the pain of reaching over and finding no one there.

### Baby Bunting

Since her husband Irwin died, Brin's family has grown. Five of her six children have married and her oldest daughter is about to give birth to the first grandchild. During the home birth, the midwife asks for a blanket to swaddle the infant. Brin reaches into the drawer and absentmindedly grabs one of Irwin's red flannel shirts.

"I feel like Daddy is here," beams Brin's daughter at the sight of her first-born wrapped in her father's Pendelton. Thus a tradition is established. In subsequent years as the other grandchildren are born, each one is wrapped in one of Grandpa Irwin's old flannel shirts.

## Sign on the Overpass

Helen and her husband, Len, live hundreds of miles from most of their family, yet they regularly make road trips to visit them. After Len dies of heart disease, Helen still wants to visit the family, but she is unaccustomed to driving alone over such a long distance. Trepidation overcomes her on her first solo journey. She feels unsure of herself and her ability to stay awake at the wheel. As her determination wavers, she approaches an overpass and sees a boldly painted message in royal blue: "HELEN I LOVE YOU!"

Buoyed by the unexpected appearance of what she interprets as a message to her, Helen's confidence rebounds. Despite logic telling her that Len hasn't personally written those words, she becomes nostalgic, thinking of Len's habit of leaving "I love you" notes for her hidden all over the house. Six hours later, Helen successfully arrives at her destination.

## Amy Jo's Dream

Two weeks after her father's death, Amy Jo has an unsettling dream. From a distance she sees her brother and sister hovering over their dad as he lies on a gurney in their front yard. Amy Jo signals to them asking if dad is alive or dead. Before they respond, Amy Jo wakes up still not sure of the answer.

Later, as she dresses for work, Amy Jo sadly reminds herself that her father is dead. As she enters her car, once owned by her dad, she discovers a cigar butt on the front seat. Cigars were her father's passion and tabooed habit. Although Amy Jo has been driving this car for weeks, she hadn't noticed the cigar before. Seeing this object of her father's affection brings Amy Jo comfort and makes her feel that Dad is still with her.

## Whistler's Mother

At a neighborhood garage sale, professional photographer Aline Smithson serendipitously finds a small print of Whistler's Mother, what looks like the exact chair from the famous painting, a leopard coat and hat, and a 1950s portrait of a cat. Spanning many months, Aline poses her good-natured elderly mother, Katrine, in over 21 ensembles seated in the position of

Whistler's Mother. In one photograph, Katrine is dressed in the leopard coat and hat and on the wall hangs the portrait of a cat. In another, she wears an Elvis wig and a white jumpsuit and on the wall hangs a black velvet Elvis painting. In other poses, she is dressed in a swim outfit, matched with a seascape; holds bread and wine as she faces a replica of the Last Supper; and is clad in a striped prisoner's uniform as she sits across from a painting of bloodhounds. Throughout the different poses, Katrine never changes her stoic expression.

After Katrine's death, Aline mourns that her mother passed away before she saw the finished witty series. "Seeing my mom's photographs hanging in galleries and being purchased pleases me so much. Now others can appreciate the playful warm woman who was my Mom," she says with pride.

## Meditation on the Good Times

Eight months after her boyfriend Parker dies, Blythe recounts to Fredda in her therapy session that she cannot stop picturing Parker's death. Those last few hours replay in her mind over and over.

Fredda guides Blythe through a visualization in which she goes back to a romantic weekend that she and Parker spent together along the Mendocino coast. As she envisions the two of them standing in the gazebo on the bluffs overlooking the ocean, Blythe can almost feel Parker's arms around her and hear him saying, "I will love you forever."

Over the next several weeks, Blythe discovers that the flashes of Parker on his death bed are less frequent. "The haunting images haven't disappeared," Blythe confides. "But I am able to recall many more positive memories now. I feel like I've reconnected with Parker's spirit in a much more loving way."

## Connecting With Dad

"I love you, Honey Bunch," are the last words Shauna's father speaks to his adored daughter just moments before he dies.

Shauna's family is nontraditional and has no funeral or memorial service for Dad. Without a formalized occasion for receiving comfort from others, she withdraws from her friends believing they cannot understand what she is going through. When Shauna reaches out to a local counseling center and they fail to return her call, she is reticent to phone again. Consequently, she receives no bereavement counseling.

Twelve years after her father's death, Shauna's grief remains unaddressed. Only when she prepares to move to a new apartment does she remember that Dad's cremains still sit in the original box in her coat closet. Taking this opportunity to create a ritual of her own, Shauna carries a small amount of Dad's ashes out to the nearby mountain trails where he loved to hike. As she sprinkles the ashes around the boulder where Dad used to sit and enjoy the view, Shauna whispers, "I love you, too, Dad."

## Grief Journal

Luanne and her sister, Heidi, relax on the porch of their summer cabin overlooking the lake. It is the first vacation they have taken together since Luanne's best friend, Kirstin, died.

"I can't believe how cathartic this is," a relieved Luanne tells her sister as she completes a page of her grief diary. "I've wanted to write about Kirstin's death for a long time, but until I had this journal I couldn't figure out where to begin."

Responding to similar sentiments expressed by grievers over the years, Fredda and her colleague Randi Pearlman Wolfson, Adult Program Coordinator at OUR HOUSE, compiled the Adult Grief Journal in 2008 and inscribed on the first page, *I never thought I would be writing in a grief journal. But here I am. You have died and I am grieving. As I write my thoughts and feelings, I am remembering you.*

Luanne finds some pages easier to complete than others and gives herself permission to skip around through the journal. She explains to Heidi, "Yesterday, I filled one of the blank pages with photographs of the two of us together and wrote about how much I miss her. Today I followed the prompt 'Music connects me with you' and my mind drifted back to Kirstin's funeral. I had forgotten that we played 'Candle in the Wind' at her service. It feels good to remember."

## Mother of the Groom

Before their marriage ceremony, Brandon and his bride, Kayla, place one long-stemmed white rose on the front row aisle seat. They share a quiet moment thinking about Brandon's mother, Lisa, who died just over a year ago.

During the ceremony, as the bride and groom stand beaming at the altar, the pastor explains to the guests, "Brandon and Kayla have placed a single white rose on the chair that would have been occupied by Brandon's mother, Lisa. In her memory, Kayla is wearing the pearl necklace that Lisa wore 29 years ago on her wedding day. Brandon and Kayla ask that we all take a moment now to remember Lisa and all those who are not here to celebrate with us on this joyous occasion."

## SUPPORT GROUPS

Although nothing can magically take away the pain you are experiencing, you will find some measure of comfort in talking to others who have also experienced a death. As described by Jo-Ann Lautman, founder of OUR HOUSE Grief Support Center in Los Angeles, "When the foundation of your home, and your life, has been shaken by death, grief groups create a sense of community and help you feel less isolated."

### Pay Now or Pay Later

For the first few months after Chalon's brother, Lionel, dies, she goes about her life like nothing has happened. She refuses to participate in any conversation about Lionel and immerses herself in her work, spending evenings and weekends at the office. Noticing Chalon's edginess, her friend Shelby urges Chalon to join a grief group. "You've got to deal with your grief, girlfriend," Shelby suggests. "Pay now or pay later, but you're going to have to pay."

Reluctant to join a group, Chalon is reassured by the fact that the other participants will be her age and all have experienced the death of a brother or sister. When she inquires at her first meeting how this is going to help her get over her brother's death, one of the seasoned members replies, "You don't get over your sibling's death. It becomes part of your life. It's like an old coat that was torn; you can repair it, but the imprint is always there. Time and talking about your grief help you get through it."

### Young Widows and Widowers

The support of a loving family and a caring community helps Shannon through the early days after the death of her 26-year-old husband, Brent. However, after a couple of months, Shannon's friends stop calling every day to check on her. They go back to their lives, raising their children, pursuing their careers, and focusing on their own priorities.

When the hospice social worker makes a follow-up bereavement call, she refers Shannon to an OUR HOUSE Support Group for young widows and widowers. At the first meeting, one woman in the group, Oriana, admits how forgetful and absentminded she has become lately. Mitch shares that he can't focus on reading material and how, even in the middle of his workday, his mind drifts back to the day of his wife's funeral. At the conclusion of the evening, Shannon tells the others, "I have been feeling like a stranger in a foreign land where I don't speak the language. But tonight I feel so supported and understood by you all."

As the group progresses over many months, the topic of funerals and burials arises. Elroy describes his visits to the cemetery, "I don't tell my co-workers where I'm going, but I visit my fiancée's grave at least once a week on my lunch break. I hope you don't think I'm strange, but I find the cemetery very peaceful."

One evening, the conversation moves to dating. Shannon confides that close friends fixed her up with a recently divorced man. "We met at a coffee house and it was pleasant until he asked, 'So, do you like to have fun?' I knew what he was really asking and I could hardly wait to leave."

They share a hearty laugh and Oriana confesses, "In those first few months I made a pass at Marty's best friend. I'm so embarrassed, but there was such a drive to make a connection. I missed Marty's touch and having someone to hold me."

When Mitch adds, "I can't imagine what it would be like to sit next to a woman in a movie theater who isn't my wife," two men and two women from the group decide to go on a practice date. The following week they talk about how their outing stirred up sentimental memories of their first date with their deceased partners. Their feelings fluctuate between nostalgia, confusion, and hope.

The group empathizes with Shannon when she relays how it took all her courage to clean out her husband's closet and give his clothes to charity. "I'm glad I saved a few things, though," she adds tearfully. "When I want to feel close to Brent, I wear one of his old rugby shirts and imagine he's nearby. It's still so hard for me to believe that I will never see him again."

After a year and a half, as the group nears its end, members recognize how, through time and mutual support, some of the tears have turned to laughter. "In many ways it's still really hard and I know that grief will be part of my life forever," observes Mitch, "but the group has helped me more than I ever could have imagined."

## Parents' Grief Group

Each Thursday evening after their grief support meeting, the eight bereaved mothers go to the nearby deli for chicken soup and comfort food. The conversation flows from tears to laughter and back again. After several months of sitting at the same booth in the back of the restaurant, the now-familiar waitress asks the women, "So who are you ladies? Do you all belong to some club?"

Ruta, who is seldom at a loss for words, retorts, "We belong to the club that no one wants to join."

The waitress is embarrassed and apologetic when Ruta explains that it is the death of their children that brings them together. "But I hear your laughter. I had no idea."

Ruta explains, "These women are my homies. We're comfortable together. There is no judgment, no pitying looks, just a lot of love and acceptance. We are living through hell, but these women make it bearable."

## Let Me Introduce You

Nine months into their grief support group, despite their diversity of experiences, the members feel a deep connection to one another. On this particular evening, Anna, a conservative attorney who usually wears a business suit and pumps, walks into the meeting wearing a cowgirl outfit complete with a Stetson hat and Western floral shirt. Manny carries a bottle of his wife's perfume. Carrie has a plate of brownies and a small urn containing her sister's ashes. Malka brings a photo album and a DVD with highlights of her father's life. Each of the participants has a chance to introduce their deceased family member to the group via treasured objects.

At the conclusion of the evening, amidst the tears and laughter, Malka exclaims, "I've gotten to know each of you so well, and now I feel like I know the people who died, too. I wish I could have known them in life."

## Coping With Grief

- Remember that there is no right or wrong way to grieve.
- Give yourself permission to grieve in your own way.
- Acknowledge that your grief will take time and follow its own course.
- Write your thoughts and feelings in a letter to the person who died.
- Express yourself creatively through art or music.
- Make a scrapbook or photo collage.
- Go for a walk in nature or get some exercise.
- Visit places that had special significance to your loved one.
- Participate in prayer, meditation, or other spiritual practices that sustain you.
- Talk to a trusted friend.
- Join a grief support group—contact the social service department of your local hospital or hospice for referrals.

- Talk with a therapist or grief counselor.
- Take care of your physical health—schedule a checkup with your doctor.
- If you feel suicidal, overuse alcohol or drugs, or are worried about your safety, immediately consult with your physician or a mental health professional.

There is no prescribed path or exact recipe for your grief journey. You will mourn in your own unique way as you grieve the death of your dear one. While you may have heard that time heals all wounds, with grief time alone is not enough. It is what you do with the time that counts. Find ways to express your thoughts and feelings, trust that the pain will ease, and be patient with yourself as you move toward hope and healing.

As you create your new life, you will discover meaningful ways to maintain a continuing connection to your loved one. You will develop a new relationship with him by keeping his memory alive in your heart and your mind. The love that you shared with him will be part of your life forever.

CHAPTER 11

# What About the Children?

*Eight-year-old Zachary has never been to a*
*cemetery but now must attend the viewing*
*of his beautiful young aunt, who has died of cancer.*
*Overwhelmed by the sight of her laid out in her casket,*
*he asks if he can go outside the building and wait for his parents.*

*As Zachary looks around and sees all the tombstones,*
*incredulously he exclaims, "Wow! There's nothing but dead*
*people here!"*

Support group member

From the time your loved one is diagnosed with a life-threatening illness you begin deliberating, "Shall I tell my child?" "Will knowing about the illness frighten her?" "Maybe I should wait and not say anything yet."

As much as you want to protect your child, she probably already senses that something is wrong. Perhaps she overhears you having a conversation that stops abruptly when she enters the room. Or she notices your tearfulness and irritability. Even your youngest child perceives changes in your behavior. Rather than add to her confusion, help your child understand the turmoil that has descended upon the family.

As you talk to your child about your dear one's illness, speak to her in age-appropriate language, using simple, concrete terms, and words she can understand. Just as you would find a way to explain to her what to expect when a baby is coming into the world, teach her about illness and death. Listen to her questions and answer them honestly. Encourage her to express her feelings. Anticipate that your child might get upset or angry, refuse to believe what you are saying, or that she may not show any outward reactions at all right now. No matter what her response, reassure your child that you are there for her. Make an effort to spend extra time with her, play with her, give her plenty of hugs, and continue to help your child feel safe and loved.

As death approaches, give your child a chance to say goodbye. Perhaps she will want to spend time with your loved one or she may prefer to draw a picture or send a message. Keeping her aware of what is happening and offering and respecting her choices will give her some measure of control during this confusing time. And when the death occurs, your child will look to you as a role model for how to react. Take this opportunity to share your feelings with each other, all the while demonstrating that you are still able to care for her. Remind your child that although someone she loves has died, that person will always be in her heart and in her memory. You can anticipate that through time your child will not only survive, but thrive.

## WHEN A FAMILY MEMBER IS TERMINALLY ILL

Help your child understand the illness. Hearing the truth from you will let your child know that you care about her and that she can trust you. You don't want her to hear harsh or inaccurate information from others. Gently introduce the possibility of death.

### My Daddy Doesn't Have Cancer

At age 5, Fabio can't remember a time when his daddy wasn't sick, but he isn't quite sure what is wrong. He and his daddy like to talk about Fabio's day at school and how much they both love soccer.

Each Sunday, Fabio's soccer coach asks if everyone is practicing between games. Most of the other children reply that their parents play with them during the week. But Fabio's father is usually too sick to even attend the games. His mom is busy taking care of the family, and, besides, she doesn't really like sports.

One day while they are warming up on the soccer field, one of Fabio's friends asks, "Is your dad coming to the game in his wheelchair? Don't you hate it that your dad has cancer?"

Fabio doesn't know what the word cancer means and doesn't like other kids talking about his dad that way. "My dad just doesn't feel well today. He doesn't have cancer."

"Uh-huh, yes he does," insists Bruno emphatically. "My mommy and daddy told me he does and he's going to die."

Tears sting Fabio's eyes and he runs off the field wondering what this is all about.

## Baba Loves You This Much

From the time Daryush is diagnosed with non-Hodgkin's lymphoma, he and his wife, Jasmina, include the children in the conversation. Eight-year-old Kamran asks lots of questions and wonders if he is going to catch dad's illness. He gets upset when dad is too tired to help him with his homework. Gila who is 3 thinks it is fun to have her daddy, whom she calls Baba, home in the afternoon when she returns from preschool. They play together on his bed and have tea parties with her dolls. It's like being at a hotel, with a TV and microwave oven on the dresser, and eating meals around a card table next to daddy's bed.

"Baba has a disease that's called cancer," explains Daryush to his children. "The cancer is very strong and it makes my body weak. That's why I don't go to work and have to spend time at the hospital getting treatments. But you don't have to worry, you cannot catch it from me."

"Are you going to die?" blurts out Kamran.

Jasmina and Daryush exchange a tender glance before Daryush continues, "If my cancer can't be cured, eventually my body will stop working and I will die."

"Like Cutesie, our bunny?" whispers Gila, climbing into her mother's arms.

"Yes," replies Jasmina. "And like Cutesie, Baba's body will be buried in the ground. We will miss him, but when we think of Baba we will all have our special memories and remember how much he loves us."

When Daryush's condition worsens and he is barely able to speak, Jasmina suggests that they make up gestures to communicate without words. From his bed, Daryush takes his turn first and makes a thumbs-up sign and Kamran shouts: "Good job!" Daryush nods his head yes.

Gila suggests: "Three blinks means 'I love you', OK, Baba?" With a faint smile, Daryush extends both his arms out to his sides and blinks three times.

"Bigger than a bread box?" Jasmina guesses.

"That's not it Mama," Gila interprets as she stretches her arms as wide apart as she can. "It means Baba loves me this much," she says, planting a kiss on her father's cheek.


## Avoiding His Mother

Teenaged Beto, an only child, has always been close with his mother. At the onset of her multiple sclerosis, Beto remains attentive even as he observes Mom's slow physical decline. As Mom becomes more disabled and has difficulty speaking, Beto uncharacteristically distances himself from her.

Luis, Beto's father, understands his wife's need for continued close-ness with their son. At the same time, Luis understands how difficult it must be for Beto to accept his mom's drastic deterioration. Although Luis tries to convey that Mom's time is limited and how meaningful it would be if Beto were to spend more time with her, Beto cannot. Instead, he dedicates all his time to practicing and rehearsing with his band and is shocked when she dies.

## Best Friends

Ten-year-old Tanesha places the floral napkin on her grandmother's bed tray while the hospice aide, Gladys, spoons chicken broth into a bowl. Before they leave the kitchen, Tanesha tells Gladys, "The girls at school are mad at me because I won't tell them what's wrong with Grandma."

Gladys pauses, understanding that it must be hard for Tanesha to explain that her grandmother is in the final stages of cancer. "You haven't told anyone?"

"Of course not. That would be weird," Tanesha glumly responds. "You can't just say your grandma is going to die."

"I think you should tell your best friends," advises Gladys. "They probably want to know what you're going through. And it will make you feel better to share your secret."

The next day at school when Tanesha sees her two best friends, Penelope and Holiday, she reveals, "My grandma has cancer and is going to die soon."

Holiday confides, "My grandma died last year. I was scared. I didn't understand what was happening."

"My grandma says she's not scared," Tanesha counters. "She says she is ready for the Lord to take her."

"We thought you were mad at us," says a worried Penelope as she links arms with Tanesha. "My mom always says best friends have to stick together. Why don't we walk home with you today?"

Tanesha smiles and says, "That would be nice."

## Talking to Your Child About Illness

- Rather than saying the person is "sick," name the disease.
- Explain the illness using age-appropriate language.
- Answer your child's questions and offer information on what lies ahead.
- Allow your child to see your emotions rather than pretending that everything is fine.

# EXPLAINING DEATH TO CHILDREN

How do you explain death to your child? You may be used to hearing people use euphemisms because they think that a child cannot understand the concept of death. While it is true that children need to be somewhere between the ages of 7 and 10 before they can comprehend that death is permanent and irreversible, there is a simple definition. Explain to your child that when someone is dead it means that his body stopped working: his heart isn't beating; he isn't breathing; his brain has stopped; and he can't see, hear, or feel anything.

## Did Pop Die?

Patrice likes living with her mom and grandparents in a big two-story house with a climbing tree in the backyard. Patrice's favorite time with her grandfather, Pop, is when he picks her up from school on Fridays and takes her for ice cream. She always orders a small vanilla cone with sprinkles and gummy bears. Pop prefers chocolate with almonds on top.

When Pop develops cancer and goes to the hospital, no one explains to Patrice why he can't pick her up for her Friday afternoon treats any more. Patrice thinks Pop must be mad at her.

One night as she lies in bed playing with her stuffed animals, Patrice overhears Mom answer the phone and grandma screaming and crying. She holds on to the wobbly banister and quietly descends the stairs to the living room. Bewildered, she looks at her mother and asks, "Did Pop die?"

Mom doesn't answer. She sends Patrice upstairs without an explanation.

## At the Museum

While her grandmother frantically looks for a parking place at the museum, 5-year-old Julia unexpectedly asks, "Bubby, why do people have to die?"

Without missing a beat, Bubby answers, "So there will be room for others to park their cars."

## Where Is Nana?

Seven-year-old Sara sits at her grandmother's funeral listening to the eulogies. At the conclusion of the service, she goes up to Rabbi Neil Comess-Daniels, creator of the children's prayer/poem/song *I Miss You*, and says, "I remember something about Nana." Pointing to her sleeve Sara recollects, "She always kept a tissue right here." The rabbi asks someone nearby for a fresh tissue, rolls it up, and places it in Sara's sleeve.

A moment later, Sara asks, "Rabbi Neil, where is Nana now?" The rabbi takes her finger and points it to Sara's heart, to her head, to the tissue rolled up in her sleeve, to her toes, to the air and the trees, to the people, and then back to her belly button, saying "Nana" with each point. Sara smiles. She knows her grandma is up, down, in the clouds, in the ground, far away, and deep inside of her.

## Daddy Is an Angel Now

Seven-year-old Carolina's father, Mario, passionately watches and plays sports, especially baseball. When Mario is hospitalized with a stroke, Carolina stays home with her Aunt Talia because the hospital prohibits visitors under the age of 16.

One afternoon Mama comes home and says, "Daddy is an angel now." Carolina sits quietly on her bed. Then after a few minutes, her eyes widen, and a smile breaks across her face as she thinks, "An Angel? That was Daddy's favorite baseball team. Why didn't he tell me he was going to be a baseball player?"

Carolina is excited to see cars in front of her house when she returns home from school several days later. It looks like a party. Daddy must be home! She races through the house where friends and relatives gather, but no Daddy. She announces to her cousins, "My Daddy is a baseball player now. He is an Angel." Carolina's cousins laugh at her and tell her she is wrong. They taunt her, "Your Dad is dead. While you were at school we went to the funeral and saw him buried in the ground."

Carolina runs out of the room crying to her Aunt Talia who picks her up and holds her. She gently explains, "Daddy had a stroke and his body stopped working. Today we buried him in the cemetery. I can take you there sometime if you ever want to go."

"But why did Mama say that Daddy is an Angel?" sobs Carolina.

"We believe that when Daddy's body died, his spirit went to heaven," explains Aunt Talia. "You can't see him, but now Daddy is your special guardian angel."

## Suggestions for Explaining Death

- Your child is trying to make sense of what you are telling her. Use the real words "died" and "death." Euphemisms can be confusing, for example:
  - Hearing "passed away" your child wonders if this is like passing a football or passing a test.

  - Hearing "Dad left us" your child wonders where Dad went and why did he leave?
  - Hearing "We lost your Mom" your child wonders why we aren't out trying to find her.
- Explain the cause of death simply and honestly; saying that someone died because he was sick is too vague.
  - Rather than, "Your dad died because he was very sick," say, *Your daddy died of a disease called cancer.*
  - Identifying the illness will ease your child's fears, and she won't have to worry that every time someone says, "I'm sick today," he is going to die, too.
- Use correct terminology when explaining what happens to the body when someone dies. *Grandpa died. That means his body stopped working, which means his heart isn't beating; he no longer breathes, sees, hears, nor feels pain.* Describing what it means to be dead is especially important when explaining burial or cremation.

## TAKING YOUR CHILD TO THE WAKE/ FUNERAL/MEMORIAL

Including your child in the funerary rituals depends upon when and where the ceremonies will take place and on the choices that you and your child make together. While it is not always possible to have her present, consider the benefits. Attending a ritual farewell allows your child to remain physically close to you, easing her fears of further abandonment. The ceremony gives her the opportunity to honor and memorialize her loved one in the presence of her family and community.

### Mariachi Band *Musica Sacra*

At his great-grandmother's wake, 4-year-old Marco stays close by his Tia Aida's side, clutching her hand, as they approach the casket.

"Is she sleeping?" Marco timidly inquires, his big eyes like saucers.

"No, Great-Grandma died," Tia Aida patiently responds. Although she has explained death to Marco multiple times, he has never seen a dead body before.

On the day of the funeral, as the pallbearers carry the casket into the church, a mariachi band plays *Amor Eterno* (Forever Love). Giant tears glisten in Marco's eyes as he looks up at his aunt and says, "She's not coming back, is she?" As Tia Aida shakes her head "no," Marco climbs up into her lap and allows her to rock him in her arms.

At the burial site, Marco places a rose on the casket and watches the box containing Great-Grandmother's body as it is lowered into the ground. For the next hour, the children play on the grassy hills of the cemetery while the family and friends reminisce. As the final send-off song *Adios* is played, Marco and his Tia Aida head back for the car.


## At the Funeral

On the afternoon that their grandfather, whom they called Papa, dies, Penny and Roger sit with their children and explain what will happen tomorrow at the cemetery. Donovan, aged 16, and Merry, aged 14, both attended their grandmother's funeral 3 years ago. Four-year-old Jack has never been to a funeral and doesn't know what to expect.

"We'll get all dressed up and go to the cemetery which is like a park," Merry begins. "Papa's body will be in a box called a casket."

"I get to read a speech about Papa," boasts Donovan, the eldest grandchild.

Penny elaborates, "We're going to sit in the chapel and listen to the minister. Your aunts and uncles and cousins will be there. Some of them will be crying, because they miss Papa. Your babysitter will be there, Jack, so you can stay with us or she can take you outside whenever you want."

Before the service, Merry hands her mom an envelope, which she has decorated with hearts to put inside Papa's casket. When the minister speaks and everyone gets quiet, Jack takes out his crayons and draws pictures of himself and Papa.

Holding back his tears, Donovan steps up to the pulpit and gives a eulogy: "Papa was a very special person. He was a lover and the kind of guy you leaned on for support. When I was little, I always used to surprise him in the morning by snuggling with him in bed. Every time he would ask for a kiss I remember a scruffy beard on my cheek. Lots of family and friends came to see Papa when he was dying. One special visitor was a service dog named Sparky. He said Sparky was such a sweet animal until the sweet animal vomited. Papa denied enjoying this special visit but in a way I think he had to appreciate it. It was good for me to talk to him while he was on his deathbed. I still know that he was able to hear my goodbye, and it made me feel good that Papa departed in peace."

### Ashes to Ashes

When Aunt Deanna dies, Will and Grace tell their children that tomorrow they will be attending a memorial service and scattering Aunt Deanna's ashes at sea.

"You mean they burned her body?" 9-year-old Devon asks his mom. "That's gross."

Realizing that they haven't taken time to help the children understand cremation, Will explains: "When Grandpa died, his body was buried in the ground. Aunt Deanna wanted to be cremated. That means her body was heated until it turned into ash."

"Did it hurt?" Devon's 6-year-old sister Marley wonders aloud.

Grace continues, "No, sweetie, it didn't hurt. Remember Aunt Deanna died before her body was cremated and she didn't feel any pain."

The next day, carrying the ceramic urn containing his sister's ashes, Will, his wife, and his children board a hired boat. As they pull away from the dock, Devon expresses his excitement, "Wow, this is cool."

When they reach the appointed location, the boat idles and Will sprinkles Aunt Deanna's ashes into the water. Marley begins to cry. Grace kneels down, wipes Marley's tears, and asks, "May I give you a hug and a kiss?" Marley nods her head yes and says, "Yes. European style, on both cheeks, just like Aunt Deanna used to do."

### Preparing Your Child for Attending Mourning Rituals

- Explain to your child:
  - Where they will be. *We will go to the church and then the cemetery.*
  - Who will be present. *All your aunts and uncles and cousins will be there.*
  - How people might react. *Mommy and Grandma will be crying.*
  - What will happen. *We will sing our favorite hymns and your uncle will give a speech about Grandpa. Then we will bury Grandpa's body in the ground.*
- Designate a caring adult who is neither overly distraught with grief nor distracted with ceremonial responsibilities to be with each child. Choose someone your child knows well and who can answer her questions. In the event that your child becomes upset, have this person be prepared to take her outside. If your child decides to return to the ceremonies she might want to sit on someone's lap, look at a book, or draw a picture.

- When possible give your child choice about whether or not to attend the services. While she may choose not to attend, chances are that if your child is not included in the mourning rituals she will draw her own conclusions about what mysterious events occurred. Your child may feel left out, angry, or even jealous of others if she doesn't participate.
- Give her an opportunity to put a memento into the casket.
- Give your child a choice about viewing the body.

## CHILDREN'S GRIEF

After your loved one dies, expect that your child will be able to handle only small amounts of grief at a time. For example, you may observe her openly expressing sadness one moment and happily playing a short time later. Developmentally, your younger child may engage in magical thinking and hold on to the hope that the person who died will come back to life. Your older child may seem to be doing well at first, yet as time goes on you may see her begin to isolate from others, neglect her school work, and engage in inappropriate or self-destructive behavior.

Regardless of your child's age, she may hide her grief in order to protect you. Since most of her friends won't have experienced a death in their immediate families, your child may feel that there is no one who understands what she is going through. "Give your child permission to express herself, whether it is sadness, fear, anger, guilt or relief," advises Lauren Schneider, Clinical Director of Child and Adolescent Programs at OUR HOUSE Grief Support Center. "Let her know that you are strong enough to hear what she has to say. And follow her intense display of grief with a stress-relieving activity like riding her bike or reading a book." Especially during this chaotic time, your child needs your acceptance, your support, and your love.

## ADJUSTING TO A NEW REALITY

### On the Train

"We're going on an adventure," announces Oakley's dad early one Saturday morning. Four-year-old Oakley misses the outings that she and her mommy and daddy used to take every week before her mommy died. Wondering if this time it will be a canoe ride or apple picking or a visit to the farm, Oakley grabs her corduroy jacket and waits for Daddy by the front door.

Daddy fills his backpack with snacks of juice, nuts, and string cheese, and they walk hand in hand down the street. "A train ride!" exclaims

Oakley as they approach the Essex Junction station. The train has rows of empty seats, and Oakley chooses one next to the window.

Oakley takes her favorite stuffed animal, Joey Kangaroo, and pretends that he is hopping from row to row. When she disturbs a woman working on her laptop computer, the woman turns to Oakley and says sharply, "Go find your mommy and sit down."

Turning her head to look at the woman, Oakley retorts, "My mommy's dead." The woman's face turns red as Oakley nonchalantly hops Joey Kangaroo to the next row.

## Mom Is Dating Already

When Chynna comes home from high school soccer practice, a few months after her father dies, she asks her older sister Jada, "Where's mom? What's for dinner?"

"We have to make our own dinner," Jada replies. "Mom's out with Brett tonight. Again. I can't believe that she met him on that widows' dating website. She would never let us go out with someone we met online."

As they reheat left-over pizza, Chynna remarks, "It seems like mom has forgotten all about dad. She took down most of his pictures. How can she bring another man into this house? I hope they aren't having sex."

Jada remarks, "I don't care what they're doing. I'm glad mom is dating. She seems happier now and it gets her off my back."

## Double Reactions

Following the death of his wife, Russell arranges for his 12-year-old twins, Dusty and Brittany, to meet with a grief counselor. During the session, Dr. Sharafi brings out a soft soccer ball labeled with an emotion on each of the differently colored sections. The girls are to toss the ball to each other and wherever the recipient's thumb lands, she must tell how that word relates to her grief. Dusty's thumb lands on SAD. "I'm sad that Mom won't be here for Christmas," she responds as she quickly throws the ball to Brittany.

"My word is HAPPY," says Brittany. "I'm happy that now Dad lets us have friends sleep over again."

"I feel GUILTY because I told Mom that I was tired of her being sick all the time," admits Dusty when it's her turn.

Both girls talk about LONELY. "It's lonely in the house without Mom," says Brittany wistfully. "I really miss her."

Dusty interjects, "Me too. Not the way she was when she was in bed but the way she used to be before she got sick."

# SADNESS

## Moving

Six-year-old Lyndon loves to stretch out on the couch where Daddy used to watch sports and read the paper before he died. Lyndon wears Dad's favorite "Go Tigers" sweatshirt and drinks milk out of Daddy's coffee mug. He misses his dad mostly at night when Dad would read him a story and stay with him until he fell asleep. Mom only has time for one story before she leaves the room. "I have a lot of work to do, but if you feel scared, turn on the flashlight that Daddy gave you," she reminds Lyndon as she tucks him into bed and turns out the light.

When Mom announces to Lyndon that they are moving to Lansing to be closer to Grandma and Grandpa and all their cousins, Lyndon protests, "We can't leave this house. I won't go."

"Don't worry, Lyndon. We'll take the couch and the television and all your toys and your bed," promises Mom.

"No," insists Lyndon. "If we move away, how will Daddy find us?"

## I Cry in My Mind

Elvis starts to cry when he tells his grandmother, "I hate it when the lady across the street says 'Your daddy died because God needed another teacher in heaven.' I need my daddy more."

Unsympathetically, Grandmother admonishes, "Stop crying, Elvis. You are the man of the house now. It's your job to be strong and take care of your mother."

Elvis stays strong in front of his mother, but a week later he gets in trouble at school when he shoves one of his classmates. Noting Elvis' uncharacteristic behavior, his teacher sympathizes, "I see that you are upset, Elvis. You must really miss your dad."

Elvis fights back his tears and looks away. His teacher persists, "Do you ever let your tears out? Does your mom know how sad you are?"

"No," replies Elvis somberly, "because I cry in my mind."

# FEAR AND ANXIETY

## My Tummy Hurts

Janos' behavior changes after his mother dies. Each day in the middle of his second grade class Janos tells the teacher, "My tummy hurts." After multiple visits to the school nurse, the teacher suggests a meeting between the boy's father and the school psychologist.

At the meeting Janos' father, Bela, describes how in the early morning when he leaves for his job as a pastry chef, Janos complains that his stomach hurts and begs his father not to leave. Yet when Bela comes home in the late afternoon, Janos' tummy ache disappears. In the evenings, when Gizella, the nanny, goes out with her boyfriend, Janos wails, "Don't go. I know you're not coming back, just like my mommy."

"The biggest fear of a child who has had a parent die, is that their surviving parent or caretaker will also die," explains the psychologist to Bela. "You can reassure Janos that most people die when they are very old. And it will help if you remind him of all the things you do to keep yourselves healthy and safe. I know you must be tired after work, but I strongly recommend that each evening you spend some special 'Janos time' with your son."

That night instead of having Gizella tell Janos a bedtime story, Bela does it himself. He recounts the story about the day Janos was born and how happy they were when Mommy brought him home from the hospital.

## Feeling Unsafe

Sixteen-year-old Latoya hides under the covers and calls her best friend, Shaniqua, "I'm scared. I think someone is trying to break into my house."

Shaniqua thinks to herself how Latoya used to be fearless, but since her father died, everything scares her. "Why don't you tell your mom?" Shaniqua counsels.

"I can't. All she does is stay in bed and watch television, and she doesn't want me to bother her." Latoya pleads, "What should I do?"

Shaniqua orders, "Open your drapes a tiny bit and look out your bedroom window. Let me know what you see."

Hesitantly, Latoya peeks out and discovers that a heavy wind is blowing leaves around the driveway and tree branches are hitting the roof. Embarrassed Latoya admits, "I guess I'm just paranoid. Now that my dad has died, I just don't feel safe any more."

## ANGER AND GUILT

When your child says "I'm so mad at Daddy for dying," and you answer, "Getting angry won't do you any good," you will not be easing her distress. If she says, "It's my fault that Daddy died," and you answer, "Your dad wouldn't want you to feel that way," you are giving your child the message that her emotions are wrong or unacceptable.

Rather than negate her feelings, strive to understand them. Your child may feel angry at the person who died for abandoning her or not taking better care of himself. She may be angry at the surviving family members for not taking better care of the person who died and sometimes wish that someone else had died instead. Her hostility may be directed at the doctors who didn't save her loved one or at God. Guilt may arise because your child blames herself for not saving the one who died or for not spending more time with him while he was alive. Your child may also feel remorseful for not being a better daughter, sister, relative, or friend.


### Am I Still a Big Brother?

Five-year-old Noah likes being a big brother. He feels grown-up and receives presents from the family when they visit. He loves holding his baby brother, Marlon, while his parents take pictures. When Marlon becomes ill and develops a high fever, his parents immediately take him to the doctor who diagnoses him with meningitis. After a week in the hospital, Marlon dies, throwing the family into chaos.

Several months later Noah tells his mom, Adrienne, "It was my fault that Marlon died. I wasn't a good big brother."

Realizing that she has been so caught up in her own emotions that she hasn't paid enough attention to Noah's grief, Adrienne consults with her therapist who recommends that Noah draw about his feelings. Noah makes a picture of himself taking a teddy bear away from Marlon. As Mom and Noah talk about the drawing they also remember all the ways Noah was a good big brother. He would make Marlon laugh, help him eat cereal with a spoon, and play with him in the bathtub.

Noah puts down his crayons and asks worriedly, "Am I still a big brother?"

"What do you think?" asks Mom.

Noah nods his head yes. "I think so too," says Mom as she gives Noah a hug.


### Anger Bags

One evening in late April, the members of the OUR HOUSE Teen Grief Group are talking about their anger. Madelina describes how mad she is at her mother for not taking better care of herself, "She knew she had high blood pressure and diabetes but she didn't take her medication regularly."

Hamilton tells the others how angry he is that he never learned CPR and feels responsible for his father's death, "By the time the paramedics arrived at my house, my dad was already unconscious. I should have been able to save him."

"Who else feels angry?" asks one of the group leaders, recognizing how important it is to normalize this common grief reaction.

Rosario offers, "I do. I feel angry all the time. I hate it that my mom died. It makes me so mad when my friends say these awful things against their moms. Or they say they wish their moms were dead. It's totally not fair."

"How could God do this to us?" Hunter demands. "My father was only forty-seven."

"No one even told me that my mom was that close to dying," accuses Jennifer. "The doctors always made it sound like she was getting better."

When the leaders introduce the project for the evening, they ask group members to write and draw about their anger on brown paper lunch bags. Hunter writes on his bag, "Who is going to teach me to drive?" Hamilton draws a picture of his father being put into the ambulance.

After sharing their projects, each teen blows into his bag, fills it with air, and then pops it, symbolically letting go of some of his angry feelings.

## SELF-DESTRUCTIVE BEHAVIORS

### Drastic Changes

After Grandfather Aga Joon dies, Pejman's behavior changes drastically. He ditches school, withdraws from social activities, and his grades decline. Aga Joon represented the one stable, comforting male in the family. He was nonjudgmental, undemanding, and gave unconditional love.

Although Pejman has experimented with drugs in the past at parties, now he smokes marijuana on a daily basis. He sneaks vodka from his parents' liquor cabinet. Without Aga Joon as his ally, Pejman loses his interest in academic achievements and wonders, "Why bother getting good grades?"

When Pejman arrives at school under the influence, the counselor calls for an emergency meeting with Pejman and his parents. The counselor suggests that Pejman attend a twelve-step program, and she makes referrals for family counseling. "We want you to get back on track, Pejman, and we know you can do it," the counselor advises.

## STAYING CONNECTED

### Message in a Balloon

Fifteen-year-old Jesus was such an avid fan of his hometown baseball team that after his death, his parents receive approval to put the team's logo on his grave marker. The family visits the cemetery each week and leaves Jesus his favorite foods, sweet bread and tamales. Sonia usually plays with her dolls while her parents talk about her big brother Jesus. She doesn't like to see her mother cry.

One Sunday morning before they go to the cemetery, Sonia's mother suggests that each family member write a prayer or a message to Jesus on brightly colored strips of paper. They place their messages into a balloon, and Sonia's dad inflates it with helium. Sonia holds tightly to the string of the balloon containing these words to her brother: *Te extrano y solamente pido que me regales un abrazo mas. I miss you and I wish I could give you a hug.* When they arrive at Jesus' grave, the family stands together as Sonia releases the balloon and watches it fly heavenward.

### Phoning Nana Bea

After his Nana Bea's funeral, 8-year-old great-grandson Avi looks sad. He asks his mother if he can still phone Nana Bea. But then he realizes he doesn't have her new phone number. He suddenly lights up saying, "Oh, I know. I'll just call 1-800-Heaven."

### Feeling Their Presence

After asking the children in the grief support group to draw pictures of where they think their deceased parents are now, the group leader asks, "Who ever feels like his parent is still with him?"

Kaspar, a very quiet and serious boy, describes, "I saw my mom standing in the trees at the funeral. She smiled at me."

"When I am in bed at night," offers Gwyneth, "my mom comes and talks to me. We say our prayers together. But I never tell my daddy because it might make him sad."

Cornell adds, "My church says my dad is in heaven, but I know he's not because he was just here in this room with us."

### Thanksgiving

"It doesn't feel right going to Aunt Crystal's house for Thanksgiving," complains Derek from the back seat of the car.

"It won't smell like it did at Grandma's," Tracey pipes up.

Mom agrees, "You're right. It will be different now that Grandma has died. So let's think of ways to remember her at the dinner table."

"I brought along Grandma's apron. I'm going to wear it when we serve the pumpkin pie," offers 15-year-old Betty Jean.

Derek gets excited, "I'll tell Grandma's story about the time she forgot to light the oven and the turkey was raw."

"Would it be okay if I say grace?" inquires Tracey. "Grandma always did."

"Yes and I know what else we can do," says Mom. "Let's set a place for Grandma, even though she won't be there. We'll ask Aunt Crystal to put a picture of Grandma in front of her plate."

Around the table when it's Derek's turn, he tells Grandma's famous story about how she almost fainted when she discovered an uncooked turkey in the oven. Derek relays the tale in such an animated fashion mimicking Grandma's old country accent that everyone collapses with laughter.

## Talking to Dad

Six-year-old Scarlett doesn't talk about her dad's death for the entire first year. It's as if it never happened.

One day, Scarlett and her mom visit the aquarium. While watching the penguins dive in and out of the water, Scarlett turns to her mother and says matter-of-factly, "Mom, you know what's good about Dad dying?"

Stunned to hear Scarlett suddenly mention her dad so casually, Mom replies, "Tell me. What's so good about Dad dying?"

Animatedly, Scarlett explains, "Now I can talk to him anytime. 'Hi Dad!'"

## Four Candles

Emile's three young sons desperately miss their mom who died 4 months ago. Creating a personalized mourning ritual, Emile purchases a box of candles and has each of his boys select his own candle holder and place it on the kitchen stove. Emile tells them, "Whenever you miss Mom, you can light your candle. That way, we will all know you are thinking about her."

Every time he sees one of the candles glowing, it signals to Emile that one of his boys might want some special attention. He finds that son, and they spend some private time together.

In relating this story to the parents in his bereavement group, Emile adds, "I forgot to tell you that I have a candle, too. And whenever the boys see my candle burning, they come and find me."

## SUPPORTING YOUR GRIEVING CHILD

### Anticipate Age-Related Grief Reactions

Children aged 2 to 5 may

- be too young to cognitively grasp that death is permanent.
- hope and believe that the person will return.
- feel responsible for the death.
- experience renewed separation anxiety.
- have trouble falling or staying asleep.
- seem unaffected in their play.

Children aged 5 to 9

- often behave as though the death hasn't happened.
- desire to conform with peers (e.g., pretend that the person is alive, at work, or on a trip).
- struggle to understand death in a concrete way.

Children and teens aged 10 to 13

- are able to understand that death is universal and permanent.
- may avoid talking about the death in an attempt to be "strong" or feel "normal."

Teens aged 14 to 18 may

- try to separate emotionally from parents as they search for their own identity.
- become isolated from family and friends.
- turn to inappropriate or self-destructive behavior to ease the pain.

### Use Helpful Phrases

**Find out where your child thinks the person who died has gone.**
Instead of saying, "She's in a better place," ask the child, *Where do you think Mommy is now?*

**Reassure your child that you and other caring adults are still in charge.**
Instead of saying, "Now, you are the man of the house," let him know, *Even though your daddy died, I am still here to take care of you and be your parent.*

**Allow your child to express her feelings of guilt, sadness, or remorse.**
Instead of saying, "It wasn't your fault," inquire of her, *What do you wish could have been different?*

**Calm your child's fears about you and others dying.**
Instead of saying, "Don't worry, nothing will happen to me," offer, *Most people die when they are very old. We take good care of ourselves so that we stay safe and healthy.*

**Allow your child to cry.**
Instead of saying, "Big girls don't cry," let her know that tears are acceptable. *I'm crying, too, because I was thinking about Grandma and how much I miss her.*

**Encourage your child to talk about and remember the person who died.**
Instead of avoiding any mention of the person, say, *I love this song, it reminds me of your mom dancing around the kitchen.*

**Include your child in decision-making whenever possible.**
Instead of assuming you know what she wants, ask, *Shall we still hang Dad's Christmas stocking on the mantle this year?*

### Pay Attention to Warning Signs

- Apathy and withdrawal from family and friends
- Indications of alcohol or drug abuse, promiscuous or sexualized behavior
- Preoccupation with thoughts about death
- Significant changes in school performance or essential daily activities

*If these signs appear, contact your doctor, local hospital, counselor, or clergy person.*

### Participation in a Support Group May Help Your Child

- Normalize her thoughts and feelings.
- Feel secure in a consistent and safe place to share memories.
- Engage in open discussion about death and ways to cope.
- Experience ways to express emotion through art, music, and play.
- Create a sense of community.

*Talking about their grief with peers who have had similar experiences, helps children heal.*

"What's wrong with Daddy?" "Why do they stop talking when I come into the room?" "Why is Mommy always crying?" "Where is Daddy now?"

Listening to your child's questions and giving her age-appropriate truthful answers without using euphemisms will allow her to better understand the events and emotions which surround her. Being honest and open with your child from diagnosis through end of life reinforces her trust in you and makes her feel safe. When you explain illness and death in a loving and gentle way, your child is not left in the dark to draw her own conclusions.

During your loved one's illness and after his death, encourage your child's expression of emotions without judging her. Reassure your child that grown-ups also cry, get angry, feel frustrated, and wish things were different. Suggest that your child find creative outlets for her feelings through drawing pictures, writing letters and poems, and retelling stories.

Although dealing with grief is a lifelong process, your child will adapt. New understandings about the illness and death will arise as she matures. As your child continues on her own path, help her maintain an everlasting connection to the person who died. Your child's life will be enriched by her loved one's memory.

# CHAPTER 12

## Supporting Those Who Grieve

*"I know just how you feel.*
*Last week we had to put down Mr. Jingles."*

Support group member

You want to support your friend or family member who is grieving. Initially, you might attend the funeral or memorial service. Your presence pays tribute to the person who died and brings comfort to the mourners. In addition, whether you attend a formal ceremony or not, there are a variety of ways to demonstrate thoughtfulness.

When speaking to your friend, how will you find the words to express your condolences? Should you mention the person who died? Will it upset him if you do? Will he appreciate your sympathy or think you are insensitive if it seems that is all you want to talk about? You may be surprised to find that what you said that seemed just perfect yesterday seems inappropriate or even offensive if you say it today. On the other hand, words that stop a conversation one week may lead to an intimate dialogue on another occasion. While you have no way of knowing exactly how what you say will be received, don't let that stop you from reaching out.

The job of your bereaved friend is to grieve. Your job is to support him. Make yourself available to help out with errands, sit with him, accompany him on a walk, or take him for a drive. You might also convey your care by making a donation in his loved one's memory. Whatever you decide to do, remember that it is never too late for acts of kindness.

## ATTENDING THE FUNERAL/MEMORIAL SERVICE

### That's What Friends Are For

Becky gets into gear when she hears that the mother of her best friend, Geneva, has died. "I'll coordinate everything," Becky offers. She notifies all their friends and divides up the responsibilities for the day of the funeral. One person prints up a map and directions from the cemetery to the house; another designs a floral display for the chapel service; Doreen begins rehearsing "To Everything There is a Season," and several others agree to bake for the reception.

On the morning of the service, a hassled Geneva calls Becky saying, "I'm not sure what to do. I'm having food delivered to my home, but I don't see how I can get back in time to have everything ready for the guests when they arrive."

Becky volunteers to stay at the house and set up the buffet and dessert tables, knowing what a relief this will be for Geneva. At the end of the day, after everyone else has left, Geneva expresses her gratitude, "I know how much you loved my mother and wanted to be at the service, Becky. I can't thank you enough for your help. I couldn't have managed without you."

"It was a labor of love," responds Becky. "What do you think friends are for? Just for going to parties?"


## Her Classmate's Funeral

Lydia, a 92-year-old independent thinker who lives by her own rules and challenges medical advice, inspires everyone in the seniors' water exercise class. Despite their casual acquaintanceship, when Lydia dies, her classmate Greta feels compelled to attend the funeral even though it is difficult for her to move about using her walker. Greta goes to the service and sits in the back row of the chapel so that she can take her cues from others about when to sit and stand.

During the ceremony, Greta learns about Lydia from her family members. Before she leaves the chapel, Greta introduces herself to Lydia's daughter, Meryl. Greta offers her condolences and relates how much Lydia has inspired her classmates with her upbeat spirit. "Your mother sets an ideal example of aging with grace," Greta tells Meryl. Hearing this praise of her mother, Meryl's eyes fill with tears. The two women shake hands, and Greta departs, happy that she made the effort to attend the funeral.


## Unbroken Promise

Brian lives out of state, and when his Grandma Ciel dies, he has to contend with the decision of whether or not to fly home for the funeral. As a struggling graduate student, airfare is a major consideration. Besides, the funeral coincides with Brian's performance in a musical trio. He meditates on his dilemma and has a fantasy conversation with his grandmother asking for her advice. Grandma tells Brian he should meet his musical commitment; he has been a good grandson during her life, and there is nothing more he can do for her. Brian feels comfortable with his decision.

The next spring while in town for a family wedding, Brian stops by to see his Uncle Larry who is terminally ill with congestive heart failure. Brian realizes that he hasn't brought his dress loafers and asks Uncle Larry if he can borrow his black wing-tipped shoes. They fit him perfectly. Playfully Brian asks, "Uncle Larry, will you leave these to me?" His uncle bargains, "Only if you promise to attend my funeral."

When Uncle Larry dies, Brian is back at the university, but he remembers his promise to attend the funeral. True to his word, Brian shows up at the service. Afterward, he collects the shoes.

### We Might Not Fit In

Kyle and Marcus read about the death of their favorite neighbor, Buncha, and the service to be held at the Thai Buddhist temple. Wanting to attend, yet apprehensive about the customs and whether they will be conspicuous outsiders, they contemplate what would be the right action. They also wonder about paying their respects at the home after the service, and if they will be expected to bring something to the house of mourning.

Reading up on customs and traditions for Thai Buddhist funerals in the book *Come as You Aren't*, Kyle learns that it is customary to present money in envelopes when visiting the home of the bereaved. Buncha's family is happily surprised that Kyle and Marcus attend the service and seem so knowledgeable about Thai funeral rituals. In appreciation, the family members place their palms together in a prayer-like fashion and slightly bow toward Kyle and Marcus, who make the *wai* gesture in return.

### Will You Attend the Funeral or Memorial Service?

- Hearing or reading about a funeral or memorial in the obituary column of a newspaper means that people are invited unless it says "Private Ceremony."
- If there is an announcement about a reception, that invitation is intended for everyone present.
- You may choose to attend the service, the burial, and/or visit the house of mourning.
- Inquire if there are expectations or restrictions on foods or gifts you bring to the mourners.

*Attending a funeral and visiting the mourners' home are signs of respect.*

## OTHER SUPPORTIVE ACTIONS

### Offer a Shoulder to Lean On

Years after her father's death, a daughter expresses appreciation for the continuing support she receives from her father's best friend:

> I recall the night before my dad's funeral when we all met at the mortuary. I was in such a world of hurt. I remember sitting down on a bench and bawling my eyes out. My mom and the others were understandably preoccupied, and I was alone. Suddenly, I felt a presence next to me. It was you. You put your arm around me and cried along with me. Yours was the shoulder I leaned on that night.
>
> ...And I'm sure I've told you this before, but it means the world to me that every time we meet, you mention my father. Perhaps out of some sense of awkwardness or an attempt to be sensitive, most people stopped mentioning him shortly after he died. You've never done that, and I can't tell you how much I appreciate it.

### Plant a Tree

Mitzi recalls how much her dear friend Herb loved her peach cobbler. He had requested that she bring him some just weeks before he died, even though he could barely manage to swallow a mouthful. The day after the funeral, Mitzi bakes one of her signature cobblers and brings it to the family. But she wants to do more.

The following spring when she is invited to join Herb's family for supper, Mitzi brings a peach tree seedling. Just before the meal is served, the family gathers in the backyard, and the tree is planted in Herb's memory.

### Nourish the Mourners

Although she loved her dearly, LaShonda cannot bring herself to attend the funeral of the beloved kindergarten teacher from the local elementary school. "I've buried my son and my husband and I can't face going to the cemetery again," she tells a neighbor.

Instead, at home in her own kitchen while the funeral is taking place, LaShonda trims a meaty ham hock and puts it in a large kettle of water. She adds corn kernels, baby lima beans, and okra and seasons her famous Okra Gumbo Soup with cayenne pepper, thyme, and salt and pepper. The next day, LaShonda delivers the soup to a grateful faculty and staff in the school office. She includes a card that says, "I hope this soup will nourish you the way Mrs. DeLong nourished the lives of our children."

## Give a Memento

Trevor, a graphic artist, has been a neighbor of Mr. and Mrs. Ortiz for the last 3 years. They share vegetables from their gardens and greet each other warmly whenever they see one another. When Mr. Ortiz dies, the Ortiz family is disappointed that Trevor doesn't attend the viewing, church ceremony, or burial. Several days later one of Mr. Ortiz' sons asks Trevor, "Why didn't you come to Dad's funeral? He really liked you."

Surprised that he would have been welcomed at what he thought was a family-only event, Trevor responds: "No one invited me." When Trevor later talks about it with his sister, she tells him that attending a funeral requires no special invitation. Trevor feels badly that he had offended Mrs. Ortiz and her children.

As a way to show his respect, Trevor draws a sketch of Mr. Ortiz standing among his corn and squash plants and takes it to the family. They are delighted to receive this thoughtful gift.

## Respect the Griever's Cherished Possessions

Three years after their son Alfie dies, Monty and Violet pack their bags for a trip to Thailand. Monty decides to wear Alfie's walking shoes. "After all, Alfie loved to travel and his shoes fit me perfectly," Monty tells his wife.

They spend 3 days at the home of Valaya and her parents in a remote city, located several hours outside of Bangkok. When it is time to leave for the airport, Monty hastily puts on his sandals. Only when it is time to board the plane does he realize that he has inadvertently left Alfie's walking shoes at Valaya's house.

Rather than have them mailed back to the United States, Monty and Violet agree that the shoes should remain where they are. In the following months, Valaya contacts Monty several times and inquires if it would be alright if her father took the shoes with him on his vacation. Deeply touched, Monty and Violet heartily consent.

Two years later, when Monty and Violet again visited in Valaya's home, they assume that Alfie's shoes have been long discarded, until the prized possessions are ceremoniously presented—clean and well cared for. Amidst everyone's tears, Violet lovingly touches and holds the shoes that once belonged to her adored son.

Valaya politely asks Monty what he would like to do with the shoes. After a brief pause, Monty replies, "If you don't mind keeping them, I would like to have them stay here with you."

With a gracious bow and a quiet "thank you," Valaya respectfully accepts the shoes back, honored to be entrusted with these precious possessions.


## Remember a Special Date

Mr. and Mrs. Simon notice photos of the high school seniors posted in the local supermarket announcing that Graduation Day will take place the following week. The Simons dread this event because their daughter Nadia, who died from injuries sustained in a car accident 6 months ago, will not be part of the ceremony.

Nadia's friends plead with the Simons to attend the graduation, and their neighbors offer to drive them to the ceremony. Reluctantly, the bereaved parents agree.

On campus, other graduates and their parents greet the Simons warmly. During the ceremony, the Student Body President makes a speech about Nadia, recognizing her school contributions and scholastic achievements. Her parents feel sad yet proud to learn how loved Nadia was. In addition, the principal posthumously awards Nadia her high school diploma and announces that a scholarship will be established in her name. The Simons are grateful that the other families have not forgotten their precious daughter and have included them in this community event.


## Pay it Forward

Trisha and Cheyenne become leaders for their daughters' Girl Scout Troop. They develop a close friendship, but lose touch with one another after Trisha and her family move to another state. Several years later, Trisha learns that Cheyenne has died of a massive stroke. Trisha wants to do something for Cheyenne's family. She makes a donation to the Heart Disease and Stroke Prevention Fund in memory of Cheyenne and sends a note to the family:

> *Cheyenne and I had many sweet moments together guiding the Girl Scouts through their badge requirements. I'll never forget her many kindnesses, especially when my whole family was sick with the flu and she arrived at the door with a roasting pan filled with hot sliced roast beef, mashed potatoes and candied carrots. Standing in*

*the doorway wearing my pajamas and bathrobe, I remember how grateful I felt seeing her there with a complete supper for my hungry family. I know I expressed my thanks to her at that time, but ever since then, when I hear about a friend or neighbor who is ill or about the family of someone who has died, I try to pay forward Cheyenne's kindness to me and cook an unexpected meal for the family.*

## Visit and Help Out

After the funeral of Galina's husband, her friend Katya says goodbye and promises, "Galina, I'm going to go now but I'll be back when the others are gone."

Katya keeps her promise and for months she phones Galina every day. Without waiting for an invitation, Katya regularly stops by with fresh flowers or vegetables from her garden and brings eggs and yogurt from the market. She takes over Galina's carpool responsibilities and runs small errands. When Katya helps Galina address and stamp thank you notes, Galina looks up and says, "I am so grateful for all the little things you do for me. I feel like you are the sister I never had."

## Helpful Actions

- Take the initiative and do something for the griever, without waiting for him to ask.
- Offer to come over for a visit, bring him something to eat, or take him out for a meal.
- Don't assume that because he said "no" once you shouldn't ask again.
- If you see something that needs to be done, ask his permission and do it!
- Help the griever remember important appointments, projects, and events and offer to accompany him.
- Offer to sit with him as he works on everyday tasks (e.g., paying bills, writing thank you cards).
- Bring photos or mementos of the person who died.
- Remember to do things for the griever even months after the death. That's when he will really need you.

*It is your presence and compassion that will help the griever more than anything.*

## WORDS AND ACTIONS TO AVOID

### Avoid Turning Away From the Griever

One morning, 4 months after her only child Caroline dies, Lorraine is ready to have her two granddaughters, aged 8 and 11, stay with her for the weekend. Lorraine thinks it will be fun for them to bake cookies together, knowing how much they enjoyed baking with their mother. Lorraine has all the ingredients, except the sugar sprinkles that the girls like to use to decorate the cookies before putting them into the oven.

Lorraine stalls all morning, postponing her trip to the market, thinking how sad it will be to shop without Caroline. At last Lorraine gets into the car, drives to the market, puts her purse into the shopping cart, and finds the baking aisle. She gets weak in the knees and feels her heart beating rapidly as she approaches the cake decorating supplies. Light-headed with so many Caroline memories, Lorraine takes a deep breath and says to herself that once she finds the sprinkles she will head straight for the express cashier lane and get out of the store.

As she stands there, Lorraine is relieved to see a neighbor walking toward her. Their eyes barely meet when the neighbor abruptly makes a u-turn and goes down another aisle. Shaken, Lorraine abandons her cart, heads for the parking lot, and drives home without her groceries.

*When you turn away from a griever, you give him the message that you don't care.*

### Avoid Judging the Griever's Appearance

Scenario 1: While Candace buys sunflowers from the grower at the Farmer's Market, she bumps into her old friend Brenda. They have not seen each other since the funeral of Candace's husband 8 months ago.

"You look great," compliments Brenda. "It's so good to see you feeling better."

"Thanks," Candace mumbles dismissively, recognizing that here is yet another person who misinterprets her outward appearance as a reflection of how she feels on the inside.

Scenario 2: During the past 9 months, Meredith has been completely focused on taking care of her terminally ill husband, Arno. After Arno dies, Meredith is exhausted, and all she wants to do is sleep. She occasionally goes out to run errands but doesn't bother to put on make up or wear anything other than old pants and a sweatshirt.

When her younger sister Geneva stops by one morning with biscotti and coffee, the dismayed look on Geneva's face communicates that she disapproves of Meredith's appearance. "You look terrible Meredith. You ought to fix yourself up. Go put on some lipstick. And get a haircut. My treat," she offers.

"I don't care how I look," Meredith counters. "Can't you for once think about how I'm feeling?"

*When you comment on a griever's appearance, you are focusing on the external and ignoring how he may be feeling on the inside.*

## Don't Forget to Mention the Deceased

The Fourth of July get-together in the park has been part of the Craddock family for as long as anyone can remember. The traditional favorite foods, a softball game, watching the fireworks, and, of course, Uncle Joe's three-legged sack race are all essential parts of the celebration. The family always teases Joe that these sack races are old-fashioned, but year after year they go along with his desire to see who will team up with whom as they laugh their way across the park.

After Joe dies, his widow Fiona attends her first Fourth of July picnic alone. To her delight, one of the grandsons has brought the sacks for the three-legged race. Everyone pairs up by height as usual and there is rollicking laughter as the members of the family race across the park. Fiona beams as she watches, with a few stray tears rolling down her cheeks. On the way home, Fiona's niece notices that her aunt is quieter than usual and seems unhappy.

"What's wrong, Aunt Fiona?" asks her niece. Through her tears Fiona answers that no one mentioned Uncle Joe all day long, not even when they were running *his* race. "Aunt Fiona, we were all thinking about Uncle Joe, but after all these months we finally saw you smiling and laughing. You looked so happy, we didn't want to upset you by mentioning his name."

*When you fail to mention the person who died, you give the message that you have forgotten him.*

## Don't Discount Anyone's Grief

Scenario 1: Phyllis walks around her apartment at the Assisted Living facility feeling lost. She isn't eating much and refuses to join in the social activities. Last week her 101-year-old mother died, and Phyllis, a spry and usually very active 82-year-old, is overwhelmed by her grief. She is dismayed when she overhears staff members say:

"Phyllis's mother was over 100 years old; what did she expect? No one lives forever."

Scenario 2: The bereavement group gathers in the church hall. Tonight the discussion turns to hurtful things that people say.

Twenty-five-year-old Blossom, devastated after the death of her younger sister recounts, "All everyone asks me is how my mom and dad are doing. What about me? Don't they recognize that I hurt, too?"

Mariah admits how her feelings are hurt because nobody offers her their condolences on the death of her ex-husband, "I was married to Sergei twice as long as his current wife. But she gets all the attention."

Katie, a young woman whose infant son died hours after his birth, adds, "If I have to hear the phrase, 'You're young. You'll have another child' one more time, I think I'll jump out of my skin."

"I started my business with Cecil and worked side by side with him for twenty-five years," Pierce explains to the group. "But my wife doesn't understand that I am still grieving. She expects me to be my old self."

*When you discount a griever's feelings, you are implying that he doesn't have the right to grieve.*

## Don't Tell People How to Grieve

Scenario 1: Other mechanics at the auto body repair shop become impatient with Alesandro. All he talks about is how much he misses Felipa, his wife, who died 9 months ago. When Paulino approaches him for a contribution to purchase a wedding gift for the upcoming marriage of their boss, Alesandro's eyes cloud over, and he begins to cry. Paulino sharply admonishes, "*Basta!* (Enough!) You have to stop your grieving and remember the good times you had with Felipa and not hold her death against the happiness of others."

Scenario 2: Tessa has dinner with longtime friends Sydelle and Warren 7 months after the death of her husband, Morley. When Sydelle talks about how she and Warren went home after Morley's funeral and discussed with each other how life goes on and how you have to grab every minute while you can, Tessa's stomach churns.

"How dare they say that to me?" Tessa asks other members of her grief support group. "They drove home together, walked into their house together, and talked about my husband together. I had to go home by myself and crawl into bed alone. Now they are suggesting that I grab on to what life has to offer? All life has to offer me right now is pain."

Scenario 3: Two years after Lotte's husband dies, she arranges to meet for lunch with her old college chums, Athena and Hillary, whose husbands are still alive.

The women become very animated when they see each other. As the maitre d' seats them at the table, Hillary notices that Lotte still wears her wedding band. Accusingly, Hillary asks, "Why are you still wearing your wedding ring? If you keep it on, you'll never meet anyone new."

"I'm not interested in finding a new husband," Lotte responds.

Athena persists, "But how can you feel like a REAL woman without a man? You know...sex and affection?"

Lotte's face turns red. "Can't I be a REAL woman without a man?"

Hillary reaches out and pats Lotte's hand. "We don't want to upset you, Honey, but isn't it time to move on?"

*When you tell grievers how they should grieve, you deny their feelings.*

## PLATITUDES TO AVOID

Grievers are often disheartened by friends and family who make comments that are well-intentioned, but not helpful. The following are examples of phrases that grievers hear, and *in italics how they might be responding internally*:

**"He's at peace—not suffering anymore."**
*Of course I am relieved that he is not suffering. I wished for that daily, but I'd take him back in any condition just to have another day together.*

**"He's in a better place."**
*Yes, that is comforting to know about HIM, but, as for me, I think the better place would be to have him right here with me.*

**"He's with God—God needed another angel."**
*What about my need for him? Why would God do this to me and my family?*

**"It was for the best."**
*Best for whom? Who makes that judgment?*

**"It was his time."**
*I wonder when you would think was the right time for the person you love to die?*

**"He wouldn't want you to be so sad."**
*I think he would understand my sadness and my need to feel what I feel.*

**"Don't worry, you're so pretty, you'll meet someone new and get married again."**
*Don't you get it? Grief isn't healed by finding a replacement.*

**"You're young; you will have other children."**
*Do you think that one child can take the place of another?*

**"I know just how you feel."**
*No you don't. You don't have a clue how I feel!*

**"It's great to see you laughing and finally over your grief."**
*I may be laughing on the outside, but on the inside I am filled with pain.*

**"Are you going to grieve forever?"**
*Well, I'm probably going to be grieving in some fashion from time to time.*

## POSITIVE EXPRESSIONS OF CONDOLENCE

*"My condolences,"* or *"I am so sorry to hear of the death of your brother."*
Saying this acknowledges the death and gives the griever an opportunity
to talk about the person who died and about how he is feeling.

*"I can't imagine what you are going through and how you are feeling. Tell
me what it's like for you."*
This demonstrates that you are truly focusing on the griever.and curious
about what life is like for him.

*"I miss your dad, too; he told the best jokes."*
When you recall fond memories of the person who died, it makes the grieving person feel good that others also cared deeply about his dear one.

*"I don't know what to say, but I am here. We can talk if you want or I can
just be here with you and we don't have to talk at all."*
Though it can sometimes feel uncomfortable to sit with someone in silence,
that may be exactly what he prefers.

*"I wonder if you feel up to taking a walk, going out to dinner or taking in a
movie with me."*
As time goes on, extending an invitation to the griever to have some enjoyment can be helpful, as long as it does not seem like a demand that he stop
grieving.

Remember that your friend will move through his grief process in his
own way, in his own time. Be there for him and accept his grief without
judgment. He will continue to need your support. Your thoughtful words
and actions will be appreciated not only now but also for many weeks,
months, and even years to come.

# CHAPTER 13

# Creating Your New Life

*"Do you believe in life after death?"*
*"Yes, I believe in life after death. MY life."*

Support group member

Creating your new life does not mean abandoning your old life. As you transition from what *was* to what *will be*, the memories and love you shared with your dear one continue to be a significant part of who you are. While you do not go back to being the person you were before your loved one died, you find a way to blend who you were with who you are becoming.

As you embark upon this new life, you stay involved with those people and activities that bring you comfort. And at the same time, you make new friends, cultivate new interests, and perhaps pursue long-abandoned goals and dreams. You gradually reinvest in life and as you do, you begin to feel hopeful about your future.

## FINDING A NEW COMPANION (WITH FOUR LEGS)

After caring for Harold in home hospice, I find myself a year after his death suddenly down in the dumps. Until now, I haven't had time to let my grief work its way to the surface. First I dealt with major obligations: planning the funeral; taking care of legal matters; donating his clothes and distributing other possessions; getting caught up with neglected household repairs; organizing his 1-year memorial service; and, on top of that, having surgery to replace my shoulder.

"Why don't you get a cat, Mom? A cat is low maintenance and great company," advises my daughter Andrea. She is responding to my sadness and entices me by saying that petting a cat can lower my blood pressure. My younger daughter, Amy, astutely recommends bereavement therapy. I follow the advice of both women. Therapy is easy; the cat is not.

I choose Tom, a big brown/gold neutered tabby, from a nearby animal shelter. I purchase a self-cleaning litter box and reorganize the laundry room to make space for it. Tom prefers my new burnt orange carpet.

I research "litter box issues" on the internet and call cat owner friends for advice. "Put foil in the corners of the room." "Try another kind of litter box." "Try another kind of litter." "Have litter boxes in different rooms." Desperate, I consult with a cat psychic but am dismayed to learn that she diagnoses cat problems by communicating with the animals over the phone. Somehow I can't see Tom confiding to a bodiless voice.

The vet tells me that cats only have litter box problems when they have physical ailments. "It's their only way of communicating." The vet also believes that Tom's emotional health contributes to his litter box issues. The doc prescribes anti-anxiety medication.

Turns out that Tom and I are a perfect match: we both take anti-anxiety pills; we both have arthritis at the base of the spine; we both are overweight; and we both are handicapped, Tom with his declawed front paws and me with three artificial joints to replace degenerated hips and shoulder.

Because I had been a caregiver to Harold for over a year, I needed nurturing. I adopted Tom to comfort me. Instead, I have become caregiver to a cat. Not fair! Nonetheless, I have grown attached to Tom. I love the way he snuggles in bed with me during our afternoon rest time as we watch Oprah. He amuses me when I call his name and he answers.

I once interviewed a former priest about why he and his wife had given a "cat mitzvah" for their 13-week-old kitten. Although the party had been carried out with tongue in cheek, the former priest responded, "It is important to recognize the joy that these creatures bring to us humans."

I couldn't have said it better. Nothing delights me more than my mornings with Tom when he curls up his over-sized body to fit in the narrow chair next to me as I have coffee and read the paper. In the evenings when I come home after being out with friends, I know that Harold will no longer be there to greet me. Yet, I still say "Goodnight, Harold" as I climb into bed and think about the wonderful life we shared. Then Tom jumps onto the covers, snuggles up, and I am content in knowing that I have created a new life.

## GIFT OF LIFE

On the night that Ethan and Sebastian meet, an unexpected topic arises. Ethan has renewed his driver's license that day, and for the first time, he has checked the box on the application saying that upon his death he wants to be an organ and tissue donor. "It's cool to think that somebody else could have my heart," he exclaims.

"Let's think about living, not dying," Sebastian redirects the conversation. As they talk about their careers and hobbies, the two men uncover mutual interests in real estate, golf, and mountain climbing. Thus begins their long-time relationship.

Fifteen years later, Ethan suffers severe brain damage following an automobile accident. Before disconnecting life support, Sebastian insures that the doctors know to honor Ethan's request, and his heart is donated to a national organ donation network.

Moved by Ethan's gift of life, Sebastian becomes an advocate for organ donation. As a volunteer, he devotes time each week to raising funds and promoting community awareness.

## HER SPIRIT LIVES IN ME

After Zoe's death, her husband Paul travels with friends to Europe and feels like he has brought her spirit with him. While in Paris, he writes a song for her with the chorus: *Love will last. Love will last. Love will last.*

When Paul returns home, he finds it difficult to sleep in the bedroom that he shared with his beloved wife and acting partner Zoe. But, he finds solace in reading and rereading the journal he kept while Zoe was dying. He writes to her expressing his gratitude, "Thank you for helping me become the person I always wanted to be. You still inspire me. Thank you for giving me the courage to go on."

No longer a duo, Paul returns to the stage as a solo act. He continues the disciplined life he had with Zoe—working, creating new material, and building his repertoire. Paul's first rehearsals are difficult because Zoe isn't there, yet he feels her presence backstage.

Paul tells their friends, "I still write letters to Zoe. I still need her. Her spirit lives on in me."

## MY NEW LIFE

Four years after the death of his wife, Jerry Wilson pays tribute to their relationship and expresses his certainty that a new life awaits him.

### A Healing Grief
Although I know that we have shared our last meal together
And we will take no more vacations, there is a yearning in me

That wishes we could play dominoes one more time
And that you would bring me ice cream when I am sick.
And so, I talk to you when these things come to mind
And I dream of you when my heart needs a reminder
Of what you looked like.

And still, sometimes, a tear comes to my eye
And a sadness to my heart knowing that I have lost some part of me.
Reluctantly I walk the paths we walked, visit places that were ours,
And talk with friends that knew me, only because I was a part of
     your life.
I go through the motions reminding myself to be present
As my soul looks for ways to escape into the past
Where you were and the pain was not.

It was you who knew the me that I do not share with others.
It was you who kept my heart in a safe place.
A nurse, a friend, a companion, the one who was my champion.
And now I must find others to talk to about the mundane things
That occupy my time, and yet another must listen to me prattle on
About some minor decision that I will make.
I learn to be alone as each sunrise shines its light on your absence.

And with each moment you move slowly toward the recesses of my
     memory.
I will not forget you because I cannot and I should not.
There are the reminders of you in each day's ebb and flow
And I choose to honor what made you singular and remarkable.
But move forward I will because you would wish it.
New chapters are waiting to be written, new life unfolds before me.
And I will find new ways to bring meaning to my life with you
     not there.

## TURNING PAIN INTO LOVE

Grace receives a double blow with the deaths of both her husband and
her mother. With the help of Alvira, a counselor from her diocese, Grace
learns that the process of healing from her losses can be a transforma-
tional journey.

   Grace works hard at turning her grief into something positive. She
spends her time helping church members who are struggling with their

own emotional crises. Eventually, Grace becomes a Spiritual Director in the Roman Catholic tradition and finds fulfillment guiding others in their spiritual practices.

## I WISH I HAD A BOOK TO READ

No one speaks to 9-year-old Beth about her father's long battle with leukemia, and when he dies, she is left to grieve on her own. Beth moves into adulthood with the grace and accomplishments of a successful young woman, but after the birth of her second child, Beth's grief erupts in full force.

A therapist who specializes in bereavement helps Beth process her long pent-up emotions. The counselor even meets Beth at her father's grave during a rainstorm. Appreciatively, Beth later thanks her counselor, "After our meeting at the cemetery and your encouraging me to talk to my dad, I finally stopped having recurring nightmares about his death."

Beth honors her father's memory by writing a book for children to help them move through their grief. "I feel like I am finally doing the work I have waited 30 years to do," she comments. "I am creating something that did not exist when my father died."

## DO-IT-YOURSELF HOME FUNERALS

After Elizabeth Knox's daughter, Alison, is killed in a car accident, she cannot bear to turn her child's body over to strangers. Elizabeth decides to take care of Alison's body at home. She believes that it is important for her sons, also involved in the accident, to be with their sister for a while rather than have her suddenly disappear. The family participates in bathing Alison, watching her, and taking in slowly the painful reality that she has passed from this life.

The family benefits so greatly from this experience that it inspires Elizabeth to create an organization CROSSINGS: Caring for our Own at Death. As a death midwife and home funeral guide, Elizabeth devotes her life to helping others who wish to take care of their loved ones' bodies themselves and plan do-it-yourself home funerals.

## IF ONLY I COULD TELL YOU

As newlyweds, Dallas and Syndee enthusiastically plan their future together. They foresee building a home, raising a family, and opening a holistic health book store. It doesn't occur to them to discuss how either one would survive without the other.

The couple's dreams are cut short when Syndee is diagnosed with cancer. The next 3 years are a whirlwind of doctor's appointments, surgery, and intense treatments, culminating in her death.

Five years later, Dallas feels he has become a different person from the man Syndee knew when she was alive. At 36, he has moved to a new city, opened the book store they had always dreamed of owning, and is learning to play the piano.

"When I look back at who I've become it's Syndee who I want to tell," says Dallas. "I sometimes feel that she would love me even more now that I've gone through this. I'm so proud of what I've accomplished. We had such a deep connection I can hear her say: 'How did my death change you? Who are you now?' I'd give anything to be able to hold her in my arms and tell her."

## YOUNG WIDOW: NAKED IN THE MEMORIAL PLAYGROUND

After her husband Stewart's death, Elizabeth Titus feels lost, isolated, and unsupported. She thinks that the stereotype of a widow is absurd—a little old lady wearing black and living all alone with a bunch of cats. Elizabeth sets out to see how other widows are reintegrating into life. She hopes their success will rub off on her.

Video camera in hand, Elizabeth flies to Florida to interview her first group of widowed men and women. Thus begins the project that leads to the creation of her documentary *Young Widow: Naked in the Memorial Playground*. "The documentary was inspired by the madness of my grief. I had no idea how I could ever have a life again," confesses Elizabeth.

Through the interviews, the widows and widowers expose their deepest sorrows. As they give a realistic face to grief, Elizabeth feels relieved to be among others on this painful journey. The interviewees express their eagerness to reveal their naked emotions and give the world an honest look into the life of a young widow. The camaraderie that develops among the participants gives them the strength to survive.

After a well-received showing of the film, Elizabeth comments: "Now that *Young Widow* is out and helping people, I realize that what I feel absolutely is gratitude. But what I feel is bittersweet. I'll never be okay that my husband died, but the depth of the experience allowed me to share with others in a true beauty-through-ashes manner. It honors Stewart and honors my struggles and honors all my widow friends. Stewart would have been so proud."

## FULFILLING A LIFELONG DREAM

When her older sister becomes a flight attendant, Rosalyn dreams of joining her in this fascinating career. But Rosalyn marries immediately after high school, has children at a young age, and works as a bookkeeper for 25 years. Life moves along pleasantly for Rosalyn until her husband, Lazlo, becomes ill and subsequently dies of lung cancer.

Three months after Lazlo's death, while net-surfing, Rosalyn discovers that there is still a chance for her to become a flight attendant. Although she worries that she may not meet the admission requirements, she asks herself, "How will I ever know if I don't try?" To her delight, the airline accepts Rosalyn's application, and after training she relocates half way across the country.

Today Rosalyn happily jets around the United States. She feels that becoming a flight attendant was meant to be. "All of life's events have fallen into place," Rosalyn tells a crew mate. "Ironically, the untimely death of my husband has allowed me to fulfill my life-long dream."

## TWELVE STEPS OF GRIEF

"I was treading water, paddling as fast as I could just to keep my head above water," Savannah tells the audience at the widows' conference four years after the death of her husband, Quincy.

Savannah, now a successful motivational speaker, uses her experience to encourage others. She recounts,

> Fine wine had always been part of our lives, but after Quincy died I found that I was drinking more than ever and using the wine to numb my pain. At the two-year mark, my grief was stuck and I was stuck in it.
>
> When I had a bad fall one night after too much alcohol, it was like something in me snapped. I realized I had to get out of the fog. I was ready to jump back into life, but I didn't know how to do it, it seemed so overwhelming.
>
> Joining a twelve-step program I discovered that the principles I was learning about sobriety really applied to my grief. Every time I read the word "alcohol," I substituted the word "grief." It all began to fit together. I learned to stay in the present and take one small step at a time.

For the first two years I couldn't remember the little things; it was too emotional. Today I can look back at my memories of our marriage with much more clarity. I still have my moments when I am flooded with missing Quincy. But more and more I am fascinated by this journey. Fascinated that I have survived.

## A NEW REASON FOR BEING

When Dinah becomes ill, her partner Eve takes her from clinic to clinic until they find a physician who understands Dinah's symptoms. Although the disease is incurable, the specialist sets Dinah on a course of treatment that extends her life by several months.

After Dinah's death, Eve wants to expand awareness about the rare medical condition that caused her lover's death. Inspired by Dinah's amazing spirit, Eve seeks a way to provide support for other patients and families to fight this disease. To her great satisfaction, a local hospital offers her the use of their conference room and promotes the first educational support group in their E-zine. Twenty people attend the first meeting and within 6 months close to 100 patients and caregivers attend regularly.

"Expanding awareness about this disease has become a mission for me," Eve says. "It puts me in contact with Dinah, like we are doing it together. The work is so spiritual. I feel a youthful burst of energy. I have become Dinah's voice, eyes, and ears. I have a new reason for being!"

## JUST US GIRLS

Mallory and her husband Herschel have been constant companions since she retired from her 30-year career as nursery school teacher. The couple plays bridge, attends concerts, and takes trips in their RV across the country. Five days after their 50th wedding anniversary, Herschel dies of heart disease.

Mallory isolates herself from friends, but after a few months of little socialization, she joins an exercise class at a Senior Center where she knows no one. Once a month, the class has a dinner to celebrate birthdays that have occurred in that month, but Mallory never attends and laughs at the idea because the meal starts at 4:30 for those who don't drive at night.

Despite qualifying as a senior herself, Mallory feels she has nothing in common with these "old ladies," some of whom use walkers and canes.

However, one night when she has nothing else to do, Mallory attends their dinner and discovers that they are fascinating women with interesting lives. One is a former nurse working in the jails, another is a retired university professor, and another an artist. More surprisingly, she realizes that she is older than most of them.

Mallory feels remorseful because she had automatically dismissed these women due to their age and infirmities. She invites some of them over for lunch, and they have a jolly time, so much so that they plan a follow-up luncheon at a Thai restaurant. Ever since, the JUGS (Just Us Girls) spend Saturday nights together trying new restaurants and attending cultural events.

## RELUCTANT RECIPIENT

Monica and Maricela, the two youngest daughters in a family of 11 children, spend their adult lives devoted to taking care of older siblings and parents. In addition to their caregiving responsibilities at home, they both maintain full-time jobs. When Monica develops breast cancer at age 55, Maricela lovingly tends to her.

After Monica's death, Maricela is informed that Monica has left money in her will to treat Maricela to a trip to Hawaii. Although she is ambivalent about accepting this magnanimous gift, Maricela feels she must honor her sister's last wishes. After a life of hardship, Maricela takes her first airplane trip and delights in soaking up the island sun, sea, and sights.

Maricela's eye-opening Hawaiian vacation whets her appetite for travel, and she subsequently explores cultures around the world. Through Monica's legacy, Maricela acquires a new passion.

## A WORK IN PROGRESS

Ginger meets Clark exactly 1 year after her husband Waylon's death. The first time Clark enters the house Ginger shared with Waylon, she feels conflicted. When they are intimate on the same couch where she had made love with her late husband, she weeps. Ginger feels guilty as if she is betraying Waylon's memory and guilty that she isn't fully present for Clark. Ginger yearns for her old life and at the same time desires to go forward in her new relationship.

When the couple marries 10 months later, Ginger celebrates having Clark as her husband. Yet her grief continues. With mixed emotions

Ginger tells Fredda, "Being married to Clark and taking his name is wonderful, yet it makes Waylon's death so concrete."

On the day marking the second anniversary of Waylon's death, Ginger sobs in Clark's arms. Clark consoles her, "I know that this is going to come and go. I don't expect to fully get it, but I understand that Waylon will always be part of who you are."

Ginger loves her new life and at the same time continues to live in two worlds. She confides, "Life is still a balancing act. But Clark is a sensitive, kind, easy going soul. We're a work in progress."

## PORTRAITS OF HOPE

"By the time she became an adult, my daughter Erika and I had become friends," says Susan Whitmore, founder and president of the Erika Whitmore Godwin Foundation. "When she died I lost my only child and my best friend. And it soon became apparent to me that the pain of my grief was going to be a million times worse than I ever imagined."

Three months after Erika's death, it suddenly occurs to Susan that there are millions of people all over the world in the same position that she is in, with nowhere to go. The idea comes to her to make a DVD about parents' grief that would help her keep Erika's memory alive and at the same time help others.

"I started to feel excited for the first time," recalls Susan describing her enthusiasm as she embarked upon the production of her DVD *Portraits of Hope: Creating a New Life After Losing a Child.* Seeing that the film reaches other bereft parents becomes Susan's passion and purpose. "The end result is that by stepping out of myself and doing something for other people who know this pain gives me so much hope and meaning in my life."

## LABYRINTH

During her husband Rusty's illness, Louisa feels guilty when her adult children express their resentment over her refusal to give up her job to become a full-time caretaker for their father. Louisa stands firm in her decision to keep working in her landscape design firm and hires a caregiver for Rusty. However, during Rusty's final weeks, Louisa sets aside her current horticultural project and remains at Rusty's side until his death.

Two years later Louisa is back in full swing as a landscape designer. Her talent for creating beautiful outdoor environments in urban spaces has earned her a reputation of which she is very proud. She receives a commission to develop a public garden within the city park. At the official opening, Louisa's children are thrilled to discover that their mother has designed a labyrinth garden dedicated to Rusty's memory. The winding circular path, bordered by lavender plants, beckons visitors into the center and back again.

"Mom, when Dad was ill, we were upset with your decision to keep working," admits Louisa's daughter. "But seeing your fabulous creation of this living memorial to Dad, we understand how your passion has sustained you."

## FREE TO BE ME

Although she imagined that she would want to marry again, Chelsea discovers that she is quite content living alone 3 years after the death of her husband Zubin. She sells Zubin's art nouveau furniture on an online auction website and redecorates the condo with antiques. When Chelsea wants to work on the weekends, she does. When she decides to catch a flight for a spontaneous vacation, she is free to go wherever she wishes. Chelsea enjoys a freedom that she never envisioned.

## LIFE'S NEW PURPOSE

On the day marking 5 years since her death, Brady visits the mausoleum and places a bouquet of red roses in the flower holder of his wife Abby's crypt. He speaks to her in hushed tones:

> "The day you died was like the first page of a book. Page one, chapter one. At first I was immobilized. I never thought I could go on without you, my darling. Yet over time I have discovered new meaning and purpose as each day takes me further into my new life.
>
> Facilitating the grief support groups I told you about has become my passion. It feels so right to accompany others through this life-altering process. It seems strange to say 'Thank you' to you Abby, but I know that this never would have happened if it weren't for your death. And as painful as it has been, I am grateful for this new direction. It is part of my path."

## MOTHER

Although Mary-Beth Manning always wanted to write about her relationship with her mother, she was not able to do so until after her mom died. "Throughout my life, my mother and I tried to be who we thought we should be so the other one would feel good," explains Mary-Beth. "I needed to protect her."

In her one-woman show, *Mother*, Mary-Beth reexperiences their relationship from a creative place. She describes how at each performance, "I know I'm going to feel pain, yet there's something pleasurable about it because it makes me feel connected to her. Feeling the grief brings my mother back. It makes her feel alive to me."

Mary-Beth recognizes how grief and joy can coexist. She lives every day with gratitude and a sense of being more present in her life. She concludes, "My mother's death matured me in ways that could never have happened if she were still alive. I look at it as my mother's last great gift to me."

## A TOAST TO THE PAST

Mitch and Oriana meet in their young widow and widower's grief support group. Gradually getting to know each other over a 2-year period, they fall in love. "I feel so comfortable around you," Oriana declares to Mitch. "You accept me for who I am, grief and all."

By the time Mitch proposes, he and Oriana both feel ready to take this next step in their lives. When Mitch breaks the news to his former in-laws, with whom he remains in close contact, his former mother-in-law jokes, "You thought one set of in-laws was a challenge? Now you'll have to balance two sets!"

The couple marries several months later on the beach at sunset, surrounded by family and friends. Radiant and glowing with happiness, Mitch and Oriana recite wedding vows expressing their deep love for each other. At the reception, the bride and groom drink a special toast to their former spouses: "To Liana and Kirk, without whom we would never have met."

## SUGGESTIONS FOR CREATING YOUR NEW LIFE

- Rekindle a long-abandoned interest.
- Go back to school or take a class.
- Return to work.
- Start a new career or business.
- Use your creative talents to tell your story through writing/scrapbooking/art/video/music.
- Explore a spiritual path.
- Reach out to friends for suggestions and inspiration.
- Reach out to acquaintances and create a new network of friends.
- Consider accepting invitations you might have previously turned down.
- Reignite your romantic life with a new partner.
- Adopt a pet.
- Try a new sport.
- Take up a new project—cooking, gardening, woodworking, or other craft.
- Participate in a book club or current events group.
- Reorganize or redecorate your home environment.
- Explore the arts—for example, learn to play an instrument, join a chorus, become a museum docent, usher at performances.
- Volunteer for a cause or an organization that has special meaning for you.

The emotional journey of *Saying Goodbye to Someone You Love* is filled with peaks and valleys. At times you feel that you are getting nowhere. At other times you recognize that you have traveled a significant distance and you are further along than you thought.

Although your dear one will have a place in your heart forever, you are now more engaged in living in the present than in the past. You notice that some things that used to upset you are less disturbing now. Other things that held little importance before have more significance today. As your life takes on new meaning and purpose, you ultimately discover that a new you is emerging.

# Discussion Guide

As we end our exploration of *Saying Goodbye to Someone You Love*, we are more convinced than ever of the importance of addressing the emotional journey through end of life and grief in an open and honest manner. If you agree, and we hope you do, you may wish to use the prompts below to initiate a conversation about this sensitive topic. The questions are designed to be used with your family and friends, in book clubs, discussion groups, and courses in death and dying.

1. Describe how your friends and family react when the topic of death arises.
2. How would you discuss end of life with someone close to you? What conversation might you have if he or she were healthy? What would the conversation be if he or she had a terminal illness?
3. What benefits might hospice afford you or your loved one? What circumstances might lead you to resist hospice care?
4. Describe how you feel when you care for someone who is ill, even if you are not the primary caregiver.
5. If you knew you were dying, what are some of the ways you would want to celebrate your life before it was over?
6. What are your thoughts about being with someone at the moment of death?
7. What do you imagine would be an ideal scenario for your own end-of-life experience?
8. Describe a memorable funeral or memorial service you have attended.
9. How do you feel about making funeral or memorial arrangements for yourself or others? What options will you consider?
10. How has grief affected you or someone you know?

11. What were your experiences with death when you were a child? How have you seen death or grief affect other children?
12. Discuss ways in which you might support someone who is grieving.
13. Give examples of how you or someone you know has created a new life after the death of a loved one.
14. How has *Saying Goodbye to Someone You Love* influenced your thoughts about end of life and grief?

We invite your comments and welcome you to share your stories with us.

Norine and Fredda
Norine Dresser: www.norinedresser.com
Fredda Wasserman: www.ourhouse-grief.org

# Resources

## REFERRALS FOR HOSPICE CARE

Consult with your doctor, health insurer, or the social services department of the
hospital.
Hospice Foundation of America: www.hospicefoundation.org

## END-OF-LIFE DECISIONS

Five Wishes: Aging With Dignity, P.O. Box 16661, Tallahassee, FL 32302-1661;
1-888-594-7437; www.agingwithdignity.org
Physician Orders for Life-Sustaining Treatment (POLST): www.polst.org

## IN PRINT

Albom, Mitch. *Tuesdays with Morrie*. New York: Doubleday Books, 1997.
Anderson, Megory and Thomas More. *Sacred Dying: Creating Rituals for Embracing
the End of Life*. New York: Da Capo Press, 2003.
Buchwald, Art. *Too Soon to Say Goodbye*. New York: Random House, 2006.
Callari, Elizabeth S. *A Gentle Death*. Greensboro, North Carolina: Tudor
Publishers, 1989.
Cannon, Yvonne. *When This You See*. San Francisco: Browser Books Publishing, 2006.
Comess-Daniels, Rabbi Neil. *I Miss You*. Santa Monica, CA. www.bethshirsholom.org
Cotter, Arlene. *From This Moment On: A Guide for Those Recently Diagnosed with
Cancer*. New York: Random House, 1999.
Dresser, Norine. *Come as You Aren't: Feeling at Home with Multicultural Celebrations*.
New York: M. Evans, 2006.
Dresser, Norine. *Multicultural Manners: New Rules of Etiquette for a Changing
Society*. New York: John Wiley and Sons, 1996.
Friedmann, Erica, Sue A. Thomas, and Timothy J. Eddy. "Companion animals
and human health: physical and cardiovascular influences." In Podberscek,

Anthony, Elizabeth S. Paul and James A. Serpell, eds. *Companion Animals & Us: Exploring the Relationships Between People & Pets.* Cambridge, UK: Cambridge University Press, 2000, 125–142.

Friedman, Robert. "Widowhood, Part 2." *Generations Magazine.* Volume 28. Winter, 2007.

Gilbert, Allison. *Always Too Soon: Voices of Support for Those Who Have Lost Both Parents.* Emeryville, CA: Seal Press, 2006.

Hartocollis, Anemona. "At the End, Offering Not a Cure but Comfort." http://www.nytimes.com/2009/08/20/healthdoctors.html

Karnes, Barbara. *Gone from My Sight: The Dying Experience.* Depoe Bay, OR: Barbara Karnes Publisher, 2005.

Kessler, David. *The Needs of the Dying.* New York: HarperCollins, 2000.

Kubler-Ross, Elisabeth and David Kessler. *On Grief and Grieving: Finding the Meaning of Grief Through the Five Stages of Loss.* New York: Scribner, 2005.

McCormack, Jerusha Hull. *Grieving: A Beginner's Guide.* Brewster, MA: Paraclete Press, 2006.

Mack, Stan. *Janet and Me.* New York: Simon & Schuster, 2004.

OUR HOUSE Grief Support Center. *My Memory Book for Grieving Children.* Los Angeles, 2007.

OUR HOUSE Grief Support Center. *My Grief Journal for Grieving Teens.* Los Angeles, 2007.

OUR HOUSE Grief Support Center. *My Grief Journal.* Los Angeles, 2008.

Pickrell John. "Timeline: HIV & AIDS." *New Scientist.* September 4, 2006.

Shaw, George Bernard. *The Doctor's Dilemma: A Tragedy* (quote spoken by Ridgeon), Act V. *New York: The Trow Press,* 1911.

Sheppard, Caroline H. *Brave Bart: A Story for Traumatized and Grieving Children.* Grosse Pointe Woods, MI: Institute for Trauma and Loss in Children, 1998.

Spector, Laurie J. and Ruth Spector Webster. *Lost My Partner—What'll I do?* Los Angeles: McCormick Press, 2008.

Tedeschi, Richard G., Crystal L. Park, and Lawrence G. Calhoun, eds. *Posttraumatic Growth: Positive Changes in the Aftermath of Crisis.* Mahwah, NJ: Lawrence Erlbaum Associates, Inc., 1998.

Terzi, Judith. "Is my mother still alive?" *Voices of Alzheimer's. The Healing Companion: Stories for Courage, Comfort and Strength.* The Healing Project, "Voices of" Series Book no. 2. New York: Lachance Publishing, 2007, pp. 217–225.

Wolfelt, Alan D. *Healing a Spouse's Grieving Heart: 100 Practical Ideas After Your Husband or Wife Dies.* Fort Collins, CO: Companion Press, 2003.

Wolfson, Randi Pearlman. *I Wish I had a Book to Read: Helping a Child's Heart Heal When Someone Special Has Died.* Los Angles: Look Up at the Moon Publications, 2007.

Worden, J. William. *Grief Counseling and Grief Therapy: A Handbook for the Mental Health Practitioner, Fourth Edition.* New York: Springer Publishing, 2009.

## MULTIMEDIA

*A Family Undertaking.* Documentary on the Home Funeral Movement, includes segment on CROSSINGS, founded by Elizabeth Knox. Fanlight Productions, 2003.

*Arrangement in Green and Black: Portrait of the Photographer's Mother Series.* Aline Smithson. www.alinesmithson.com. Silvershotz, 2007.

*Calm Your Mind and Nourish Your Soul.* Audio CD. Fredda Wasserman. Guided Meditation, 2005. www.freddawasserman.com

*Graceful Passages: A Companion for Living and Dying.* Produced by Michael Stillwater and Gary Remal Malkin. Companion Arts, L.L.C. 2000.

*Jonna's Body, Please Hold.* DVD. Jonna Tamases, writer and performer. Directed by Adam Bluming. Mad Lively, 2007. www.jonnasbody.com

*Mother.* Mary-Beth Manning, playwright and performer. Directed by Dhianna Castle, October 2, 2009.

*Portraits of Hope: Creating a New Life After Losing a Child,* 2004. DVD. www.griefHaven.org

*Speed Grieving.* DVD. Reiner, Alysia, performer/creator/producer. Directed by Jessica Daniels. Performers: Alysia Reiner, David Alan Basche, James Naughton. Kampfire Films & Too Wonderful 2 Be Limited, 2009.

*Where the Ocean Meets the Sky.* DVD documentary. Directed and Photographed by Barry Berona & Greg Daniels. Produced by Pia Clemente. Liquid Media Productions, 2008.

*Young Widow: Naked in the Memorial Playground.* DVD documentary. Directed by Elizabeth Titus, 2008. Young Widow Productions, 2008.

## OTHER RESOURCES

CaringBridge: connects family and friends during serious health events; www.CaringBridge.org

Life Journeys: creates video biographies of people facing serious illness; www.lifejourneys.com

OUR HOUSE Grief Support Center: provides support groups, education, and resources; www.ourhouse-grief.org

Sacred Dying Foundation: creates vigils and rituals for the dying; www.sacreddying.org

Prayer Shawl Ministry: creates shawls for the dying; www.shawlministry.com

The Go Wish Game. Produced by CODA. www.codaalliance.org

# Index